# Introduction to English Civil Law

## for German-Speaking Lawyers and Law Students

## Vol. 2

## 2011

Begründet von

**Dr. iur. utr. Rainer Wörlen (†)**

ehemals Professor an der Fakultät Wirtschaftsrecht

Fachhochschule Schmalkalden

fortgeführt von

**Dr. iur. Kristina Balleis**

**Dr. phil. Alexandra Angress**

Professorinnen an der Fakultät Wirtschaft und Recht

Hochschule Aschaffenburg

**ALPMANN UND SCHMIDT Juristische Lehrgänge Verlagsges. mbH & Co. KG**

**48149 Münster, Annette-Allee 35, 48001 Postfach 1169, Telefon (0251) 98109-33**

**AS-Online: www.alpmann-schmidt.de**

Liebe Leserin, lieber Leser,

wir sind stets bemüht, unsere Produkte zu verbessern. Fehler lassen sich aber nie ganz ausschließen. Sie helfen uns, wenn Sie uns über Druckfehler in diesem Skript oder anderen Printprodukten unseres Hauses informieren.

E-Mail genügt an „druckfehlerteufel@alpmann-schmidt.de"

Danke
Ihr AS-Autorenteam

**Prof. Dr. iur. Kristina Balleis**
**Prof. Dr. phil. Alexandra Angress**
Introduction to English Civil Law, Vol. 2
for German-Speaking Lawyers and Law Students
4th revised edition 2011
ISBN: 978-3-86752-131-4

Verlag Alpmann und Schmidt Juristische Lehrgänge
Verlagsgesellschaft mbH & Co. KG, Münster

# Vorwort

Am 3. November 2009 verstarb *Rainer Wörlen* unerwartet im Alter von 63 Jahren. Als ob er – wie *William Shakespeare*, der den „Paisley Snail" Case vorweggenommen hat (siehe dazu S. 29 f.) – eine Vorahnung gehabt hätte, hat er in der Vorauflage aus dem Jahre 2005 folgendermaßen zum letzten Kapitel „Law of Succession" übergeleitet:

"Unfortunately, an individual's life must come to an end as inevitably as any book. For human beings the end is death. We do not know exactly what will happen to us after death. The only thing we can be sure of is that "Death brings heirs." The end of a book does not have to mean its death. Books may live endlessly. ..." – „Menschen sterben, Bücher können weiter leben".

*Rainer Wörlen* hat eine große Zahl didaktisch herausragender Lehr- und Lernbücher hinterlassen. Wer ihn persönlich gekannt hat, weiß, dass seine Leidenschaft den beiden Bänden zum Englischen Zivilrecht („Introduction to English Civil Law – for German-Speaking Lawyers and Law Students, Vol. 1 + 2") galt. Das geniale Konzept dieser beiden Bücher, dem (deutschen) Leser eine fremde Rechtsordnung zu erschließen und zugleich die fremde (Rechts-) Sprache zu vermitteln, geht auf diese Begeisterung zurück. Wir haben es uns zur Aufgabe gemacht, dieses Konzept im Sinne *Rainer Wörlens* fortzuführen, welches in seinem nachfolgend abgedruckten Vorwort zur ersten Auflage ausführlich beschrieben ist. Diese Lektüre, insbesondere des Abschnittes „IV. Zur Arbeitsweise mit diesem Buch" sei allen Lesern, die mit dem Buch gewinnbringend arbeiten wollen, nachdrücklich ans Herz gelegt.

Band 2 führt in fünf verschiedene Bereiche des englischen Zivilrechts ein. Dabei steht im Vordergrund, dem Leser die zugrunde liegenden Rechtskonzepte anschaulich zu vermitteln, da sie oftmals nicht mit den uns vertrauten deutschen Konzepten vergleichbar sind. Die Neuauflage versucht sich dem Vergleich der beiden Konzepte vorsichtig anzunähern.

Seit der mittlerweile vergriffenen 3. Auflage ist einige Zeit vergangen, weshalb eine grundlegende Überarbeitung angebracht erschien. An manchen Stellen wurden die Akzente verschoben, an anderen inhaltliche Neuausrichtungen vorgenommen und Bereiche wie *property* und *trusts* vertieft. Aufgenommen wurden einige bislang nicht berücksichtigte *statutes*, z.B. *Consumer Protection Act 1987, Commonhold and Leasehold Reform Act 2002, Civil Partnership Act 2004, Gender Recognition Act 2004* und *Protection from Harassment Act 1997.* Aus der aktuellen englischen Gesetzgebung waren unter anderem einzuarbeiten: *Charities Act 2006, Perpetuities and Accumulation Act 2009, Human Fertilisation and Embryology Act 2008* und *Child Maintenance and Other Payments Act 2008.* Im „Family Law" waren ferner die fortgeschrittenen Reformdiskussionen in Sachen *cohabitation* und *divorce* zu gegenwärtigen.

Vollständig überarbeitet wurden auch die sprachliche Fassung sowie die Vokabelübersetzungen. Dabei haben wir zusätzlich englische Fachbegriffe gekennzeichnet, für die es kein exaktes juristisches Pendant im Deutschen gibt. Wo angebracht, wurden *cases* zugunsten der Lesbarkeit verkürzt oder neu formuliert.

Neu ist auch die Bearbeitung im Team. *Kristina Balleis* verantwortet als Juristin in erster Linie die fachlichen Inhalte, *Alexandra Angress* als Sprachwissenschaftlerin die sprachliche Fassung. Beraten und unterstützt wurden wir durch *William Herbert*, M.A. (Hons) (Cantab.), Solicitor aus Birmingham. Ihm gebührt unser allererster und aufrichtigster Dank. Als langjähriger Freund *Rainer Wörlens* und Begleiter der Vorauflagen wie auch als Mitglied der Deutsch-Britischen Juristenvereinigung e.V. lag ihm das „Weiterleben" und die juristische sowie sprachliche Qualität dieses Buches besonders am Herzen. Federführend hat er „Property Law" betreut, aber auch am „Tort Law" intensiv mitgearbeitet, zahlreiche hilfreiche Anregungen gegeben, geduldig und unermüdlich viele „kleine und große" Fragen der Autorinnen beantwortet und dabei viele Stunden seiner Freizeit geopfert. Er hat auch den Kontakt zu britischen Juristinnen und Juristen hergestellt, mit denen wir uns unter seiner engagierten Koordination unter anderem vor Ort in Birmingham beraten konnten.

Besonderer Dank gebührt Solicitor *Alison Turnbull*, LL.M., LL.B., von der Birmingham City University, School of Law, die dort Senior Lecturer in Law ist und sich der Lehre von *tort law* verschrieben hat. Ihr akademischer Input hat die Überarbeitung des vom *case law* dominierten Kapitels „Tort Law" außerordentlich befördert.

Darüber hinaus danken wir *Keith Dudley (T.E.P.)*, *Christopher* und *Nicola Howdle*, beide B.A. (Hons) und *Michael Follis*, LL.B. (Hons), alle Solicitors aus Birmingham, die in ihrem jeweiligen Fachgebiet (*law of succession*, *law of trusts* und *family law*) dazu beigetragen haben, die entsprechenden Kapitel auf den neusten Stand zu bringen.

Für all die erfahrene großzügige Hilfe aus England danken wir herzlich. Etwaige Fehler oder Ungenauigkeiten haben gleichwohl wir allein zu verantworten. Konstruktiv-kritische Anregungen und „Fehlermeldungen" nehmen wir deshalb dankbar und gern entgegen. Sie erreichen uns per Mail unter kristina.balleis@h-ab.de und alexandra.angress@h-ab.de oder mit der Post unter der Anschrift: Fakultät Wirtschaft und Recht, Hochschule Aschaffenburg, Würzburger Str. 45, 63743 Aschaffenburg.

Aschaffenburg, im Juni 2011 *Kristina Balleis & Alexandra Angress*

# Preface

On November 3, 2009 Rainer Wörlen died unexpectedly at the age of 63. Like William Shakespeare who anticipated the Paisley Snail case (cf. page 29 f.), he must have had some premonition when writing the following introduction to his chapter on the Law of Succession in the review copy of this book in 2005:

"Unfortunately, an individual's life must come to an end as inevitably as any book. For human beings the end is death. We do not know exactly what will happen to us after death. The only thing we can be sure of is that "Death brings heirs." The end of a book does not have to mean its death. Books may live endlessly. ..." – „Menschen sterben, Bücher können weiter leben".

Rainer Wörlen has bequeathed a plethora of excellent didactic textbooks. Anyone who knew him personally knows that Rainer Wörlen was passionate about his two volumes on English Civil Law. The ingenuity of the concept of these two books – to introduce to the German reader a foreign legal system and, at the same time, the legal language and terminology – is the result of his enthusiasm and commitment.

We have therefore taken it upon us to continue to develop this concept in the same way as Rainer Wörlen described it in detail in the preface to his first edition. We warmly recommend to all the rewarding experience of reading this preface, particularly part IV. "On how to work with this book".

Volume 2 provides an introduction to five different areas of English Civil Law. The concrete illustration of legal concepts underlying the legal system is the focus of this book, as it is often difficult to find corresponding German legal concepts. This new edition is a first tentative approach to compare both English and German legal concepts.

Some time has passed since the third edition became out of print, hence the need for a fundamental revision of certain topics. A shift in emphasis has been made in certain areas; new thematic guidelines have been introduced in others, and areas such as Property and Trusts have been developed further. New legislation has been taken on board such as *Charities Act 2006, Perpetuities and Accumulation Act 2009, Human Fertilisation and Embryology Act 2008* and *Child Maintenance and Other Payments Act 2008.* In addition, commentary has been included on *Consumer Protection Act 1987, Commonhold and Leasehold Reform Act 2002, Civil Partnership Act 2004, Gender Recognition Act 2004* and *Protection from Harassment Act 1997.* Furthermore, we have referred to current proposals for reform of the law on cohabitation and divorce in our chapter on Family Law.

The linguistic style of this introduction has been completely revised as well as the vocabulary section. In addition, we have highlighted legal concepts and terms of English Law that have no direct German equivalent. Cases have been shortened or re-written when considered appropriate in order to be more user-friendly.

The team working on this new edition is also new: Kristina Balleis, professor of law at Aschaffenburg University of Applied Sciences, has been responsible for the content of this edition, and Alexandra Angress, professor of Business English at Aschaffenburg

University of Applied Sciences, has been in charge of the linguistic style. Our special and sincere thanks go first and foremost to William Herbert, M.A. (Hons) (Cantab.), Solicitor in Birmingham, who has advised and supported us throughout. As a long-standing friend of Rainer Wörlen and member of the British-German Jurists Association, he values the legal and linguistic quality of this publication and has closely followed the preparation of the publication. He has coordinated the chapter on Property and has also worked on Tort as well as supporting the authors with various helpful recommendations and ideas. He has patiently answered our questions great and small, sacrificing many hours of his free time. Mr Herbert has also established contact with other English lawyers whom the authors have had the privilege to meet and to consult in Birmingham thanks to his initiative and commitment.

Special thanks go to Alison Turnbull, LL.M., LL.B., Solicitor, Senior Lecturer at the School of Law, Birmingham City University who specialises in Tort Law. Her academic input regarding case law has considerably advanced our revision of the chapter on Tort.

Furthermore, we would like to thank Keith Dudley (T.E.P.), Christopher Howdle, B.A. (Hons), Nicola Howdle, B.A. (Hons) and Michael Follis, LL.B. (Hons), all four solicitors in Birmingham who, with their expertise in their respective fields, have supported us in updating the chapters on Succession, Trusts and Family, respectively.

We are grateful for all the generous support from our colleagues in the UK. At the same time, we are solely to blame if there are any mistakes or inaccuracies. We therefore warmly welcome constructive criticism and feedback. You can reach us via e-mail at kristina.balleis@h-ab.de and alexandra.angress@h-ab.de and at the following address: Fakultät Wirtschaft und Recht, Hochschule Aschaffenburg, Würzburger Str. 45, D - 63743 Aschaffenburg.

Aschaffenburg, June 2011 Kristina Balleis & Alexandra Angress

# Vorwort zur ersten Auflage

## – zugleich (unter IV.) eine Arbeitsanleitung –

I. Wenn man als Deutscher ein englischsprachiges Buch über englisches Zivilrecht schreibt, hat das ganz besondere – persönliche und sachliche – Gründe. *„Persönlich"* habe ich in zahlreichen Aufenthalten im "United Kingdom" und auf Malta (dessen Amtssprache, bei allerdings unterschiedlichem Rechtssystem, Englisch ist) eine besondere Affinität zu den Bewohnern „dieser Inseln", zu ihrer Landschaft sowie zu ihrer Sprache und dem englischen Recht entwickelt. Die Faszination, die das englische Rechtssystem auf einen ausländischen Juristen ausüben kann, ist schwer in Worte zu fassen, man kann sie nur „fühlen", muss sie „erlebt" haben. Z.B.: Wenn man Sitzungen des "High Court"[1] in den "Royal Courts" am "Strand"[1] im Herzen von London oder des "House of Lords"[1] im Parlamentsgebäude "live" verfolgt, bei *Clive Max Schmitthoff* weiland eine vierwöchige Vorlesung "Introduction to modern English law" gehört, einige der ehrwürdigen "Inns of Court"[1] besucht hat und anlässlich eines Empfangs in der "Law Society"[1] dem schon zu Lebzeiten legendären *Lord Denning* (der am 05.03.1999 im Alter von 100 Jahren starb) die Hand reichen durfte.

II. Eine *sachliche* und zutreffende Begründung gibt *Graf von Bernstorff*[2] in *seinem* Vorwort:

»Das englische Recht ist für international tätige Unternehmen und Juristen sowie für rechtsvergleichend arbeitende Studenten von großer Bedeutung. Die wichtigsten Finanzplätze der Welt finden sich in Staaten, die „englischem" Recht folgen. Die Staaten des *Commonwealth* folgen bis heute den Grundprinzipien englischen Rechts, sodass die in diesem Buch niedergelegten Ausführungen in vielerlei Hinsicht auch in anderen Ländern der Welt nutzbar sind. Internationale Verträge unterliegen häufig englischem Recht. Die Außenhandelspraxis arbeitet überwiegend auf der Basis englischen Rechts. Kurzum: die Praxis hat sich mit dem englischen Recht immer wieder auseinanderzusetzen.«

Außerdem:
»Da der Commonwealth heute über 1,5 Milliarden Menschen umfasst, unterliegt jeder vierte Mensch dem englischen Recht, das ... die wohl wichtigste Rechtsordnung der Welt darstellt«.[3]

Für Juristen, die sich auf internationalem Parkett bewegen wollen, sind gute Kenntnisse der englischen Sprache und Grundkenntnisse des englischen Rechts unerlässlich. Dieser Erkenntnis haben eine Vielzahl deutscher Universitäten und Fachhochschulen Rechnung getragen: an manchen rechtswissenschaftlichen Fakultäten und Fachbereichen wurden Lehrstühle für „angelsächsisches" oder „anglo-amerikanisches" Recht errichtet,

---

1 Was sich hinter diesen Namen verbirgt, könnten Sie nach der Lektüre von Vol. 1 dieses Werks wissen.

2 Vgl. "Bibliography" (= Literaturverzeichnis).

3 *Bernstorff, S.1.*

und vielerorts werden Kurse von Muttersprachlern ("native speakers") in englischer Rechtssprache sowie Vorlesungen über englisches Recht gehalten.

III. Das vorliegende Werk entspricht weitgehend meiner im *Fachbereich Wirtschaftsrecht* der Fachhochschule Schmalkalden gehaltenen Vorlesung "Introduction to English civil law", die sich mit zwei Semesterwochenstunden auf drei Semester erstreckt. Als Zivilrechtler habe ich mich auf das englische *"civil law"* beschränkt, da ich vom öffentlichen Recht, inklusive Strafrecht, nichts (mehr) verstehe...

Es gibt bereits einige Lehrbücher und Grundrisse zum englischen und anglo-amerikanischen Recht, die von deutschen Autoren in deutscher Sprache geschrieben wurden (vgl. "Bibliography"→ *Bernstorff, Blumenwitz, Henrich, Reimann*). So qualitätsvoll (wie insbesondere das – auf das US-amerikanische Privatrecht beschränkte – Buch von *Reimann*) diese Bücher auch sind, sie sind nicht in der Lage, *Recht und Sprache gleichermaßen zu vermitteln.* Die englischen Rechtsbegriffe werden überwiegend als bekannt vorausgesetzt und selten erklärt, sodass man diese Bücher obwohl auf Deutsch geschrieben - ohne englisch-rechtliche Vorbildung und ohne ein spezielles englisch-deutsches Rechtswörterbuch zu benutzen, kaum verstehen kann.

Es gibt bereits auch eine Reihe von Lehrbüchern über „anglo-amerikanische Rechts*sprache*" (vgl. "Bibliography" → *Byrd, Heidinger/Hubalek, Riley*), die als Sprachlehrbücher von hoher Qualität sind. Sie sind – da sie nur Fragmente aus englischer Rechtsliteratur und Rechtsprechung wiedergeben können – naturgemäß nicht geeignet, *ein Rechtsgebiet geschlossen darzustellen*.

Dieses Buch ist eine **Kombination aus einem englischsprachigen Lehrbuch über englisches Zivilrecht und einer Einführung in die englische Rechtssprache**. Es ist damit, insbesondere auch durch die Präsentation von deutschen Übersetzungen neben dem englischen Text, ein Novum.[4]

IV. **Zur Arbeitsweise mit diesem Buch:**

Der vorliegende Band II (= Vol. 2) ist die Fortsetzung von „Introduction to English Civil Law, Vol. 1" mit den Kapiteln „Classification and sources of English Law, The administration of law, The legal profession, How to find the law, Persons in law, The law of contract". Die in Vol. 1 vermittelten Kenntnisse sind in diesem Vol. 2 nicht zwingend, aber dringend erforderlich.

Alle Worte, die im Text unterstrichen sind, erscheinen in deutscher Übersetzung auf dem rechten Rand jeder Seite. Dabei wurde nicht immer die „wörtliche", sondern die jeweils am geeignetsten erscheinende „freie" Übersetzung gewählt. Es wurden nicht nur spezifische Rechtsbegriffe übersetzt, sondern auch eine Vielzahl von Wörtern der Umgangssprache, von denen ich glaube, dass sie nicht unbedingt zum Wortschatz eines Lesers gehören, dessen Schulenglisch nicht besser als „befriedigend" war. (Als solcher sollte man allerdings wissen, dass z.B. das Verb *"to seek"* heißt, wenn *"sought"* am Rand mit *„suchen"* übersetzt wird). Wiederholungen sind dabei bewusst vorgenommen. Sehr

4 *Ähnlich:* Der kurze und sehr gute „Legal Reader" von *Donald R. Black* (vgl. „Bibliography"), der auf insgesamt 133 Seiten eine kurze Einführung in das angloamerikanische Recht(ssystem) gibt, die Vokabeln dabei aber in gesonderten Listen ausweist.

treffend weist *Black* in der Einführung zu seinem „Legal Reader" auf die Binsenwahrheit (= *truism*) hin: *„Repetitio mater studiorum est"* (= *„repetition is the mother of learning"* – „Wiederholung ist die Mutter des Lernens"). *Black's* moderner Abwandlung dieser Binsenwahrheit schließe ich mich gerne an: *„Understanding is the key of learning"*! Wiederholung wiederum fördert das Verständnis! Aus diesem Grund wird am Ende von Teilabschnitten deren Inhalt jeweils anhand von grafischen Übersichten zusammengefasst, sodass Sie sich die wichtigsten Begriffe und Rechtsinstitute sowie ihre Bedeutung nochmals einprägen können, bevor Sie mit dem Lesen und Lernen (= Studieren) fortfahren. Nehmen Sie sich dabei nicht zuviel vor, sondern arbeiten Sie langsam und gründlich! Da man eine *Sprache* intensiver lernt, wenn man sie nicht nur liest und spricht, sondern auch *schreibt*, empfehle ich Ihnen, sich – wie zu Schulzeiten – ein *Vokabelheft* anzulegen, in dem Sie nach der Lektüre von Teilabschnitten (spätestens am Ende jeden Kapitels) alle Ihnen unbekannt gewesenen Vokabeln notieren und abschnittsweise *auswendig lernen*!

Von einem (ursprünglich beabsichtigten) alphabetisch geordneten englisch-deutschen Vokabelverzeichnis am Ende des Buchs habe ich abgesehen: Das lästige Nachschlagen soll ja gerade auf ein Minimum reduziert werden.

Sollten Ihnen an der einen oder anderen Stelle meine *rechtlichen* Ausführungen nicht ausreichen, empfehle ich, das jeweils angesprochene Thema in einer der im Literaturverzeichnis erscheinenden Gesamtdarstellungen zum Englischen Recht oder gar in einem der großen englischsprachigen Standardwerke zu dem jeweiligen speziellen Rechtsgebiet nachzuarbeiten. Die wichtigsten dieser Werke sollten in Ihrer Hochschul- oder Seminarbibliothek vorhanden sein. Um Ihnen die Auswahl zu erleichtern, wird am Ende jeden Kapitels unter "Further reading" Literatur zur Vertiefung zitiert, die ich bei der Anfertigung dieses Kapitels benutzt habe.

Da es sich bei diesem Werk um eine Einführung in das *englische* Zivilrecht und *nicht* um ein *rechtsvergleichendes* (vgl. hierzu das vorzügliche Standardwerk von → *Zweigert/ Kötz*) Werk handelt, habe ich Hinweise auf Ähnlichkeiten mit und Unterschiede zu dem deutschen Bürgerlichen Recht *kursiv* nur spärlich, zumeist auf Fußnoten verteilt.

Für Hinweise und Anregungen aus dem Leserkreis bin ich stets dankbar.

Schmalkalden, im Januar 2000

*Rainer Wörlen*

## Chapter Seven

## Chapter Eight

## Chapter Nine

## Chapter Ten

## Chapter Eleven

| | |
|---|---|
| Abt. | Abteilung |
| AG | Aktiengesellschaft |
| allg. | allgemein |
| a. | am |
| Aufl. | Auflage |
| | |
| b. | bei |
| B. | Bestimmtheit |
| B.A. | Bachelor of Arts |
| BGB | Bürgerliches Gesetzbuch |
| | |
| Cantab. | *Latin*: cantabrigiensis (= of Cambridge) |
| CD | Civil Defence |
| cf. | confer (vgl.) |
| C.J. | Chief Justice |
| Co | Company |
| | |
| dies. | dieselben |
| d.h. | das heißt |
| | |
| E.C.T. | electro-convulsive-therapy |
| EGBGB | Einführungsgesetz zum BGB |
| engl. | Englisch |
| etc. | *Latin*: et cetera (= and so on) |
| e.g. | *Latin*: exempli gratia (= for example) |
| ed./Ed. | edition (Aufl.) / Editor (Hrsg.) |
| | |
| f./ff. | following; für / following page |
| | |
| GCSE | General Certificate of Secondary Education |
| ggü. | gegenüber |
| | |
| hist. | historisch |
| Hons. | with honours |
| Hrsg. | Herausgeber |
| | |
| i.e. | *Latin*: id est (= that is to say) |
| IELS | Institute of English Language Studies |
| Inc. | incorporated (company) |
| | |
| J. | Justice |
| jmd. | jemand |
| jur. | juristisch |

| | |
|---|---|
| lat. | lateinisch |
| L.J. | Lord Justice |
| LL.B. | Bachelor of Laws |
| LL.M. | Master of Laws |
| Ltd | limited (company) |
| | |
| M.A. | Magister Artium |
| M.R. | Master of the Rolls |
| | |
| o. | oder |
| | |
| p. | page |
| PCE | Perchlorethen |
| plc | public limited company (AG) |
| pty. | party / proprietary |
| | |
| R. | *Latin*: Regina (= the Crown) |
| Re | in that matter |
| rw | rechtswidrig |
| | |
| s. | see / section / siehe |
| s.a. | see above |
| schott. | schottisch |
| s.o. | siehe oben |
| ss. | sections |
| sub nom. | *Latin:* sub nomine (= under the name of) |
| St | Saint |
| StGB | Strafgesetzbuch |
| StPO | Strafprozessordnung |
| | |
| T. | Treuhandverhältnis |
| T.E.P. | Trust & Estate Practitioner |
| typ. | typisch |
| | |
| u. | und |
| UK | United Kingdom |
| usw. | und so weiter |
| | |
| v | versus |
| vgl. | vergleiche |
| vol. | volume |
| | |
| WEG | Wohnungseigentumsgesetz |

## I. English (and Anglo-American) law in English


*Adams* — Law for Business Students, 6th revised ed., Pearson Education Ltd, Harlow 2010

*Baker* — An Introduction to English Legal History, 4th ed., Oxford University Press, Oxford 2002

*Barker & Padfield* — Law Made Simple (Made Simple Series), 12th ed., Reed Elsevier, Oxford 2007

*Bell* — Real Property (Cracknell's Companion Cases & Statutes), 4th ed., Old Bailey Press, London 2004

*Bermingham* — Tort (Nutcases), 5th ed., Sweet & Maxwell, London 2008

*Bermingham* — Tort (Nutshells), 8th ed., Sweet & Maxwell, London 2008

*Black* — Black's Legal Reader – An Introduction to the Anglo-American Law and Legal System, 1. Aufl., Hannover 1998/99

*Borkowski* — Textbook on Succession, 2nd ed., Oxford University Press, Oxford 2002

*Boucher & Corns* — GCSE Law Casebook, 3rd revised ed., Blackstone Press, London 1995

*Burn* — Cheshire and Burn's Modern Law of Real Property, 17th ed., Oxford University Press, Oxford 2006

*Chang* — Equity and Trusts (Nutcases), 5th ed., Sweet & Maxwell, London 2010

*Chang* — Land Law (Nutcases), 5th ed., Sweet & Maxwell, London 2009

*Cooke* — Law of Tort, 9th ed., Pearson Education Ltd, Harlow 2010

*Cracknell* — Equity and Trusts (Cracknell's Companion Cases & Statutes), 4th ed., Old Bailey Press, London 1995

| | |
|---|---|
| *Cracknell* | Torts (Cracknell's Companion Cases & Statutes), 9th ed., Old Baily Press, London 2000 |
| *Cracknell* | Succession: The Law of Wills and Estates (Cracknell's Statutes), 5th revised ed., Old Bailey Press, London 2004 |
| *Cretney (Ed.)* | Cretney's Principles of Family Law, 8th ed., Sweet & Maxwell, London 2008 (by *Masson, Bailey-Harris, Probert contributors*) |
| *Davey & Wicks* | Butterworths Property Law Handbook, 8th ed., LexisNexis Butterworths, London 2009 |
| *Deakin, Johnston & Markesinis* | Markesinis and Deakin's Tort Law, 6th ed., Oxford University Press, Oxford 2007 |
| *Denham* | Law: a modern introduction, 4th ed., Hodder & Stoughton Educational, London 1999 |
| *Dobson* | Sale of Goods and Consumer Credit, 6th ed., Sweet & Maxwell, London 2000 |
| *Dodds* | Family Law (Cracknell's Law Students' Companion), 4th revised ed., Old Bailey Press, London 1997 |
| *Douglas & Lowe* | Bromley's Family Law, 10th ed., Oxford University Press, Oxford 2006 |
| *Duddington* | Land Law (Law Express), 3rd ed., Pearson Education Ltd, Harlow 2011 |
| *Edwards & Stockwell* | Equity and Trusts (MyLawChamber Pack), 9th ed., Pearson Education Ltd, Harlow 2010 |
| *Finch & Fafinski* | Tort Law (Law Express), 3rd ed., Pearson Education Ltd, Harlow 2011 |
| *Geldart, Geldart & Geldart* | Introduction to English Law, Originally Elements of English Law, 11th ed., Oxford University Press, London 1995 |
| *Giliker & Beckwith* | Tort, 3rd ed., Sweet & Maxwell, London 2008 |

| | |
|---|---|
| *Haley* | Equity & Trusts (Nutshells), 8th ed., Sweet & Maxwell, London 2010 |
| *Haley* | Land Law (Nutshells), 8th ed., Sweet & Maxwell, London 2010 |
| *Harpum, Bridge & Dixon* | Megarry & Wade: The Law of Real Property, 7th ed., Sweet & Maxwell, London 2008 |
| *Harpwood* | Modern Tort Law, 6th ed., Cavendish Publishing Ltd, London 2005 |
| *Harris* | An Introduction to Law (Law in context), 7th ed., Cambridge University Press, Cambridge 2007 |
| *Harvey & Marston* | Cases and Commentary on Tort, 6th ed., Oxford University Press, Oxford 2009 |
| *Hayton, Matthews & Mitchell* | Underhill & Hayton: Law of Trusts and Trustees, 17th ed., LexisNexis, Butterworths, London 2006 |
| *Hedley* | Tort, 6th ed., Oxford University Press, Oxford 2008 |
| *Herring* | Family Law (Law Express), 3rd ed., Pearson Education Ltd, Harlow 2011 |
| *Heuston & Buckley* | Salmond and Heuston on the Law of Torts, 21st ed., Sweet & Maxwell, London 1996 (cited as "Salmond and Heuston")* |
| *Hudson* | Equity & Trusts, 4th ed., Cavendish Publishing Ltd, London 2005 |
| *Jones* | Textbook on Torts, 8th ed., Oxford University Press, Oxford 2002 |
| *Kerridge* | Parry and Kerridge: The Law of Succession, 12th ed., Sweet & Maxwell, London 2009 |
| *King* | Probate Practitioner's Handbook, 5th revised ed., The Law Society, Londen 2006 |


* In England bezieht man sich üblicherweise nicht auf den aktuellen Autor, wenn das Werk schon durch den Namen des ursprünglichen Autors bekannt ist. Bei großen Standardwerken haben wir uns daran gehalten; i.d.R. aber berufen wir uns auf den aktuellen Autor, der leichter im Literaturverzeichnis zu finden ist.

*Kidner* Casebook on Torts, 11th ed., Oxford University Press, Oxford 2010

*Lawsen & Rudden* The Law of Property (Claredon Law Series), 3rd ed., Oxford University Press, Oxford 2002 (by *Rudden*)

*Lunney & Oliphant* Tort Law – Text and Materials, 4th ed., Oxford University Press, Oxford 2010

*Lyall* An Introduction to British Law, 2nd ed., Nomos, Baden-Baden 2002

*Matthews, O'Cinneide & Morgan* Hepple and Matthews' Tort – Cases & Materials, 6th ed., Oxford University Press, Oxford 2008

*Oakley* Parker and Mellows: The Modern Law of Trusts, 9th ed., Sweet & Maxwell, London 2008

*Pearce, Stevens & Barr* The Law of Trusts and Equitable Obligations, 5th ed., Oxford University Press, London 2010

*Pettit* Equity & the Law of Trusts, 11th ed., Oxford University Press, London 2009

*Pollock, Sir* A First Book of Jurisprudence. For Students of the Common Law (originally published: Macmillan, London-New York, 1896), F.B. Rothman, Littleton, Colo., 1996

*Riddall* Land Law, 7th ed., Oxford University Press, London 2004

*Riddall* The Law of Trusts, 6th ed., LexisNexis Butterworths, London 2002

*Rogers* Winfield and Jolowicz on Tort, 18th ed., Sweet & Maxwell, London 2010 (cited as "Winfield and Jolowicz")

*Rose (Ed.)* Blackstone's Statutes on Contract, Tort and Restitution 2008-2009, 19th ed., Oxford University Press, London 2008

*Shears & Stephenson* James' Introduction to English Law, 13th ed., Oxford University Press, Oxford 2005 (cited as "James' Introduction ... ")

| | |
|---|---|
| *Standley* | Family Law, 7th ed., Palgrave Macmillan, Basingstoke 2010 |
| *Stapleton* | Product Liability (Law in Context), LexisNexis Butterworths, London 1994 |
| *Stevens, Pearce & Jackson* | Land Law, 4th ed., Sweet & Maxwell, London 2008 |
| *Tayfoor* | Law Cartoons: Tort, Sweet & Maxwell, London 1995 |
| *Templeman & Bell* | Land: The Law of Real Property – Old Bailey Press: Casebook, 2nd ed., London 1999 / Revision Work Book, 3rd ed., London 2004 / Textbook, 4th ed., London 2004 |
| *Templeman & Burr* | Conveyancing – Old Bailey Press: Casebook, 2nd ed., London 2004 / Revision Work Book, 1st ed., London 1997 / Textbook, 4th ed., London 2003 |
| *Templeman & Cutler* | Equity and Trusts - Old Bailey Press: Casebook, 3rd ed., London 2003 |
| *Templeman & Dodds* | Family Law – Old Bailey Press: Casebook, 3rd ed., London 2004 / Revision Work Book, 4th ed., London 2004 / Textbook, 4th ed., London 2003 |
| *Templeman & Doherty* | Equity and Trusts – Old Bailey Press: Revision Work Book, 4th ed., London 2004 |
| *Templeman & Halliwell* | Equity and Trusts – Old Bailey Press: Textbook, 4th ed., London 2003 |
| *Templeman & Pitchfork* | Obligations: The Law of Tort – Old Bailey Press: Casebook, 3rd ed., London 2004 / Revision Work Book, 3rd ed. / London 2004 / Textbook, 4th ed., London 2003 |
| *Templeman & Spedding* | Succession – Old Bailey Press: Casebook, 2nd ed., London 2000 / Revision Work Book, 3rd ed., London 2003 / Textbook, 3rd ed., London 2001 |
| *van Gerven, Lever & Larouche* | Tort Law (Common Law of Europe Casebooks), reprint edition, Hart Publishing, Oxford 2001 |

*Weir* — A Casebook on Tort, 10th ed., Sweet & Maxwell, London 2004

*Wild & Weinstein* — Smith & Keenan's English Law, 16th ed., Pearson Education Ltd, Harlow 2010

*Wilman* — Brown: GCSE Law, 9th ed., Sweet & Maxwell, London 2005

*Wragg* — Family Law (Nutshells), 8th ed., Sweet & Maxwell, London 2010

## II. English (and Anglo-American) law in German

*Bernstorff, Graf von* — Einführung in das englische Recht, 3. Aufl., C. H. Beck, München 2006

*Blumenwitz* — Einführung in das anglo-amerikanische Recht, 8. Aufl., C. H. Beck, München 2010

*Henrich & Huber* — Einführung in das englische Privatrecht, 3. Aufl., Recht und Wirtschaft, Darmstadt 2003

*Reimann* — Einführung in das US-amerikanische Privatrecht, 2. Aufl., C.H. Beck, München 2004

*Sacco* — Einführung in die Rechtsvergleichung, Nomos, Tübingen 2010

*Sachsen Gessaphe, Prinz von* — Rechtsvergleichung, C.H. Beck, München 2010

*Zweigert & Kötz* — Einführung in die Rechtsvergleichung auf dem Gebiete des Privatrechts, 3. neubearb. Aufl., Mohr Siebeck, Tübingen 1996

## III. English legal terminology

*Byrd* — Einführung in die Anglo-Amerikanische Rechtssprache, Band I, Introduction to Anglo-American Law & Language, 3. Aufl., C.H. Beck, München 2011

*Byrd* — Einführung in die Anglo-Amerikanische Rechtssprache, Band II/Vol. II Contracts and Torts, Introduction to Anglo-American Law & Language, 2. Aufl., C.H. Beck, München 2010

*Chartrand, Millar & Wiltshire* — English for Contract and Company Law, 3rd ed., Sweet & Maxwell, London 2009

*Heidinger & Hubalek* — Angloamerikanische Rechtssprache Band 1: Praxis-Handbuch für Rechtsanwälte, Wirtschaftsjuristen und Wirtschaftstreuhänder, 4. Aufl., LexisNexis ARD ORAC, Wien 2004

*Heidinger & Hubalek (Hrsg.)* — Angloamerikanische Rechtssprache Band 2: Praxis-Handbuch für Rechtsanwälte, Wirtschaftsjuristen und Wirtschaftstreuhänder, LexisNexis ARD ORAC, Wien 2011

*Linhart* — Englische Rechtssprache – Ein Studien- und Arbeitsbuch, C. H. Beck, München 2008

*Sims* — English Law and Terminology, 3. Aufl., Nomos, Tübingen 2010


## IV. Dictionary of legal (and commercial) terms


*Alpmann (Hrsg.)* — Langenscheidt Alpmann, Fachwörterbuch Kompakt Recht, Englisch, 2. Aufl., Langenscheidt Fachverlag, Berlin – München – Wien – Zürich – New York 2009

*Collin, Janssen & Kornmüller* — PONS Fachwörterbuch Recht Englisch-Deutsch, Deutsch-Englisch, 2. Aufl., PONS GmbH, Stuttgart 2005

*Dietl & Lorenz* — Wörterbuch für Recht, Wirtschaft und Politik = Dictionary of Legal, Commercial and Political Terms Band I: Englisch-Deutsch, 7. Aufl., C. H. Beck, München 2011

*Dietl & Lorenz* — Wörterbuch für Recht, Wirtschaft und Politik = Dictionary of Legal, Commercial and Political Terms Band II: Deutsch-Englisch, 5. Aufl., C. H. Beck, München 2005

| | |
|---|---|
| *Flory & Froschauer* | Grundwortschatz der Rechtssprache. Deutsch-Englisch/Englisch-Deutsch, 3. Aufl., Luchterhand, Neuwied 2005 |
| *Köbler* | Rechtsenglisch – Deutsch-englisches und englisch-deutsches Rechtswörterbuch für jedermann, 7. Aufl., Vahlen, München 2007 |
| *Romain, Bader & Byrd* | Wörterbuch der Rechts- und Wirtschaftssprache Teil 1: Englisch-Deutsch, 5. Aufl., C.H. Beck, München 1999 |
| *Romain, Byrd & Thielecke* | Wörterbuch der Rechts- und Wirtschaftssprache Teil 2: Deutsch-Englisch, 4. Aufl., C. H. Beck, München 2002 |

# Chapter Seven

## Tort Law[1]

Deliktsrecht/Recht der unerlaubten Handlung

## I. The meaning of the term tort

Begriff

Lunney & Oliphant's Tort Law (p.1) introduces the concept of tort as follows:

"The law of tort – the word derives from the French for 'wrong' – is the law of civil liability for wrongfully inflicted injury .... Tort itself is a very old concept, older even than the concept of crime .... Tort was a form of legalised selfhelp .... The other civil jurisdictions in Europe ... take varying positions, some more closely aligned with the French approach, some with the German. The English Law of Tort stands in stark contrast."

Haftung

Thus, an English-German dictionary of legal terms defines *tort* as „unerlaubte Handlung, (zivilrechtliches) Delikt, Vergehen", accordingly. The adjective *tortious* is translated as „unerlaubt, deliktisch". A *tortious act* means „unerlaubte Handlung" (in terms of German civil law). There is also the term „unerlaubte Handlung" as a translation for *trespass* (meaning also: „Besitzstörung, Übertretung, Zuwiderhandlung, unbefugtes Betreten"). This reveals that the **torts** and **trespasses** of English civil law are only, in part, congruent with the German „unerlaubte Handlung".

Rechtswörterbuch

verdeutlichen

teilweise – deckungsgleich

According to German civil law (*§ 823 ff. BGB*), „unerlaubte Handlung" means an unlawful, culpable act, which injures the rights of another person who thereby suffers damage.

gemäß

widerrechtl. – schuldhaft – verletzen

Rechte (und Rechtsgüter!) – Schaden erleiden

The **meaning** of *tort* is **wider**. *Tort* includes facts and situations which, in German law, not only entitle a claimant to an action for damages, but also give rise to other claims, such as, for example, a claim for restitution, a claim for an injunction or a claim for interference with possession.

Tatbestand

berechtigen – Schadensersatzklage

zur Folge haben

Herausgabeanspruch – *hier*: Unterlassungsanspruch – Besitzstörung

**Tort law** is a **collection of separate torts** which have grown over time to produce a patchwork of liabilities. The result of their historical evolution over a long period of time is that these separate torts are not systemised.

sich entwickeln/anwachsen

Flickenteppich von Haftungstatbeständen

in ein System bringen/systematisieren

1 There is an (ongoing) academic dispute over the terminology of "law of tort" versus „Law of torts" (plural). In order to avoid this unsettled question and in accordance with numerous relevant textbooks, the authors have decided to use the term "Tort Law" as headline for the following chapter.

herrühren/stammen – mittelalterlich

The oldest torts (e.g. *trespass* or e.g. *detinue* – cf. vol. 1, chapter 2, p. 28 "writ of detinue") derive from medieval common law.

altertümlich/veraltet
Genugtuung – geschädigte Partei – Kläger/Antragsteller/Beschwerdeführer – Billigkeitsrechtsprechung – Mangel/Unzulänglichkeit – Klageschrift/schriftl. gerichtl. Anweisung

The archaic common law with its few remedies was, in many cases, not able to give satisfaction to the injured party (i.e. the claimant). This led to a *jurisdiction in equity* being developed by the Lord Chancellor.[2] Do you remember the deficiency of the old common law: "No writ, no remedy"? (If not, cf. vol. 1, chapter two, p. 27).

Universal-/Allzweck-
zivilrechtlicher Verstoß/Unrecht
Verletzung/Schaden
Körperverletzung
*etwa*: bloßes Betreten eines Grundstücks – *etwa*: unbefugtes Betreten von Vieh – Geltungsbereich

The most important all-purpose writ which covered common civil wrongs in medieval law was **trespass**. A writ of trespass was available for all *direct injury to persons, goods, or land*. Thus, suffering injury oneself, e.g. by battery, damage to personal goods, to gates, hedges, land, or mere entry upon land or cattle trespass, fell within the ambit of *trespass*.

betrügerisch/unehrlich
verdreht/entstellt
bezeichnen – Straftat

The **word tort** derives from the Latin "tortus", meaning crooked or twisted, and the French "tort", meaning wrong. In English law, the word *tort* is used to denote *civil* wrongs, as opposed to *criminal acts*.

We can summarise so far that **trespass** is a **particular type of tort**. So how can we define *tort* in modern terms?

Lehrbuch
*hier*: unterschiedlich
feststellen
in erster Linie
wiedergutmachen/abhelfen
Aufgabenkreis/Gebiet
zuweisen – Verantwortlichkeit – schädliches Verhalten

Let us consult two of the leading textbooks on the law of tort: Salmond & Heuston and Winfield & Jolowicz. According to Salmond, a *tort* is "a civil wrong for which the remedy is a common law action for unquantified damages, and which is not exclusively the breach of a contract or the breach of trust or other merely equitable obligation." Winfield asserts that "tortious liability arises from the breach of a duty primarily fixed by law; such duty is towards persons generally, and its breach is redressable by an action for unquantified damages". According to Lord Denning[3] "the province of a tort is to allocate responsibility for injurious conduct."

## II. Trespass

Oberbegriff

The term *trespass* comprises several torts. There is no corresponding umbrella term in German. The *three types of trespass* are:

2 Der Lord Chancellor war bis 2006 Sprecher/Vorsitzender des House of Lords. Heute ist er nicht mehr Oberhaupt der Justiz und übt nur noch exekutive Tätigkeiten aus, ist z.B. auch Justizminister (seit 2007). Zur allgemeinen Gerichtsorganisation in England vgl. vol. 1, chapter 2, p. 30, 38 ff.

3 Lord Denning, gestorben 1999, war wohl der einflussreichste englische Richter des 20. Jahrhunderts und Master of the Rolls.

- trespass to the person
- trespass to goods
- trespass to land.

## 1. Trespass to the person

Verletzung der Rechte einer Person

This tort covers a selection of ways in which an individual may suffer interference from others. At common law, it comprises *three forms:* **civil assault** – as distinguished from criminal assault -, **battery** and **false (unlawful) imprisonment**.

erfassen
umfassen
Bedrohung – Körperverletzung
Freiheitsberaubung

There is also a new statutory tort of *harassment* which tends to be viewed as a form of trespass to the person. It has been used in a variety of situations, e.g. stalking, domestic violence, neighbour disputes and protest situations. This tort was created by the *Protection from Harassment Act 1997*.

Belästigung

### a) Civil assault

Bedrohung

Contrary to common belief, to *assault* someone is to cause him intentionally *to expect* immediate harm or offensive physical violence. If you do actually *touch* that person, that is *battery*. One legal definition of *civil assault* is that it is "an act of the defendant which causes the claimant reasonable apprehension of the infliction of a battery on him by the defendant" (Winfield & Jolowicz).

allgemeine Auffassung – angreifen/tätl. bedrohen – bewusst/vorsätzlich
körperliche Gewalt
Befürchtung/Besorgnis
Zufügung

There are several ways in which you can assault someone, even without touching him. For example by threatening words ("Your money, or your life!"),[4] by shaking your fist in a threatening manner as a boxer, or by pointing a weapon at him. It is also possible to assault someone with a harmless object, since the essential element in assault is the **reasonable expectation of violence**, in the terms of reasonable *fear,* the word used in old cases.

drohend(en)
mit der Faust drohen
eine Waffe richten auf

When, for example, A points a gun at B, which A knows to be unloaded, though B does not, and it is so near that it might produce injury if it were loaded and went off, this constitutes an *assault*. An extreme example is found in a criminal case reported in *The Times* on 21 January 1991, where a man was jailed for six years for attempting

bewirken
losgehen – darstellen
einsperren – versuchen

4 In the days of horse-drawn travel, this was the threat voiced by a highwayman when he held up a stagecoach.

Wegelagerer
Postkutsche

begehen
Gefängnisaufenthalt – strafbare Handlung/Vergehen/Delikt

to rob a bank with a banana. The robbery was committed on the day he had finished a prison sentence for a similar offence.

Körperverletzung

## b) Battery

Anwendung
Rechtfertigungsgrund
darstellen/begründen – spucken
(aus)gießen – einen Stuhl wegziehen

*Battery* is the **direct** and **intentional application of physical force** to another person without lawful justification. *Any physical contact* may constitute *force*. So battery may be committed by spitting at someone, pouring water over him, snatching a chair away as he sits down or throwing a stone at him.

*hier*: Umfang – Alltag
Drängeln – Menschen(warte)schlange
stillschweigende Einwilligung

However, a certain amount of contact in everyday life would not constitute a battery. For instance: jostling in a queue or stepping on someone's foot in a crowd does not constitute battery, because it is considered that one has given implied consent to such things happening.

schon der/die/das bloße – unerlaubte Berührung – unabhängig von
gleichkommen – körperlich
*hier*: vernünftiger Mensch/verständige Person

On the other hand, mere unauthorised touching would constitute battery, regardless of the motive. A kiss given by a stranger constitutes battery, as it amounts to intentional bodily contact and a reasonable person would not have consented to the act.

Freiheitsentziehung/-beraubung

## c) Unlawful imprisonment

Zufügung
Einschränkung der Bewegungsfreiheit
widerrechtlich – berauben
gefallen – nötig sein
Einschließung – Gefängniszelle
Freiheitsentzug – unangemessen/unzumutbar – (be)hindern
jdm. etw. freistellen

*Unlawful (or false) imprisonment* consists of the infliction of complete bodily restraint on another without lawful justification. This may happen whenever a person is wrongfully deprived of his liberty to go where he pleases. Thus, there need be no imprisonment such as incarceration in a prison cell. The mere holding of the arm of another against his will is sufficient. The imprisonment, however, must be for an unreasonable length of time and must be a **total loss of freedom.** Thus, to restrain a person from going in three directions but, at the same time, leaving him free to go in a fourth, is not unlawful imprisonment.

*hier*: stilllegen
Einzäunung
versperren
weitergehen – Hindernis

*Example – Bird v Jones (1845)*

A bridge company lawfully blocked a public footpath on Hammersmith Bridge in London by creating an enclosure for spectators to pay to watch a boat race taking place on the River Thames. Mr Bird claimed he was entitled to use the footpath and so did not have to pay to enter the enclosure, but was stopped by two policemen who barred his entry to the enclosure. Mr Bird was told he might proceed to another point around the obstruction

but that he could not go forward. He declined and after half an hour, attempted to force his way forward. He injured Mr Jones in the process, and was arrested. He claimed that he had been unlawfully imprisoned by the police officers.
***Held:*** that there was no **unlawful imprisonment** since Mr Bird was free to go another way.

ablehnen/sich weigern – versuchte sich mit Gewalt einen Weg zu bahnen – dabei ... verletzen – für Recht erkennen

It is possible that the person imprisoned might even be unaware of it at the time. So a person can be imprisoned whilst asleep, whilst in a state of drunkenness or whilst in a state of insanity. There is **no need for the person affected to know** about the constraint.

Unzurechnungsfähigkeit/Geisteskrankheit

*Example – Meering v Graham-White Aviation Co Ltd (1919)*

An employee was suspected of stealing a keg of varnish from his employer. Two works security officers asked the employee to go with them to the works' office to answer questions. The employee, not realising that he was suspected, agreed to go with them and even suggested a short cut. He remained in the office for some time during which security officers stayed outside the room without his knowledge. He later claimed that he had been unlawfully imprisoned, and the question arose whether the person claiming *unlawful imprisonment* must actually know the other person is restraining his freedom.
***Held:*** that the employee had been imprisoned and his **knowledge was irrelevant** to the question of liability. The extent of his knowledge might, however, be relevant when it came to calculating the amount of his damages.

Fässchen – Lack – Werks- – verdächtigt – zustimmen – Abkürzung – aufkommen – überhaupt/eigentlich/wirklich – Haftbarkeit/Verantwortlichkeit

**All forms of trespass to the person**, civil assault, battery and unlawful imprisonment, are – unlike negligence, which we will deal with further below – **actionable *per se***. That means that there is **no need to prove damage** in order to bring a claim. Liability arises if the defendant commits the relevant act without any requirement that the claimant suffers harm. The claimant, however, must prove, that the defendant *intended* to do what he did (intention or intent) or was at the very least *reckless* that what he was about to do would have the consequence which happened (recklessness).

anders als/im Gegensatz zu – (ein)klagbar/belangbar als solche – um zu/zwecks – *hier*: entstehen – Absicht/Vorsatz – allermindestens – *wörtlich*: sorglos/unbekümmert – *hier*: grobe Fahrlässigkeit

Jagdgesellschaft
Verletzung
*hier*: Schaden
ab-/bestreiten/in Abrede stellen
behaupten
fahrlässig

Beweislast/pflicht
*hier*: liegen bei/tragen
juristische Vorfrage

in der Tat/sogar – *hier:* zurücknehmen

*Example – Fowler v Lanning (1959)*

There was a shooting party on a farm in Dorset. Mr Fowler was injured, and claimed against Mr Lanning for his injuries and other losses, on the ground that he had been injured by Lanning. Lanning denied that he was liable, because Mr Fowler had not alleged that he, Lanning, had intended to injure him or had been negligent.

***Held:*** that in an action for *trespass to the person*, it was necessary to prove intent or negligence on the part of the defendant. The **onus of proof** in respect of the defendant's intent or negligence **lies with the claimant**. The court in this case was asked to decide this as a preliminary point of law. As Fowler had not claimed in his action that Lanning had intentionally or negligently injured him, his claim was in effect cancelled before it could get fully to court.

vorsätzlich – grob fahrlässig

Note that the report of this case talks of the need to prove that the injury had been caused *intentionally* or *negligently*, but the modern law in relation to trespass is that the injury must have been caused either **intentionally** or **recklessly**. A person injured only negligently may, however, have a claim for the tort of negligence – see below.

Verteidigungsvorbringen/Rechtfertigungsgrund

### d) Defences

Einwilligung
Notwehr
*etwa*: vorläufige Festnahme

There are primarily *three possible defences* available in an action for *trespass to the person*:

- **consent** (which may be express or implied),
- **self-defence** and
- **lawful arrest**.

freiwillig
Begehung

It goes without saying that a person who has voluntarily *consented* to the commission of a tort may not sue on it. **Consent** (in Latin: "volenti") is a *general defence* available when a claimant gives his consent with prior knowledge of the risk involved.

verhältnismäßig
zur Verteidigung

Einzelfallumstände

**Self-defence** must be proportional to the attack, which means that no more force may be used in defence than is reasonably necessary. What is reasonable is a matter for the court to decide on the particular facts of each case.

Haftbefehl – Straftat
befürchten
schuldig

A private individual has certain limited powers to **arrest** someone – i.e. without warrant – when either a more serious criminal offence has been committed and he has reasonable grounds to suspect that the person whom he wishes to arrest is guilty of having committed the offence, or if he has reasonable grounds to suspect that the person he wishes to arrest is actually committing a more serious criminal offence – *s.24A Police and Criminal Evidence Act 1984* (cf. *§ 229 BGB* or *§ 127 StPO* in German law). There are also several other conditions in the legislation, and of course the powers of the police are considerably wider.

## 2. Trespass to goods

verbotene Eigenmacht ggü. beweglichen Sachen

According to the *Torts (Interference with Goods) Act 1977, s.1,* **wrongful interference with goods** includes (1) trespass to goods, (2) conversion of goods and (3) negligence or any other tort so far as it results in damage to goods or to an interest in goods.

*etwa*: rechtswidrige Sachstörung
*etwa*: Unterschlagung
Waren/Güter/Artikel

**Wrongful interference by trespass to goods (1)** is a wrong against the *personal property* (see more details in chapter 8, section II.2) of another, more precisely against his *possession* of goods. Goods are moveable assets.

bewegliche Sache

*Trespass to goods* is essentially a **tort against possession**, which means that it is not necessary that the possessor also be the owner. Possession under English law is a difficult topic, which is considered more fully in the next chapter on property law, section III.2. For the moment, it will be sufficient to say that a person possesses goods when he has some form of control over them, together with the intention to exclude others from possession and to hold the goods on his own behalf. Possession must exist at the moment when the wrongful interference is committed. However, possession does not necessarily involve an actual grasp of the goods; often a lesser degree of control will be sufficient.

Thema/Gegenstand
ausführlicher
ausreichend
ausschließen
für sich selbst
Zugriff

*Example – The Tubantia (1924)*

The claimant, a marine salvage company, was trying to salvage the cargo of the *SS Tubantia* which had sunk in the North Sea. He had discovered the wreck and marked it with a marker buoy. His divers were already working in the hold, when the defendant, a rival salvage company, appeared on the scene and started to send divers down to salvage the cargo from the wreck.
***Held:*** that irrespective of who was the owner of the property salvaged, the claimant was sufficiently in *possession* of the wreck to found an **action in trespass**.

Schiffsbergungsgesellschaft – bergen
Wrack – Markierungsboje
*hier*: Rumpf/Lagerraum
konkurrierend
begründen

The *wrongful interference by trespass to goods* must be **direct** and effected **by force**.

gewaltsam

schnappen – treten
löschen – Tonbandaufnahme
kratzen – Blech

This may consist of moving an object or throwing something at it. Examples of *trespass to goods* are: to snatch someone's hat, to kick someone's dog, to erase a tape-recording, to throw another's book out of the window or to scratch the panel of a car.

streng (*hier*: ohne Verschuldensnachweis) – einreichen – unrechtmäßige Besitzergreifung

The liability in such cases of *trespass to goods* would **not** appear to be **strict.** Most actions under the tort *trespass to goods* are brought as a result of **intentional dispossession.** Mere negligence may not suffice, however. This follows a similar development in the tort of *trespass to the person* which began with the decision in *Fowler* v *Lanning (1959),* dealt with above.

Let us take a look at other forms of *wrongful interference with goods:*

Unterschlagung
sich einmischen/behindern

Gegenstand von – Abzahlungskauf

*hier*: Besitzanspruch/unbestreitbarer Rechtstitel – Eigentum(srecht)

**Wrongful interference by conversion (2)** arises when the defendant intentionally interferes with goods in a way that may be regarded as *complete denying* the claimant's rights of possession or use. Mere interference with possession is not enough. If, for example, a car – subject to a hire-purchase agreement – is sold to a private person, the seller would, in such a case, have given the buyer a good title and at the same time denied the hire-purchase company the right of ownership of the car. In that case, the hire-purchase company can sue the seller for *conversion*.

Abholung
Lastwagenfahrer

mit leeren Händen
auf Herausgabe

zurückerwerben
aufrechterhalten

| *Example – Jarvis v Williams (1955)* |
|---|
| Jarvis agreed to sell some bathroom fittings to Peterson. At Peterson's request he delivered them to Williams. Peterson refused to pay the price and Jarvis agreed to take them back if Peterson would pay for collection. Peterson accepted this offer and Jarvis sent his lorryman, with a letter of authority, to collect the fittings but he was told that he could not take them, so he returned empty-handed. Jarvis claimed against Williams in conversion for the return of the goods.<br>***Held:*** that on the delivery to Williams, the property in the goods passed to Peterson, and the arrangement for re-collection did not revest the property in Jarvis. It follows that, at the time of collection, Jarvis had no right of property in the goods to sustain an **action in conversion**. |

| *Example – Parker v British Airways Board (1982)* |
|---|
| The claimant was in B.A.'s first-class lounge at Heathrow airport, London waiting for a flight. He found a gold bracelet on the floor and gave it to an employee of B.A. together with his name and address, asking that it should be returned to him if not claimed. It was not claimed but B.A. sold it. The claimant sued in **conversion**.<br>***Held:*** that the claimant was entitled to the proceeds of sale. |

Armreif

wegen Unterschlagung klagen

Erlös

In general, liability for *wrongful interference by conversion* is **strict** and it is not necessary for the claimant to prove that the defendant had a wrongful intention, though sometimes it may be a defence for the defendant to say that he acted honestly.

Loss of goods by the **negligence** of the defendant **(3)** is not *conversion* but the claimant may now sue under the provisions of the *Torts (Interference with Goods) Act 1977* for damage to goods caused by negligence.

Another form of *wrongful interference with goods* is the **detention of goods.** *S.2 (1)* of the *Torts (Interference with Goods) Act 1977* abolishes the old tort of detinue (as yet mentioned above), which was a tort relating to detention of goods. Mere detention can now amount to conversion. In other words, detinue and conversion are merged.

Vorenthaltung

abschaffen

verschmelzen

## 3. Trespass to land

Besitzstörung an Land /verbotene Eigenmacht ggü. unbewegl. Sachen

### a) Definition and examples

*Trespass to land* is the **unlawful entry** of a person or thing **onto land** or into buildings **in the possession of another**. Salmond & Heuston define *trespass to land* as: "Entering upon land in the possession of the claimant or remaining upon such land or placing any object upon it, in each case without lawful justification".

Eindringen/Betreten

**Examples** of trespass to land are: leaving parcels on the wrong person's doorstep, leaning a ladder against the wall of the neighbour's house, throwing something into or entering oneself into another's forecourt and removing a dustbin.

Paket

Türschwelle – anlehnen

Vorhof/Vorgarten – entfernen – Mülleimer

unbefugt betreten/eindringen
Eingriff in – wie gering auch immer

To *trespass on land*, one does not even need to step onto the land. Putting one's hand through a window would be enough. Every invasion of property, however small, is a *trespass to land*.

Pächter/Mieter – einstöckig
gerichtliche Verfügung
Werbeschild – anzeigen
vorkragen/hereinragen – Luftraum
1 inch = 2,54 cm
Entfernung

| *Example – Kelson v Imperial Tobacco Co (1957)* |
|---|
| The claimant was the tenant of a one-storey tobacconist's shop and brought an action against the defendants, seeking an injunction requiring them to remove, from the wall above the shop, a large cigarette advertising sign displaying the words 'Players Please'. The sign projected into the airspace above the claimant's shop to the extent of some eight inches. The claimant claimed that the defendants, by fixing the sign in that position, had trespassed on his airspace.<br>***Held:*** that the invasion of airspace by a sign of this nature constituted a *trespass* and, **although the claimant's injury was small**, it was an appropriate case in which to grant an injunction for the removal of the sign. |

freiwillig
willentlich – Irrtum/Missverständnis
mähen

It is, however, important to note that if a person is pushed or thrown onto land, he is not there voluntarily so cannot be held liable; on the contrary, it is the person who pushed him there who may be liable. If the trespass is done deliberately, mistake is no excuse. The defendant need not be aware that he is trespassing. So, for example, if you mow grass thinking it is yours when, in fact, it belongs to your neighbour, you would be committing a *trespass to land*.

Mündung
entladen – wieder flottmachen
Flut
Vorküste
*hier*: schlüssig/zulässig sein
geltend machen
üblich/vorherrschend
daraus folgend/*hier*: eine Folge sein
Revision

| *Example – Southport Corporation v Esso Petroleum Co (1957)* |
|---|
| The Esso company's tanker became stranded in the estuary of a river. The master of the tanker discharged oil in order to refloat the ship. The action of the wind and tide took the oil onto the Corporation's foreshore and caused damage. The Corporation sued in trespass and negligence. At first instance, the court thought that trespass would lie, but the Court of Appeal contended that there could be no trespass because the injury was not direct, but was caused by the tides and prevailing winds; in trespass, **the injury must be direct** and not consequential.<br>***Held:*** that there was no *trespass*. *Note* that there was also an appeal based on *negligence*, but the defendants were held not to have been negligent. |

*Trespass to land* can even be committed without physically touching the land. Moreover, one should also note that, with regard to ownership of land, the air above it also belongs to it – to such height as is necessary for the ordinary enjoyment of the land. Thus, it constitutes an *actionable wrong* to fly a kite, or send a message by carrier pigeon, or ascend in an aeroplane, or fire a bullet over it, as in the so called "Tasmanian cat case": *Davies* v *Bennison (1927)*, where the defendant shot a cat on the claimant's roof. The claimant was entitled to damages for *trespass to land* as well as for the value of the cat.

Drachen steigen lassen
Brieftaube – aufsteigen – eine Kugel abfeuern
Dach
und auch/ebenso wie/sowie

*Example – Woollerton and Wilson v Richard Costain (Midlands) Ltd (1969)*

In this case, the first instance court granted the owners of a factory and warehouse in Leicester (in central England) an injunction restraining the defendants from trespassing on and invading airspace over their premises by means of a swinging crane.
***Held*** (on appeal by the defendants): that the injunction was suspended for twelve months to enable the defendants to complete their work, the defendants having offered to pay for the right to continue to trespass and to provide insurance cover for neighbouring properties. It was also held that, for a claim for trespass to be successful, no actual harm to the claimant is needed.

eindringen
Gelände – schwingender Kran
aufschieben
Versicherungsschutz

The **four elements of trespass to land** can be summarised as follows:

- **direct** interference with the land,
- **voluntary** interference,
- **no need of awareness** of trespass on the part of the defendant and
- **no requirement for harm or damage**.

The last element shows that this kind of tort is also **actionable *per se*** in the same way as *trespass to the person*.

## b) Defences

Entry onto land does not constitute the tort of *trespass to land* if it is justifiable. There are *four main defences* to *trespass to land*:

berechtigt/gerechtfertigt

- **consent:** a person who has permission to enter is not a trespasser;

- **contractual licence**: such as payment of an entry fee or purchase of tickets for a sporting event;
- **lawful authority:** particular people may have permission to enter such as court bailiffs and the police (*Police and Criminal Evidence Act 1984*);
- **necessity:** this justifies trespass in emergency situations to deal with a perceived threat.

Gerichtsvollzieher

Notlage/Notstand

vermutete/subjektiv wahrgenommene Gefahr

### c) Remedies

Rechtsmittel/-behelf/Rechtsschutzmöglichkeit/Klagebegehren

The following remedies are available to a claimant:

- **damages:** this is, in general, the amount by which the value of the land is diminished as a result of the trespass, but not the cost of reinstatement;
- **injunction:** this may be used to stop the defendant from continuing or repeating the trespass; the claimant may apply to the court for both damages and an injunction;
- **self-help:** the occupier of the land may eject a trespasser after first requesting him to leave and giving him reasonable time to do so; no more force may be used than is reasonable in the circumstances, otherwise, the occupier himself may be sued for assault and/or battery. Self-help can also be used to remove objects placed on or over one's land, e.g. to cut down branches from overhanging trees, but the branches so removed should be returned to the owner of the tree;
- **possession order:** if a trespasser has full possession of land, an order for possession must be obtained to restore possession of the land to its rightful owner.

jdm. zur Verfügung stehen

Schadensersatz

geringer werden/vermindern

Wiederinstandsetzung

einstweilige/gerichtliche Verfügung

ersuchen

Selbsthilfe – hinauswerfen – Besitzstörer – auffordern

Äste

gerichtliche Anordnung der Wiederinbesitznahme – jmd. wieder zu etwas verhelfen

**Diagram 38**

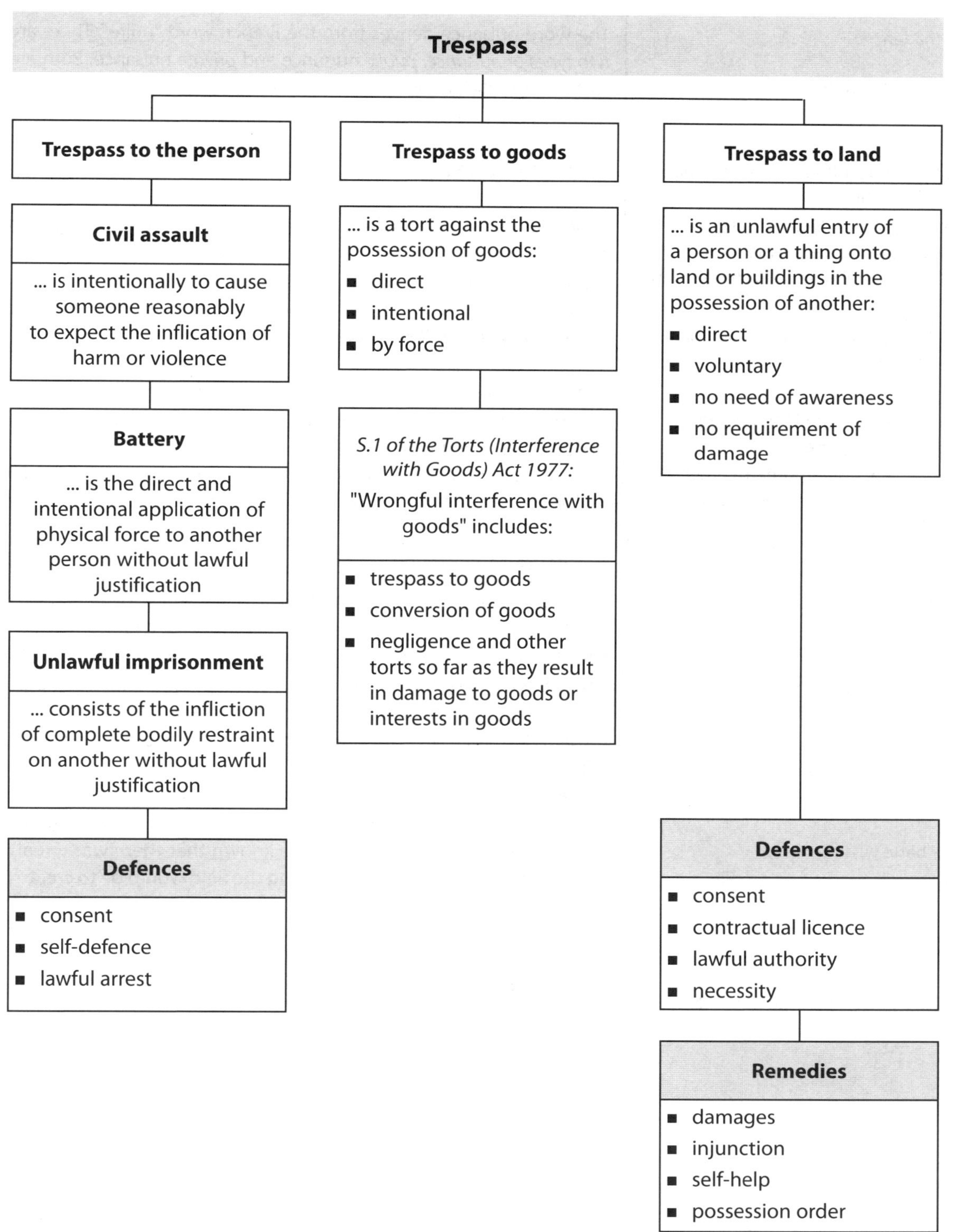
Trespass
Trespass to the person
Civil assault
... is intentionally to cause someone reasonably to expect the inflication of harm or violence
Battery
... is the direct and intentional application of physical force to another person without lawful justification
Unlawful imprisonment
... consists of the infliction of complete bodily restraint on another without lawful justification
Defences
consent
self-defence
lawful arrest
Trespass to goods
... is a tort against the possession of goods:
direct
intentional
by force
S.1 of the Torts (Interference with Goods) Act 1977:
"Wrongful interference with goods" includes:
trespass to goods
conversion of goods
negligence and other torts so far as they result in damage to goods or interests in goods
Trespass to land
... is an unlawful entry of a person or a thing onto land or buildings in the possession of another:
direct
voluntary
no need of awareness
no requirement of damage
Defences
consent
contractual licence
lawful authority
necessity
Remedies
damages
injunction
self-help
possession order

## III. Nuisance

Beeinträchtigung/Störung
schaden
Strafdelikt/Verbrechen

The word nuisance derives from the French word "nuire". There are *two types of nuisance: public* nuisance and *private* nuisance. Both are **torts**, but public nuisance is also a crime.

### 1. Public nuisance

Störung der öffentlichen Sicherheit und Ordnung

Tun oder Unterlassen – gefährden
etw. stören/beeinträchtigen/in Konflikt geraten mit – Wohlbefinden
Gruppe
erheblich/wesentlich – beeinträchtigen/betreffen

*Public nuisance* consists of an unlawful act or omission endangering or interfering with the lives, comfort, safety, property, or common rights of the public. Whereas *private* nuisance may affect only one person, *public* nuisance is something which requires that **a class of people be materially affected.**

erzeugen – in großem Umfang
behindern/sperren
unhygienisch/verdorben – errichten
Fabrik – emittieren – übermäßig

Examples of the tort (and crime) of *public nuisance* are: organising a pop music festival which generates large-scale noise and traffic, obstructing a highway or making it dangerous for traffic, selling unhygienic food, throwing fireworks into the street or erecting a factory which emits excessive smoke.

| *Example – R.* v Shorrock (1993)* |
|---|
| The defendant let a field on his farm for a weekend for £2,000. He did not know for what purpose the field was let and he went away for the weekend. The field was used for an "acid house party" which was attended by more than 3,000 people and created a great deal of noise. The police received nearly 300 complaints. The defendant was convicted of causing a public nuisance and fined. ***Held*** (by the Court of Appeal): that it was not necessary for the Crown** to prove that the defendant had actual knowledge of the nuisance, as he ought to have known that there was a real risk that the consequences of letting the field would be to create this sort of nuisance. |

vermieten
aufsuchen/besuchen
eine Menge an – Beschwerden
verurteilt
mit Geldstrafe belegen
er hätte wissen müssen

* R. means Regina.

** The Crown, represented by the Director of Public Prosecutions (cf. vol. 1, p. 71), is the prosecutor, because public nuisance is a crime.

Staatsanwalt/Vertreter der Anklage

| Example – *Attorney-General* v *Gastonia Coaches (1976)* | |
|---|---|
| Gastonia were coach operators and owned 22 coaches, of which 16 were parked in residential roads adjoining the Gastonia offices. No matter how carefully these coaches were parked, they inevitably interfered with the free passage of other traffic.<br>***Held*** (in an action by the Attorney-General): that Gastonia were committing a *public nuisance*. An injunction was issued preventing Gastonia from parking the vehicles on the highway. Damages were also awarded to Gastonia's neighbours who had suffered from the emissions of exhaust gases, excessive noise and obstruction of their drives. | Busunternehmer<br>Wohnstraße – angrenzen<br>behindern<br>Generalstaatsanwalt<br>ausfertigen/*hier*: erlassen<br>Auspuffgas<br>Behinderung der Zufahrt |

The Attorney-General is a Government minister, and he has power to protect a group of people who are suffering from breach of the criminal law, in this case the **crime** of public nuisance, which is a matter of *public law*. However, public nuisance is also a **tort**. Where **particular harm** (e.g. personal injury, discomfort, damage to property or economic loss) is suffered by individual persons who are different from that of the general public, those individual persons can also bring a *private law* claim for damages. This **requirement of special damage** for a claim on the ground of public nuisance limits the multitude of claims that would succeed if public nuisance were actionable on the basis of interference only.

spezifische Beeinträchtigung
Allgemeinheit/Öffentlichkeit

| Example *Castle* v *St Augustine's Links (1922)* | |
|---|---|
| On 18th August 1919, a taxi was driving along the road from Deal to Ramsgate (in the south-east England, not far from Canterbury and Dover). The road led past a golf course. A golf ball was hit off the course and struck the windscreen of the taxi, breaking it. A piece of glass from the broken windscreen injured the driver's eye and he had to have his eye removed. The driver claimed against the owner of the golf course.<br>***Held:*** that the proximity of the hole to the road constituted a **public nuisance**, and so the owner of the golf course was liable for the injury caused. The injured driver was awarded damages of £450. | Golfplatz<br>entfernen |

To summarise: There are two requirements that must be satisfied regarding *public nuisance*:

(1) the nuisance has affected **a class of people** and
(2) the claimant has suffered **special damage**.

Before dealing with *private nuisance* let us recapitulate that the distinction between these torts – public and private nuisance – is based upon *the effect* of the nuisance, *not the nature* of the nuisance itself.

verbotene Besitzstörung (des Einzelnen)

## 2. Private nuisance

The tort of *private nuisance* consists of unlawful interference with a person's *land* or his use or enjoyment of it. Here, a **person with a proprietary right or interest must be affected.**

### a) Requirements

unzumutbar/unangemessen
zum Nachteil/Schaden von
sich richten nach – vernünftiger Mensch/verständige Person
Arglist/Böswilligkeit – vorübergehend

"The very essence of private nuisance ... is the unreasonable use by a man of his land to the detriment of his neighbour", as Lord Denning stated in *Miller* v *Jackson (1977)*. What is *reasonable* is based on the conduct of **the reasonable person**. It will depend on such factors as time, place, presence or absence of malice and whether the effects are temporary or permanent.

Thus, there are two initial requirements for *private nuisance*:

(1) **the protection of land or property**
(2) from **unreasonable interference**
(3) besides the third requirement, the **damage**.

That is to say, in contrast to trespass (cf. above), private nuisance is **not actionable *per se***. Some **damage** must have occurred to enable the claimant to sue.

etw. beeinträchtigen/stören
auf etwas hinauslaufen
lästige Gerüche – Flecken
Wäsche – Abwasser ansammeln

There are many ways of interfering with someone's enjoyment of his land which may amount to nuisance: for example, excessive noise, offensive smells, factory pollution leaving dirty marks on washing or allowing sewage to collect on land.

The basic rule is that you should **use your property without causing harm to any other person** (as a German law student or lawyer, at this point you should remember *§ 903 S. 1 BGB*, which contains the same maxim).

| *Example – Kennaway v Thompson (1980)* |
|---|
| The defendants represented a club at which motor-boat racing and water-skiing were carried on. In 1972 the claimant moved into a house which she had had built near to the lake on which the above activities were carried out, as they had been since the early 1960s. After the claimant moved in, the nature of the club's activities increased in frequency and noise because large powerboats took part in international meetings. Those were preceded by periods of noisy practice. The claimant sought *damages for nuisance and an injunction*.<br>***Held:*** that at first instance only damages were awarded – £1,000 for the past nuisance and £15,000 in respect of future nuisance – since the court regarded it as oppressive to issue an injunction to prevent the club from continuing its activities on the ground that this was contrary to the public interest.<br>The Court of Appeal allowed the claimant's appeal and awarded an injunction, stating that the public interest should not prevail over the private interest of a person affected by a continuing nuisance. Accordingly the claimant was entitled to an injunction under which the club was ordered to curtail its activities, restricting noisy meetings to a limited number of occasions. |

vertreten

Rennboot

vorausgehen

zusprechen/gewähren

unterdrückend/einschränkend

einschränken

In this case the court stated: "The question is whether the neighbour [i.e. the defendant] is using his property reasonably, having regard to the fact that he has a neighbour [i.e. the claimant]. The neighbour who is complaining must remember, too, that the other man can use his property in a reasonable way and there must be a measure of give and take, live and let live".

leben und leben lassen

## b) Unreasonable use of land

In considering whether an act or omission is a nuisance, the courts have taken the following factors into account when determining whether or not the particular **use of land is unreasonable** (we will see below that in the case of the tort of negligence, the claimant has to prove that the defendant's *conduct* is unreasonable).

beachten/berücksichtigen

### *aa) Health and comfort*

Gesundheit und Wohlbefinden

There need be no direct injury to health. It is sufficient that a person has been prevented, to an appreciable extent, from enjoying the ordinary comforts of life. This is because the purpose of the tort of nuisance is to protect a person's interest in his *land* rather than in

hindern – spürbar/merklich

his *person*. If injury has been suffered, the claim would be in *negligence* (see below) rather than in *nuisance*.

### *bb) Character of the neighbourhood*

Gegend
Wohngebiet
belebt/geschäftig/betriebsam

The standard of comfort that a person is entitled to expect will vary from area to area (character of the neighbourhood). For someone living in a quiet residential area, he is entitled to expect that it will remain that way, so an activity which disturbs that will constitute a nuisance. If the same activity were to be carried out in an area which was already noisy and bustling, it would not constitute a nuisance.

An exception to this is the access of light to a building. All buildings are entitled to the same amount of light; an activity which interferes with this would constitute a nuisance wherever the building is situated.

### *cc) (Excessive) sensitivity of the claimant*

Empfindsamkeit
besonders/eigen/auffällig
nur, weil
übermäßig/über Gebühr

A person cannot take advantage of his peculiar sensitivity to noise and smells. An act which would not disturb a *reasonable person* will not be a nuisance just because the particular person concerned, or his property, is unduly sensitive.

Kartonage
vermieten – Stockwerk
lagern

| *Example – Robinson v Kilvert (1889)* |
|---|
| The owner of a house used the cellar to manufacture cardboard boxes, which involved heating the cellar with hot dry air. The owner had leased out the floor above to a tenant who used it to store a particular type of brown paper. The hot air from below raised the temperature of the ground floor and damaged the brown paper because this type of brown paper was peculiarly sensitive to heat. The tenant claimed that the activity below constituted a *nuisance*.<br>***Held:*** that the person below was not liable. The activity would not have damaged ordinary brown paper; it was just that the paper in this case was a **particularly sensitive** type. |

### *dd) Public benefit*

öffentliches Interesse

The general utility of the alleged nuisance does not exempt from liability. This means that what the defendant is doing – even if it is or can be useful to society – does not necessarily mean that it is not a nuisance. In this case the court will do a "balancing act" between the claimant and the defendant.

allgemeiner Nutzen – behaupten – freistellen

Pig sties, breweries, quarries, tanneries and fish and chip stalls can be useful and necessary for the community, but if their operation causes discomfort to the claimant, they constitute a nuisance. The fact that the trade or industry is of public benefit is not a defence in law.

Schweinestall – Brauerei – Steinbruch – Gerberei – „Pommesbude“
Betrieb – Unbehagen/ Unwohlsein
Gewerbe – im öffentlichen Interesse

| *Example – Adams v Ursell (1913)* |
|---|
| A new occupier took over the house next door to the claimant and used it as a fish and chip shop. The claimant complained about the smell of frying fish and hot fat permeating every room in his house like a fog every time the fish and chip shop was open. ***Held:*** that this activity constituted a *nuisance*, even though cheap take-away food such as fish and chips was popular and served a need in the working-class area which the shop served. |

durchdringen
Nebel

Moreover, if an activity constitutes a nuisance, it is irrelevant that it was already being carried on before the claimant came to the area. The defendant cannot allege that the claimant came to the area knowing that the nuisance was in existence:

| *Example – Bliss v Hall (1838)* |
|---|
| Mr Bliss and his family moved into a house near to a candle-maker who had been carrying on his business there for 3 years. Mr Bliss complained that the terrible smell from the candle-making business constituted a nuisance. The candle-maker argued that he was already carrying on this business before Mr Bliss moved in, and so Mr Bliss should not be entitled to complain. ***Held:*** that this was **not a valid defence** for someone who was causing a *nuisance*. |

betreiben
sich beschweren

(Fort)Dauer

### *ee) Duration*

einmaliges Ereignis
unmaßgeblich – darlegen
*hier:* Ausmaß

A single event is not a nuisance and a temporary interference may be too trivial to constitute a nuisance. The claimant must show that there is some degree of repetition of the offending act.

vorher

| *Example – Bolton v Stone (1951)* |
|---|
| A cricket field was near a road and it was proved that in 35 years only six to ten cricket balls had been known to have been hit into the road. No-one had previously been injured until the claimant was struck by a ball.<br>***Held:*** that this event **did not occur often enough** and therefore was not a *nuisance*. |

Arglist/Böswilligkeit

### *ff) Malice of the defendant*

niederer Beweggrund – Grundlage/Basis – Verletzungshandlung

*etwa:* johlend applaudieren – „auf die Pauke hauen"

verderben

Sometimes **malice** or **evil motive** may become the foundation of the offending act. This is one of the rare occasions in law where malice on the part of the defendant contributes to liability. To shout, shriek, and whistle and "to paint the town red" may be a reasonable use of your own property, but if it is done with the express purpose of spoiling your neighbour's musical evening, it may be a nuisance, as we will see below *(Christie* v *Davey (1893))*.

An *evil motive* is illustrated in our next case.

Züchter – Silberfuchs – errichten
Anschlagtafel

Baugrundstück – schädlich

abfeuern – 12-Kaliber-Gewehr
Fähe (*Jagd*)/Füchsin

sich paaren – werfen – verschlingen

| *Example – Hollywood Silver Fox Farm v Emmett (1936)* |
|---|
| The claimant was a breeder of silver foxes and erected a notice board on his land stating: "Hollywood Silver Fox Farm". The defendant owned a neighbouring field, which he was about to develop as a building estate, and he feared that the notice board would put off potential buyers of the new houses. He asked the claimant to remove it, and when this request was refused, he sent his son to discharge a 12-bore gun close to the claimant's land, with the object of frightening the vixens during breeding. The result of this activity was that certain of the vixens did not mate at all, and others, having whelped, devoured their young.<br>The claimant brought his action alleging nuisance. The defence was that the defendant had a right to shoot as he pleased on his own land. |

**_Held:_** the defendant's **evil motive** behind what he had been doing turned what would otherwise have been an innocent use of land, into a *nuisance*.

### *gg) Variety* — Vielfalt

The modes of annoyance are infinitely variable: bell-ringing, circus performances, the excessive use of radio, stenches, filth or opening a sex-shop in a residential area may all constitute nuisances.

Belästigung – Glockengeläut
Zirkusvorstellung – Gestank – Dreck

*Example – Christie v Davey (1893)*

A music teacher occupied a semi-detached house. She and her daughter gave piano, violin and singing lessons in the house for four days a week amounting to 17 hours in all. There was also music and singing at other times, and occasional musical evenings. The neighbour, a woodcarver who was also an amateur musician himself, found the noise annoying and started a campaign of retaliation in an effort to persuade the music teacher to stop her activities. He wrote abusive letters. He played the concertina, horn, flute, piano and other musical instruments, blew whistles, knocked on trays or boards, hammered, shrieked and shouted. The music teacher brought an action against the neighbour in *nuisance*.
**_Held:_** that she succeeded – the neighbour's actions were being made **wilfully for the purpose of annoyance**. The activities of the music teacher herself were not an unreasonable use of their house, and so did not constitute nuisance on her part.

Doppelhaushälfte
Holzschnitzer
störend/lästig
Vergeltung/Heimzahlung
beleidigend/ausfällig
Ziehharmonika
(Triller)Pfeife – Tablett – Brett
absichtlich – zum Zwecke von – Belästigung/Störung

### *hh) Several wrongdoers* — mehrere Schädiger

A nuisance may result from the act of several wrongdoers. If, for instance, A, B and C are the persons involved, any of them may be proceeded against. The claimant may sue all jointly or separately, for example A, for the total damage. If this is done, A will have the right to a contribution from B and C.

verklagen – gemeinsam
Ausgleichsanspruch gegen

## 3. The parties to an action — Klageparteien

Let us now answer the question of *who may sue and who may be sued?*

The person who occupies the land affected by the nuisance is the person *who may bring the action*.

The principle that no other person injured on the property has a claim in nuisance is illustrated by the following case.

| *Example – Malone v Laskey (1907)* |
|---|
| The defendants owned a house which they leased to a firm named Witherby & Co, who sub-let it to the Script Shorthand Company. The claimant's husband was employed by this company, and was allowed to occupy the house as an emolument of his employment. A flush cistern in the lavatory of the house was unsafe, the wall brackets having been loosened by the vibration of the defendants' electric generator next door. The claimant told Witherby & Co of the situation, and they wrote to the defendants, who sent two of their plumbers to repair the cistern free of charge. The work was carried out in a negligent manner and, four months later, the claimant was injured when the cistern came loose. The claimant sued the defendants in nuisance, and in negligence. ***Held:*** that there was no claim in *nuisance* against the defendants. The claimant was not a tenant, and **only the tenant could sue in nuisance**, but **not other persons** present on the premises, though such persons may have a claim where the nuisance is a public nuisance. |

untervermieten — Entlohnung — Spülungskasten — Wandhalter — Klempner — kostenlos/umsonst – *hier*: schlampig — sich lösen

A landlord may, however, *sue* in some cases, for example, where a permanent injury is caused or will be caused to his property.

Grundeigentümer/Verpächter/Vermieter

The person *to be sued* is the one who created the nuisance, i.e. the occupier (a person who exercises an element of control over premises) of the land – from which the nuisance emanated.

ausgehen

But a landlord also may be liable if *he* created the nuisance and then leases the property, or if he authorises a tenant to commit or continue the nuisance.

Mieter/Pächter

| *Example – Harris v James (1876)* |
|---|
| A landlord was *held* liable for the nuisance created by his tenant's blasting operations at a quarry because he had let the property for that purpose. The tenant, therefore, inevitably created a nuisance. |

Sprengung – Steinbruch — unvermeidlich

## 4. Defences

It is, of course, a defence to rebut the allegation that a nuisance was caused and to prove that the act complained of is not an unreasonable interference with the use or enjoyment of land.

widerlegen – Behauptung
über etwas klagen

The law recognises, as mentioned above, that in everyday life, generally there must be some element of "give and take", e.g. noise caused by the carrying out of repairs. Repairs carried out in the middle of the night, however, might not be reasonable.

*hier:* berücksichtigen/anerkennen
Vornahme – Reparatur

There are some similarities with the defences to the *trespass to land* (see above section II.3.b), p. 12). Both torts disturb the occupier of land. The main difference between them is that trespass of land is a *direct* interference, whilst nuisance is an *indirect* one.

Ähnlichkeit
stören/belästigen
wohingegen/während

**Defences to nuisance** are:

- the **consent** of the claimant, which is a general defence always applicable to each type of tort;
- **statutory authority**, which means that it is a defence to show that a statute authorises the act or omission in question;
- **prescription** (***note***: applicable to private nuisance only): It is possible to acquire the right to commit a private nuisance by *prescription*. This means: when a person has been carrying on an activity continuously for at least 20 years, he may be considered to have acquired the right to continue to do so and the activity will not then constitute a nuisance. However, this defence will rarely succeed, since what the defendant must prove is 20 years tolerance of the interference. So it is not surprising, that the leading case dates from the 19th century:

gesetzliche Erlaubnis
*hier:* ständige Rechtsausübung
erlangen
Grundsatzentscheidung/Präjudiz

*Example – Sturges v Bridgman (1879)*

The defendant, a confectioner and baker in Wigmore Street, London, had used a pestle and mortar for some twenty years on his premises. The claimant, a doctor, built consulting rooms in his garden next to the confectioner's premises. Noises and vibration interfered with the claimant's practice and, accordingly, he sued the defendant in nuisance.
***Held:*** that although the defendant could acquire a prescriptive right to create a nuisance, the nuisance in this case arose only when the doctor's consulting room was built.

Konditor
Stößel – Mörser
Behandlungszimmer
demzufolge/folglich
*hier*: auf ständiger Rechtsausübung beruhend

Geringfügigkeit – winzig
Maxime/Grundsatz
Kleinigkeit

- **triviality,** where the damage caused was minute or minimal, or perhaps amounted to only a temporary interference. The maxim (in Latin) here is *de minimis non curat lex* ("the law does not concern itself with trifles").

## 5. Remedies

The principal remedies for nuisance are *damages* and *injunction*. Generally, an injunction will not be granted if damages are awarded. The injunction's objective is to balance the interests of the claimant and defendant. The injunction may reflect this by limiting the nuisance rather than prohibiting it entirely (see above, *Kennaway* v *Thompson (1980)*, p. 17).

### a) Damages

in die Ausgangslage versetzen

The **usual common-law remedy** for a breach of the civil law is to award damages to the claimant to compensate him for his loss. If the claimant can establish that a nuisance has been committed, he has a right to damages as monetary compensation. The principle is that the award of damages should return the claimant to the position that he would have been in, if the tort had not occurred.

### b) Injunction

wieder auftreten

An injunction is an order of the court that the defendant must stop the activity which constitutes the nuisance. Although that is usually one of the orders which the claimant wants from the court, an injunction is an **equitable remedy** and is therefore available only at the **discretion of the court**. The claimant must show that the nuisance is likely to recur and do irreparable damage to him. The court can refuse to grant an injunction if it feels that damages would be an adequate remedy.

### c) Abatement

Beseitigung/Bekämpfung/Herabsetzung/Linderung

The injured party may abate the nuisance himself i.e. by removing it, provided that no unnecessary damage is caused and that no injury arises to an innocent third party, e.g. a tenant. This remedy is the exercise of the right of **self-help**, which can be invoked when the nuisance can be terminated without entering another person's land. It applies, for example, to over-hanging trees or roots. However, the branches which are cut off still belong to the owner of the tree and so should be returned to him. If the nuisance cannot be abated without entering the other's land, permission must be obtained, unless there is an emergency.

beseitigen
vorausgesetzt, dass
Selbsthilfe – aufrufen/sich berufen auf
betreten
falls nicht/es sei denn – Dringlichkeit/Notfall

## 6. Differences between trespass to land and nuisance

We have already stated that the **torts** of *trespass to land* and *nuisance* are similar in that they **both affect land**, trespass to land in a *direct* manner and nuisance *indirectly*. Yet there are some other differences which can be summarised as follows:

betreffen

| Trespass to land | Nuisance |
|---|---|
| ▪ Actionable *per se* | ▪ Requires proof of damage (not actionable *per se*) |
| ▪ Unlawful *entry* of a person or a thing on another's land | ▪ No entry necessary |
| ▪ May consist of *one* act only | ▪ Usully *more than one* act is necessary |
| ▪ Trespass is only a *civil* tort | ▪ *Public* nuisance is a tort *and* a crime |

Diagram 39

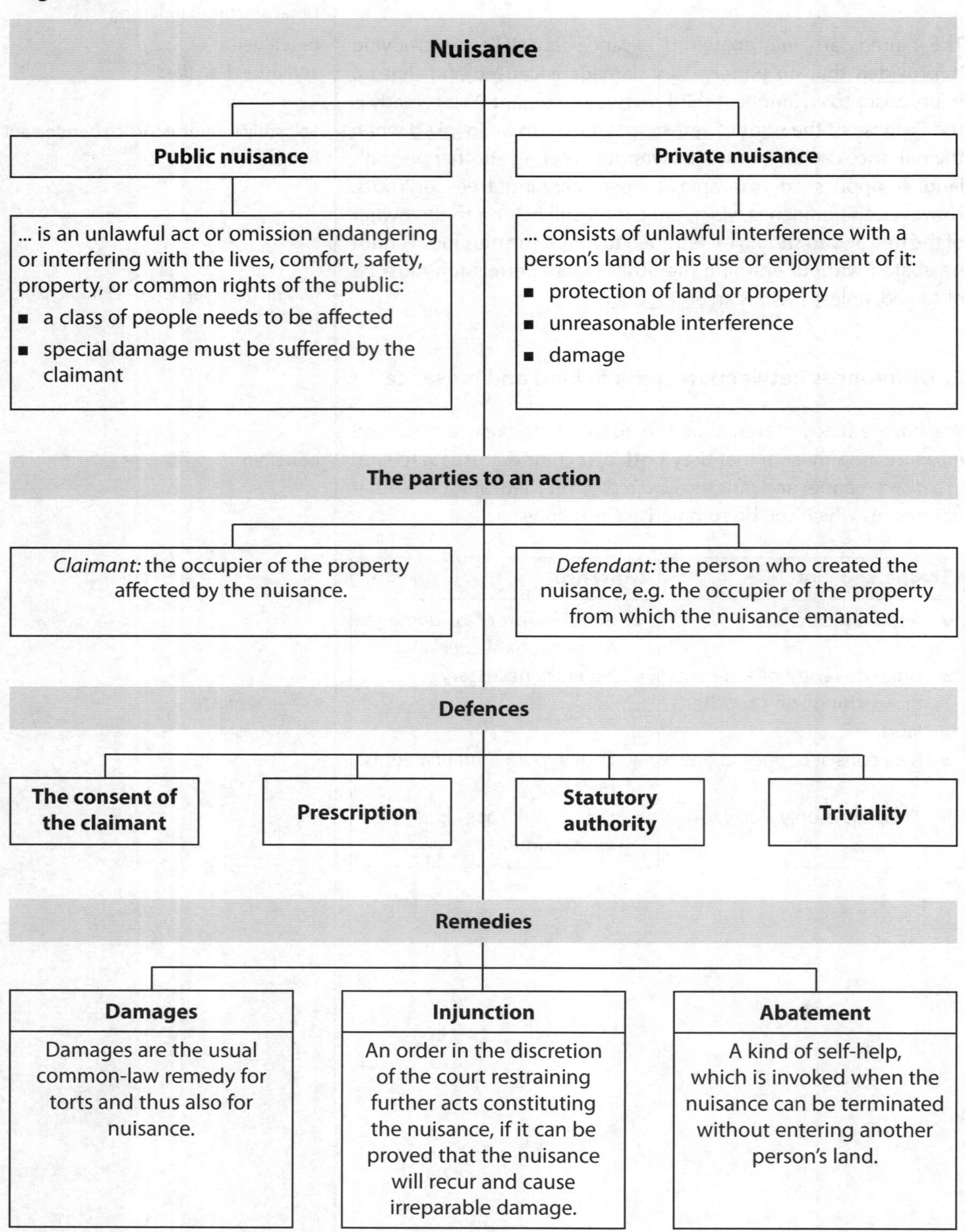
Nuisance
Public nuisance
... is an unlawful act or omission endangering or interfering with the lives, comfort, safety, property, or common rights of the public:
▪ a class of people needs to be affected
▪ special damage must be suffered by the claimant
Private nuisance
... consists of unlawful interference with a person's land or his use or enjoyment of it:
▪ protection of land or property
▪ unreasonable interference
▪ damage
The parties to an action
Claimant: the occupier of the property affected by the nuisance.
Defendant: the person who created the nuisance, e.g. the occupier of the property from which the nuisance emanated.
Defences
The consent of the claimant
Prescription
Statutory authority
Triviality
Remedies
Damages
Damages are the usual common-law remedy for torts and thus also for nuisance.
Injunction
An order in the discretion of the court restraining further acts constituting the nuisance, if it can be proved that the nuisance will recur and cause irreparable damage.
Abatement
A kind of self-help, which is invoked when the nuisance can be terminated without entering another person's land.

# IV. Negligence

Haftung für Fahrlässigkeit/Fahrlässigkeit

## 1. Introduction

There are two concepts underlying the term of negligence.

Konzept/Idee/Begriff

According to the first concept, negligence is a **separate tort** with a corresponding **title of liability**. The **tort of negligence** is committed by a person (the *defendant*) who is in breach of a legal duty of care which he owes to another (the *claimant*), and that breach results in damage to the claimant, undesired by the defendant (see Winfield & Jolowicz). This *legal* meaning of negligence will be dealt with in this chapter.

*etwa*: Haftungstatbestand
Verletzung einer rechtlichen Sorgfaltspflicht
Schaden herbeiführen – ungewollt/nicht vorsätzlich

There is another concept to the term negligence in English law which is mentioned here to avoid confusion: Negligence – in its everyday meaning – is also a **type of fault**. It is used to describe the state of mind which is necessary for the defendant to have in order to be liable for certain torts. On a sliding scale, (1) a defendant can have *intended* to cause damage, (2) he can have been *reckless* as to whether his conduct caused the damage, (3) his conduct can have been *negligent* (in other words, careless), resulting in damage being suffered, and (4) none of these can be applicable, but the damage was still suffered *through no fault of the defendant*.

Verschuldensform
Geistes-/Bewusstseinszustand
um ... zu – Gleitskala
beabsichtigen
*etwa*: gleichgültig (grob/bewusst fahrlässig) ggü. der Frage, ob ... – fahrlässig (leicht, mittel)
unverschuldet

An example of category (1) is assault or battery (see above), which both require *intention*. It is quite common for torts which require proof of intention, that *recklessness* – category (2) – is sufficient, e.g. in the case of assault or battery. An example of category (3) is *negligent* misstatement. An example of category (4) is the rule in *Rylands* v *Fletcher*, which imposes liability without the defendant having been at fault – also known as *strict liability* (see section VI below).

üblich
fahrlässige Falschangabe/Falschdarstellung – Haftung auferlegen/Verantwortlichkeit begründen – schuldig sein

The **tort of negligence** is a relatively recent creation of English law. Negligence as a tort in its own right is the result of development – over the course of English legal history – of trespass and trespass on the case. In the 19th century, courts first dealt with the tort of negligence and, more than 100 years later, the House of Lords in the landmark case of *Donoghue* v *Stevenson (1932)* put the tort of negligence firmly on the map of English law.

modern/neu
eigenständig
allg. Schadensersatzklage wegen rw oder fahrlässig begangener Handlungen, durch die dem Kläger Schaden entstanden ist – Grundsatzentscheidung – *hier*: zum festen Bestandteil machen

Today a high proportion of all actions in the courts involving torts are claims in the **tort of negligence**.

Anteil – beinhalten

Merkmale

## 2. Elements of the tort of negligence

zerlegt werden

The definition of tort of negligence can be broken down in four component parts:

schulden – Sorgfaltspflicht
Sorgfaltspflichtverletzung

(äquivalenter) Kausalzusammenhang

abseitig/entfernt liegend

(1) the defendant owed a **legal duty of care** to the claimant,
(2) there was a **breach of that duty** by the defendant,
(3) as a result of that breach, the claimant suffered damage – **(factual) causation** –, and
(4) the damage suffered was reasonably foreseeable, i.e. not too remote – **remoteness (legal causation)**.

The claimant has to prove each of these four elements.

rechtlich/von Rechts wegen

### a) The legal duty of care

verletzt/geschädigt

angemessene Sorgfalt an den Tag legen – Schaden – in jedem Sachverhalt

The first element of negligence is the *legal duty of care* owed to the injured party. This means that, due to the particular relationship between the defendant and the claimant, there is an obligation for the defendant to take proper care to avoid causing injury to the claimant in all the circumstances of the case.

berechtigt – so nachlässig, wie es ihm gefällt

In the famous case *Le Lievre* v *Gould (1895)*, Lord Esher said: "A man is entitled to be as negligent as he pleases towards the whole world, if he owes no duty to them."

Basis/Grundlage – Haftung – sofern nicht/außer wenn – anklagen

This is true and it is good law. On your own private property, you do not owe a duty to anyone and you can be as negligent as you please. Negligence is not a foundation of liability unless the person whose conduct is impeached is under a *legal duty to take care* vis-à-vis the person who has suffered damage.

begründen
Schutzverhältnis

In real life it can be difficult to decide whether such *a legal duty of care* exists. There are two ways in which *a duty of care* may be established:

- there is a **special relationship** between the defendant and the claimant which gives rise to a duty of care *(aa)*, or
- outside of these recognised duty situations, the duty must be established according to the **principles developed by case law** *(bb)*.

#### *aa) Special relationships*

anerkennen

The courts recognise the existence of a *duty of care* in some sort of "special" relationships such as between one road-user and another, solicitor and client, doctor and patient, employer and employee and manufacturer and consumer.

If a *duty of care* is not established by one of these categories mentioned, individual circumstances will be taken into account to determine whether a *duty of care* exists:

Einzelfallumstände
ermitteln/eruieren/bestimmen

***bb) The neighbour principle***

In *Donoghue* v *Stevenson* the House of Lords formulated the "neighbour principle" to adress the question of when a *duty of care* is owed between a defendant and a claimant. The case is also known as the case of *"The Paisley Snail"*.

This case is of fundamental importance for the development of negligence as an independent tort as such and for the evolution of the English law of tort.

| *Example "The Paisley Snail" – Donoghue v Stevenson (1932)* |
|---|
| Mrs Donoghue went with a friend to a café in Paisley, near Glasgow. The friend placed the order – Mrs Donoghue had a "ginger beer float", which is ice cream with ginger beer poured over it. She proceeded to eat it. When the rest of the bottle of ginger beer was poured into a glass, out came the remains of a decomposing snail. The bottle was of opaque stone rather than transparent glass, so neither Mrs Donoghue nor her friend could have known it was there, nor could the owner of the cafe. Mrs Donoghue was taken ill, poisoned by the drink or sickened by the thought of it, or both.<br>Mrs Donoghue claimed against Stevenson as the manufacturer of the drink, that he had been negligent in preparing and checking the drink before putting it on sale. Stevenson's defence was that, *even if he had been negligent*, he did not **owe a duty of care** to Mrs Donoghue. Note that as Mrs Donoghue was not the person who had bought the drink, she could not bring a claim under any contract for the sale of goods. The case came to court on this point of law, so for the purposes of this judgment it is assumed that Stevenson had in fact been negligent.<br>The House of Lords decided 3:2 in favour of Mrs Donoghue. The most famous speech in the judgement is the one given by Lord Atkin. He said, in response to Stevenson's defence, as follows – and it is worth setting out this extract at length: |

Bestellung aufgeben
Ingwer – gießen/schütten – fortfahren
zersetzt
undurchsichtig
Hersteller
wegen/um…willen
annehmen
in Erwiderung
es ist es wert – behandeln
ausführlich

"The law appears to be that, in order to support an action for damages for negligence, the claimant has to show that he has been injured by the breach of a duty owed to him in the circumstances by the defendant to take reasonable care to avoid such injury. In the present case, we are not concerned with the breach of the duty; if a duty exists, we will assume for the purposes of this case that it has been broken.

We are solely concerned with the question whether, as a matter of law in the circumstances alleged, the defendant owed any duty to the claimant to take care. It is remarkable how difficult it is to find in the English authorities statements of general application defining the relations between parties that give rise to the duty.

weglassen/aussparen

And yet the duty which is common to all the cases where liability is established must logically be based upon some element common to the cases where it is found to exist. To seek a complete logical definition of the general principle is probably to go beyond the function of the judge, for the more general the definition, the more likely it is to omit essentials or to introduce non-essentials.

sich zufrieden geben mit

nur – Beispiel

bezeichnen

Missetäter

At present, I content myself with pointing out that in English law there must be, and is, some general conception of relations giving rise to a duty of care, of which the particular cases found in the books are but instances. The liability for negligence, whether you style it such or treat it – as in other legal systems – as a species of "culpa", is no doubt based upon a general public sentiment of moral wrongdoing for which the offender must pay.

But acts or omissions which any moral code would censure cannot in a practical world be treated so as to give a right to every person injured by them to demand compensation. In this way rules of law arise which limit the range of claimants and the extent of their remedy. The rule that you are to love your neighbour becomes in law, you must not injure your neighbour; and the lawyer's question, "Who is my neighbour?" receives a restricted reply.

in Betracht/Erwägung ziehen

You must take reasonable care **to avoid acts or omissions which you can reasonably foresee would be likely to injure your neighbour.** Who then, in law is my neighbour? The answer seems to be – **persons who are so closely and directly affected by my act that I ought reasonably to have them in contemplation as being so affected when I am directing my mind to the acts or omissions which are called in question**.

> It is a proposition, which I venture to say, no one who was not a lawyer would for one moment doubt. It will be an advantage to make it clear that the law in this matter, as in most others, is in accordance with sound common sense*".

Behauptung – wagen/riskieren

* Some slight alterations to the language have been made in this extract.

William Shakespeare, writing in the early 17th century, had the foresight to see this coming – *The Winter's Tale* Act 2 scene 1 line 37:

Blick in die Zukunft/Voraussicht

*There may be in the cup*
*A spider steep'd, and one may drink, depart,*
*And yet partake no venom, for his knowledge*
*It is not infected; but if one present*
*The abhorr'd ingredient to his eye, make known*
*How he hath drunk, he cracks his gorge, his sides*
*With violent hefts. I have drunk, and seen the spider.*

Here the corresponding translation by Dorothea Tieck.[5]

*Wohl kann sich eine Spinne*
*Verkriechen in den Becher, und man trinkt;*
*Man geht, und spürt kein Gift; nicht angesteckt*
*Ward das Bewusstsein, aber hält uns einer*
*Die ekelhafte Zutat vor, und sagt uns,*
*Was wir getrunken, sprengt man Brust und Seiten*
*Mit heft'gem Würgen: – ich trank und sah die Spinne.*

The events in this case *"The Paisley Snail"* took place in Scotland, and Scots law is not part of the English legal system. The House of Lords (nowadays the Supreme Court), however, is the final court of appeal for both England and Scotland, and applies English or Scots law as appropriate. In this case, their Lordships expressly stated that they considered both English and Scots law to be the same on this point.

wendet entsprechend englisches oder schottisches Recht an

This decision was a landmark in the evolution of the English law of tort, providing the foundations for a **general duty of care** in negligence.

Meilenstein
liefern – Grundlage/Basis – allgemeine Sorgfaltspflicht

Two essential statements can be derived from this decision (see the words emphasised in bold by the authors): On the one hand, the duty of care requires a certain **proximity** between the two parties.

Fettdruck
Nähe/Nachbarschaft

5 Dorothea Tieck (* März 1799 in Berlin; † 21. Februar 1841) hat mit ihrem Vater Ludwig Tieck und Wolf Heinrich Graf von Baudissin zahlreiche Werke William Shakespeares übersetzt.

gewisses Maß an Kontrolle

In order to satisfy this requirement for proximity it is upon the claimant to show that the defendant had a certain degree of control over and responsibility for the potentially dangerous situation. On the other hand, the duty of care is restricted by the test as to whether the **harm was reasonably foreseeable**.

There have been many decisions based on the case of the *"Paisley Snail"*, for instance:

*Example – Grant v Australian Knitting Mills Ltd (1936)*

hier: sich zuziehen
Hautentzündung – Wollunterhose
Krankheit
unsichtbar – Übermaß – schwefelsaures Salz/Sulfit – Unterwäsche
vorbringen
unterscheiden/abweichen von
innerlich – tragen
äußerlich

The claimant, who had a perfectly normal skin, contracted dermatitis through wearing woollen underpants which had been manufactured by the defendant. The disease was caused by invisible excess of sulphites which had been negligently left in the underwear during the manufacturing process. The defendant contended that *Donoghue* v *Stevenson* could be distinguished on the ground that the ginger beer was to be consumed internally whereas the underpants were to be worn externally.

Es kann kein zwingender Unterschied gemacht werden ... – schädlich/ungesund – haftbar/verantwortlich
verdeckter Mangel

***Held:*** following *Donoghue* v *Stevenson*, the defendant was liable in **negligence**. No distinction can be logically drawn between a noxious thing taken internally and a noxious thing applied externally. Nor can the claimant be held accountable as the latent defect could not have been discovered by a reasonable examination – like the snail in the opaque glass.

An dieser Stelle lässt sich zusammenfassend festhalten, ... – Fall/Beispiel

To summarise so far, in order to decide whether a **duty of care is owed** in any given instance, the judge will ask himself the following questions:

einigermaßen/halbwegs
hier: eng/nah

- Was the harm **reasonably foreseeable**?
- Is there a sufficiently **proximate relationship** between the parties?

neu überdenken/nachprüfen

In *Caparo Industries plc* v *Dickman (1990)* the basic concept of the **neighbour principle** was reconsidered more recently.

in Betracht ziehen
vielmehr
Sorgfaltspflicht auferlegen

The court confirmed the *two requirements* established in *"The Paisley Snail"* (see above), but it was also considered that there is in fact a *third factor to take into account*, which is:

- Would it be **fair, just and reasonable to impose a duty of care**?

Rechnungsprüfer/Bilanzbuchhalter

The following case considers the liability of an auditor for financial loss suffered by investors. It also sets out the main points which a court must consider to establish whether a *duty of care* exists.

*Example – Caparo Industries plc v Dickman and Others (1990)*

Caparo, which already held shares in Fidelity plc, eventually acquired the controlling interest in the company. Caparo later alleged that certain purchases of Fidelity shares and the final bid were made after relying on Fidelity's accounts, which had been prepared by Touche Ross & Co, the third defendants.
The accounts, Caparo alleged, were inaccurate and misleading in that an apparent pre-tax profit of some £1.3 million should in fact have been shown as a loss of £400,000. It was also alleged that, if the supposed true facts had been known, Caparo would not have made a bid at the price it did and might not have made a bid at all.
***Held:*** The Court of Appeal decided that while Touche Ross did not have a *duty of care* towards members of the public in regard to the Fidelity accounts, it did owe a *duty of care* to Caparo because Caparo was already a shareholder in Fidelity when it made the final purchase of shares and the bid.
The two main judges in the House of Lords provided an interesting contrast: Lord Bridge concentrated more on the case law and the dissenting judgment of Lord Denning in *Candler* v *Crane, Christmas & Co (1951)*, who thought that the defendant accountants in that case should have owed a *duty of care* to Candler because they had prepared allegedly negligent financial statements on the basis of which they knew Candler might invest. Therefore Lord Bridge distinguished between a wider *duty of care* to avoid causing injury to certain persons/ property, and the duty to avoid causing others to suffer purely economic loss. Thus he held that there is no *duty of care* to members of the public at large who rely on a company's accounts in deciding to buy shares in the company.
Lord Oliver however was concerned with establishing the purpose of an audit under the *Companies Act 1985.*
The purpose for which the auditors' certificate was made and published was that of providing those entitled to receive the report with information to enable them to exercise the powers which their respective proprietary rights in the company conferred on them and not for the purposes of individual speculation with a view to profit.
The *duty of care* was one owed to the shareholders as a body and not to individual shareholders. It was **not** held to be **fair and reasonable** to expect the auditors to owe *a duty of care* to anyone else who may use the accounts in order to form a view of the value of the company.

letztendlich

Kauf – Anteil/Aktie – letztes Angebot/ Angebot – vertrauen auf – Berechnung/Bericht/Darstellung

in Gefahr

Generally speaking, the tort of negligence can only be fulfilled by *actively doing something* rather than by failing to act In general, you do not owe a duty to the world to take *positive action* to prevent harm. There is, for example, no obligation to rescue someone you see in peril. In some special relationships, however, you do have a **duty to act positively** because of the greater power of control you hold. Such relationships could arise between prison officers and prisoners, employers and employees, occupiers and visitors (see below in section 4, the *Occupiers' Liability Acts*) or parents and children.

A similar situation is to be found in the following case:

Schüler – Kindergarten/Vorschule – unterhalten/leiten

Lehrerin – verantwortlich

sich kümmern um

unverschlossenes Tor – kleine Straße
Lastwagen –ausweichen
aufprallen – Telegraphenmast

Träger/Betreiber/Leitung
Sachverhalt
*hier*: für fremdes Verschulden haften

Vorkehrung/Sicherheitsmaßnahme

| *Example – Carmarthenshire County Council v Lewis (1955)** |
|---|
| A boy aged 4 years was a pupil at a nursery school run by the Council who were the local education authority. The boy and another little child were made ready to go out for a walk with the mistress in charge, who left them for a moment in order to get ready herself. She did not return for 10 minutes, having attended to another child who had cut himself. During her absence, the boy got out of the classroom and made his way through an unlocked gate, down a lane, and into a busy highway. He caused the driver of a lorry to swerve so that it struck a telegraph pole, as a result of which the driver was killed. His widow brought an *action for damages of negligence* against the Council as the operator of the nursery school.<br>***Held:*** in the circumstances of the case the mistress had not been negligent, and so the Council as her employer could not be vicariously liable for her negligence (see section VII below). However, the Council had itself been negligent because it had **not taken reasonable precautions** to keep young children who used the premises from getting out into the highway. |

* This case was brought under the Fatal Accidents Act 1976, which allows the dependants of the deceased person to bring a claim.

öffentliche Ordnung/Grundprinzipien von Recht und Ordnung

Since the law of negligence is not based on statute, the courts have the flexibility to take **public policy** considerations into account when they have to decide whether it would be **fair, just and reasonable to impose a duty of care.** So – on the one hand – the courts can protect certain classes of defendant from liability and – on the other hand – also provide additional help to certain classes of claimant in bringing an action.

*Example – Ashton v Turner (1980)*

After spending the evening together drinking heavily, the claimant persuaded his friend to join him in a burglary. They were disturbed and chased; their car crashed at high speed and the claimant – the passenger – sustained serious injuries. The friend was convicted of burglary, dangerous driving and driving with more than the permitted amount of alcohol in his blood. The claimant sued him, *inter alia*, in negligence for his injuries.
***Held:*** that the defendant was not liable in *negligence*. As a matter of **public policy**, the law would, in certain circumstances, refuse to recognise the existence of *a duty of care* owed by one participant in a crime to another participant in the same crime, in respect of an act done in connection with the commission of that crime. This was such a case.
*Note* that even if the court had decided that a *duty of care* was owed, the maxim *ex turpi non oritur actio* applied and afforded the friend a complete defence.

Einbruch
verfolgen/jagen
verurteilen
*lat.*: unter anderem
liefern
*etwa*: Rechtfertigungsgrund, der zur völligen Haftungsfreistellung führt

The maxim *ex turpi causa non oritur actio*[6] constitutes a general defence which is available when a claimant gives his consent with prior knowledge of the (criminal) risk involved; in this case, the tort arises in the course of an unlawful (usually criminal) act/activity.

*lat.*: „aus einer verwerflichen Sache entsteht keine Klage" i.S.v „Wer sich ungesetzlich/unmoralisch verhält, hat keinen Grund zu klagen."

The other defence similar to *ex turpi* is the maxim *volenti non fit injuria*, where the claimant has consented to the risk in question. In this case the risk is voluntarily assumed.

*lat.*: „Dem Einwilligenden geschieht kein Unrecht."

Both defences are complete ones, i.e. the claim will therefore fail.

Here is another example of the court taking into account **public policy** considerations:

*Example – Hill v Chief Constable of West Yorkshire (1988)*

The claimant was the mother of the last victim of a serial murderer, the "Yorkshire Ripper". She claimed damages on the basis that the police had negligently failed to apprehend the murderer before her daughter was killed.
***Held:*** that notwithstanding that *harm* was **reasonably foreseeable**, there was **insufficient proximity** between the police and the victim. The House of Lords further stated that a *general duty of care* to protect all members of the public from the

verhaften
ungeachtet dessen, dass
weiterhin

6 *In Latin:* "from a dishonorable cause an action does not arise"; vgl. auch: „Mitgegangen, mitgefangen, mitgehangen" ... (Simrock, Die deutschen Sprichwörter, Reclam-Nachdruck 1995, Nr. 7044).

nicht durchführbar/ unpraktikabel
äußerst schädlich für

consequences of crime would be impracticable and, on grounds of **public policy**, deeply damaging to police operations.*

Urteil/Entscheidung
gültig

* After the judgments of the European Court of Human Rights in *Osman (1998)* and of the House of Lords in *Barret* v *Enfield (1999)*, this decision can no longer be considered good law.

### *cc) Exceptions*

ersatzpflichtig/einklagbar

Not every type of damage caused by the defendant's negligent act is always recoverable. The following exceptions illustrate that particular circumstances (economic loss, negligent misstatement, nervous shock) call for the application of particular legal principles.

(reiner) Vermögensschaden/wirtschaftlicher Schaden

*(1) (Pure) economic loss*

(durchaus) missverständlich sein
Vermögen
im Rechtssinne – Sachschaden

A question which has often come before the courts is how to deal with a loss which is *purely economic loss*. This expression as stated by Winfield & Jolowicz "is liable to mislead": if a car is destroyed, that is *economic* in the sense that the owner's assets are thereby diminished. However, in legal terms, it is classified as damage to property and the owner is entitled to its value as damages.

fraglos/unzweifelhaft – dem Wesen nach – keine Schwierigkeiten haben zu gestatten – Ersatz – Körperschaden

Verdienstausfall – Arztkosten

Even if the loss is unquestionably only financial in nature, the courts have no difficulty in allowing its recovery if it is a consequence of physical injury or damage to the claimant's property. As we have seen in *Donoghue* v *Stevenson*, the claimant could have recovered lost earnings and medical expenses.

Grundprinzip
zuordenbar/zuschreibbar

Gewinnausfall – Betriebsverlust
Kapitalverlust

The key principle is that there is a distinction between ***pure*** *economic loss* – not attributable to physical harm caused to the claimant or his property – and *economic loss* which is the result of physical damage to person or property. *Economic loss* is recoverable, **pure economic loss**, however, is **not recoverable in tort**. The latter includes loss of profits, loss of trade and loss of investment revenue.

aufgraben
Stromkabel – verursachen – Schmelzwerk – stilllegen – Stromunterbrechung – fand ein Schmelzvorgang statt – fest werden lassen – Schmelzofen

*Example – Spartan Steel & Alloys Ltd* v *Martin & Co (Contractors) Ltd (1973)*

A builder, in the course of digging up a road, negligently cut a power cable, causing the nearby smelting works to be shut down. At the time of the power cut, there was a "melt" in progress and, to stop the steel solidifying, it had to be drawn out in the furnace. This reduced its value by £368.

> The foundry claimed the reduction in value of the melt and for the profit which would have been made had the process been completed. They also claimed for the loss of profit from 4 further melts which would have been processed but for the 14-hour power cut.
> ***Held:*** that the foundry (the claimant) should recover the reduction in the value of the solidified melt and the profits the claimant would have made from *that* sale. However, they obtained nothing for the loss of profits on the 4 further melts which could not have been processed before the electricity was restored: that was **pure economic loss** independent of the property damage, and therefore **non-recoverable in tort**.

Gießerei – Minderwert – Schmelzmasse
beenden
ausgeführt werden – ohne
Stromversorgung
wiederherstellen
Sachschaden

The reason why *pure economic loss* is **not recoverable in tort** is that allowing such claims may result in "liability in an indeterminate amount for an indeterminate time to an indeterminate class of people", i.e. in *potentially limitless liability* – see Cardozo, C.J. in *Ultramares Corporation* v *Touche (1931)*, an American case which is cited with approval in the English courts.

unbestimmt
Beifall/Gutbefund/Anerkennung

Compensating for economic loss in contractual matters is an entirely different case; in the latter, pure economic loss can be recovered because the parties are in contract with each other and there has been a breach of contract.

*(2) Negligent misstatement*

fahrlässige Falschangabe/-darstellung

The courts have been careful to examine whether it is right for a *duty of care* to be owed for negligent misstatement, since in cases involving negligent misstatement, there is not likely to be any physical loss, only economic loss.

wahrscheinlich nicht geben

The extent to which there can be a *duty of care* in relation to negligent *misstatements*, as opposed to negligent *acts*, is a problem that the courts have had to address in the recent past.

in jüngster Vergangenheit/vor kurzem

Formerly, the general rule was that a person was liable for negligent *acts* but not for negligent or unintentional *statements*, however inaccurate or misleading. Thus in *Candler* v *Crane, Christmas & Co (1951)* mentioned above, it was held that an accountant who negligently prepared certain accounts for a particular transaction was under no liability in tort in respect of those accounts, even though a claimant, in reliance on the accounts, invested money in the company and suffered financial loss as a consequence.

früher
Tat/Handlung – Äußerung
Bilanzbuchhalter/Rechnungs-/Wirtschaftsprüfer – Abrechnung/Rechenschaftsbericht – im Vertrauen auf
finanzieller Schaden

noch einmal durchdenken/ überprüfen – verwerfen/aufheben
fahrlässige Falschangabe/-darstellung

However, the House of Lords reviewed this area of the law and overruled it in the following case (which has been dealt with already in the context of "negligent misrepresentation" in vol. 1, p. 181 f.).

Since the following landmark decision, liability in tort can be founded on *negligent misstatement* in appropriate circumstances.

| *Example – Hedley Byrne & Co Ltd v Heller & Partners Ltd (1964)* |
|---|
| Hedley Byrne & Co Ltd were advertising agents who wished to do business with a company and had to pay that company a substantial sum in advance. Byrne wanted to check that company's creditworthiness. They therefore contacted the company's bankers, Heller, for a reference. Heller wrote a favourable reference, but headed the document "without responsibility". Byrne acted on the report and gave substantial credit to the company, but the company became insolvent shortly afterwards and Byrne suffered substantial losses. They claimed that the reference was misleading and sued Heller in *negligence*.<br>***Held:*** that a banker would normally be liable in negligence in this type of situation. A *duty of care* will arise where a person provides information or **advice, to someone who he knows (or should know) will be relying on it,** and the person giving the advice is so placed that the other **person could reasonably rely on his judgment** or skill or on his ability to make careful enquiry.<br>*Note*: In this particular case, as the information was given expressly *"without responsibility"*, this *duty of care* could not arise. Therefore the bankers were not in fact held liable for Hedley Byrne's losses, because of the disclaimer of liability. |

Werbeagent
Kreditwürdigkeit
betiteln/ausfertigen
sich richten nach/befolgen
beachtlich/beträchtlich
irreführend
vertrauen auf
Ermittlung/Nachforschung
Haftungsausschlussklausel

Urteilsgründe

The ratio of *Hedley Byrne* can be summarised as follows. One can recover *economic loss* caused by **negligent misstatement**, so long as

- a *special relationship* exists,
- the claimant *relies* on the defendant's skill and knowledge, and
- it was *reasonable* for him to rely on the advice.

Fachkenntnis und Wissen
Rat(schlag)

As this opened a new area of tortious liability, the House of Lords imposed strict limitations upon the situations which would give rise to such liability by establishing the need for a *special relationship* between the parties, in which it was *reasonable* for the person who suffered the economic loss to have *relied on the advice* of the other party.

Such *special relationships* have been held to arise, for example, between a solicitor and his client, a bank clerk advising a borrower on a mortgage loan, an environmental health inspector and the owners of a guest house, and a friend purchasing a car on his friend's behalf, as in the following example:

Hypothekenkredit

| *Example – Chaudry v Prabhakar (1988)* |
|---|
| Ms Chaudry, a junior accountant, wanted to buy her first car. She asked Mr Prabhakar, a friend who had some knowledge of cars, though not a mechanic (he worked in a grocer's), to find a suitable car that had not been involved in an accident. The friend found her a VW Golf which he recommended. It was subsequently discovered to have been involved in a serious accident, had been poorly repaired after the accident and it was unroadworthy.<br>***Held:*** that the friend was **liable for his misleading advice**, even though he had acted solely out of friendship.<br>*Note*: that Stocker L.J. stated, however, that: "in the absence of other factors giving rise to such a duty, the giving of advice sought in the context of family, domestic or social relationships will not in itself give rise to any duty in respect of such advice." In such situations it would **not be reasonable to respect the advice to be relied on**. |

Lebensmittelladen

dürftig repariert

nicht verkehrssicher

entstehen lassen

suchen – innerhalb

The criteria from *Hedley Byrne* v *Heller* were restated in *Caparo Industries plc* v *Dickman (1990)* – see above: the House of Lords held that the auditors of a company's accounts did not owe a *duty of care* in negligence to persons who might buy shares in that company in the future. Lord Bridge stated that to be liable, the auditors must know who is relying on the statement and to what use it is being put.

Argument/Maßstab/Kriterien – bekräftigen

Wirtschafts-/Bilanz-/Rechnungsprüfer – Unternehmensbilanz

wofür es gebraucht wird

On the other hand, someone who is giving advice free of charge may owe a *duty of care* where the circumstances make it clear that considered advice is being sought.

kostenlos/umsonst

wohlüberlegter Rat

In the case of *White* v *Jones (1995)*, for example, the House of Lords decided that liability for negligent advice would be established in tort where the claimant can prove that advice was communicated in circumstances where the two parties were in a *special relationship* and it was *reasonable* for the claimant to have *relied on that advice*.

*Example – White v Jones (1995)*

In a family dispute, the father changed his will in March 1986 so that his daughters received nothing. 6 months later, a reconciliation took place and, in July 1986, the father gave his solicitors (the defendant) instructions to draw up a new will giving his daughters £9,000 each. The solicitors delayed carrying out the father's request and, after a month, he renewed his instructions. The solicitors had still failed to act by the time the father, who was 78, died in September 1986.

***Held:*** the daughters were entitled to recover *damages* from the father's solicitors for negligence. A professional person such as a solicitor, according to the House of Lords, has to "act with due expedition and care" on behalf of his clients. In the case of writing a will, the intention of the client is to benefit the beneficiaries, and so the solicitor also owes the beneficiaries a *duty of care* if he is negligent in implementing the instructions of his client.

Versöhnung
eines neues Testament aufsetzen
sich verspäten – ausführen
unterdessen
gebührend
ausführen/umsetzen

In other words, the principle of this case is: reliance on a statement of promise by the claimant is not essential to establish a duty of care; the assumption of responsibility by a solicitor towards a client extends to the intended beneficiary. Therefore to sue for *economic loss* caused by *negligent advice* one must prove both (1) a **special relationship** with the advisor and (2) also that it was **reasonable** to have **relied on that advice**.

Übernahme
sich erstrecken auf – vorgesehen/geplant/bestimmungsgemäß/beabsichtigt

*(3) Nervous shock*

Nervenschock

Another exception which, at first, does not seem to have much in common with economic loss is *nervous shock* or *psychiatric injury*. Both increase the prospect of potentially countless claims as a single incident could affect a multitude of people.

Aussicht/Wahrscheinlichkeit erhöhen – unzählig

One means of limiting the potential number of claimants is the stipulation that the *psychiatric injury* suffered must be a **medically recognised condition**, e.g. post-traumatic stress disorder, pathological grief, personality disorder or miscarriage. Not medically recognised are distress and simple grief.

Mittel/Weg
Bedingung/Maßgabe
in der Medizin feststehendes Krankheitsbild – posttraumatisches Stresssyndrom – Trauer als Krankheitsbild – Persönlichkeitsstörung – Fehlgeburt – Verzweiflung – einfacher Kummer

Moreover, the psychiatric damage must be caused by **sudden witnessing** – by sight or sound – a horrifying event.

In addition to these *two particular* preconditions (medical recognition and sudden witnessing), the *four general* preconditions for constituting a tort of negligence also must be fulfilled (duty of care, breach of the duty, factual causation and remoteness).

To be recoverable, the *damage* not only has to be *reasonably foreseeable*, but the claimant also must

- be a close relative of the victim, an unwilling participant in the event or a passive, unwilling witness (**special relationship** between claimant and victim), and
- be **proximate** in both time and space to the scene of the incidence (see below "aftermath test").

naher Verwandter – unfreiwillig Zeuge

in zeitlicher und räumlicher Nähe

*Example – McLoughlin v O'Brian (1983)*

The claimant's husband and children were involved in a serious road accident. The claimant was told of the accident about two hours later by a neighbour who took her to hospital to see her husband and her daughters. There she learnt the horrific news that her youngest daughter had been killed, and she saw her husband and the other children, and witnessed the nature and extent of their injuries. They were still in the same state as at the scene, covered in oil and mud. As a result of what she saw, combined with the horrific news of the death of her daughter, she suffered severe *nervous shock*.

***Held:*** that, although distance and time were factors to be considered, they were *not* legal restrictions. The mother was entitled to damages for *nervous shock*, even though she was not present at the accident, because she came upon the **immediate aftermath of the accident** and the nervous shock was a **reasonably foreseeable** consequence of the injuries to her family caused by the defendant's negligence.

Verkehrsunfall

wie am Unfallort

Öl und Dreck

erleiden – ernst/heftig/schlimm

rechtliches Hindernis

die unmittelbaren Auswirkungen vorfinden

**Reasonable foreseeability** of nervous shock alone is not enough. In addition to reasonable foreseeability of the damage the factors mentioned above must also be considered: the **relationship** between the victim and the claimant, the **proximity** of the claimant in time and space to the scene of the accident and the means by which the shock is caused. There is no need for the claimant to be present at the time of the incident, but he must come upon the immediate aftermath. This so-called "**aftermath test**" was adopted by Lord Wilberforce in *McLoughlin* v *O'Brian* and also applied in the following case.

unmittelbare Folgen/Auswirkungen

übernehmen

anwenden

*Example – Alcock v Chief Constable of South Yorkshire (1992)*

Actions for *nervous shock* were brought against the police arising from a disaster at the Hillsborough football stadium in Sheffield. The arrangement for letting a large number of late-arriving supporters into the stadium went wrong. The police mistakenly opened a gate, intended only as an exit, into a cordoned-off area

entstehen aus

Unglück/Katastrophe

Anhänger – versehentlich

abgesperrter Bereich

überfüllt
zerquetschen

of the terraces which was already overcrowded. 95 people were crushed to death. The tragedy was caught on live television as it was happening and no-one was able to stop it.

Claims were brought by relatives and friends of the victims who had suffered psychiatric illness as a result of their experiences. A number of them had been in other parts of the stadium from where they had witnessed the events. Others had seen the disaster live on television. Some of the claimants had identified bodies at the mortuary; others suffered solely from being told the news. The claimants based their claim on the argument that the sole test for *a duty in nervous shock* was **reasonable foreseeability.**

Leichenhalle

das einzige Kriterium

***Held:*** the only persons who could bring a claim for *nervous shock* are those who can satisfy all the following conditions (1) they have **close ties of love and affection with the victim**; (2) they must have been **present at the accident or its immediate aftermath**, and (3) the psychiatric injury must have been **caused by direct perception of the accident or its immediate aftermath** and not upon hearing about it from someone else.

Band

Wahrnehmung

## b) Breach of the duty

Once it has been established that there *is* a duty of care owed by the person who caused the injury or damage (the defendant), to the person who suffered it (the claimant), the next question is whether there has been a *breach* of that duty? In other words, whether the defendant has not come up to the *standard of care* required by law.

erfüllen/gerecht werden – Sorgfaltsmaßstab

### *aa) Standard of care – the reasonable person*

verständiger Mensch/vernünftige Person/*hier*: Durchschnittsbürger

A defendant will be in *breach of duty* if he has acted *negligently*, which means that he has not acted in a reasonable way, but carelessly. The question which arises is then how a **reasonable person** would have acted in the defendant's position? According to Baron Alderson in *Blyth* v *Birmingham Waterworks (1856)*, negligence may be explained as "the omission to do something which *a reasonable man*, guided upon those considerations which ordinarily regulate the conduct of human affairs, would do or doing something which *a prudent and reasonable man* would not do".

nachlässig/unsorgfältig

Unterlassen
von Überlegungen geleitet sein
normalerweise regeln – Verhalten in menschlichen Angelegenheiten – umsichtig und vernünftig

The **standard of the reasonable person**, of course, varies with each individual situation but, as a general rule, the standard is that of a person who uses ordinary care and skill. In other words: all our actions are compared to those of an *ordinary reasonable man*, who is neither careless nor overly careful. The reasonable person is *average*, not perfect.

die im Verkehr erforderliche Sorgfalt – variieren/sich ändern

gewöhnliche Sorgfalt und Geschick

übermäßig sorgfältig

In the early $20^{th}$ century judges gave an example of the *ordinary reasonable man* as "a man on the Clapham omnibus". Clapham is a district of south London which, in those days,[7] was an ordinary but respectable suburb where the reasonable man would be found going about his daily life, such as travelling to and from work by bus.

Instead of asking the question "what did this *particular* defendant foresee in this particular situation?" the general (objective) question is "what would a *reasonable* person have foreseen in this particular situation?"

| *Example – Condon v Basi (1985)* |
|---|
| During a football match, the defendant recklessly tackled the claimant, breaking his leg. The defendant was sent off by the referee.<br>***Held:*** that the defendant was liable in *negligence*, the foul falling below the **standard of care** reasonably expected in any match. |

unbesonnen/rücksichtslos – angehen/angreifen – jmd. des Spielfelds verweisen – Schiedsrichter

Foul

unterschreiten

### *bb) Special standards of care*

There are certain situations in which the courts apply a different standard of care from that of the reasonable person, since the application of the latter would not be suitable.

geeignet/sachdienlich/angemessen

Such a situation is when the defendant has a **particular skill or professional expertise**:

7 Despite changes in the character of cities over the years, this expression is still regularly used by English lawyers. Note the old-fashioned word which the judges use for "bus".

trotz

sich unterziehen – Elektroschock-therapie – Beckenbruch

Entspannungsmedikament
Sicherungsmaßnahme – (Zeugen-) Aussage machen – Praxis
*hier*: Gruppe

*Example – Bolam v Friern Hospital Management Committee (1957)*

A patient agreed to undergo electro-convulsive therapy (E.C.T.). During the treatment he suffered a fracture to the pelvis. The issue was whether the doctor was negligent in failing to give a relaxant drug before the treatment, or in failing to provide means of restraint during the procedure. Evidence was given of the practices of various doctors in the use of relaxant drugs before E.C.T. treatment. One body of medical opinion favoured the use of relaxant drugs, but another body of opinion took the view that they should not be used because of the risk of fractures.
***Held:*** that the patient's claim failed. A defendant is not negligent if he acts in accordance with the practice accepted at the time as proper by a responsible body of professional opinion skilled in a particular form of treatment.

ausgebildet/qualifiziert – praktischer Arzt – Chirurg

This leading case in the area of clinical negligence establishes the general principle that the appropriate test for judging the acceptable **standard of professional behaviour** is *not* that of the ordinary man: the defendant is judged by the standard of the *ordinary skilled person* in that trade or profession. Thus: a doctor must show the skill of a reasonably competent doctor, a surgeon must show the skill of a reasonably competent surgeon, etc.

Fahrschüler – messen an/beurteilen nach

In contrast to cases of skilled or professional defendants, there are cases where the defendant has a **particular lack of skill**. The inexperience or lack of skill of the defendant is not taken into account in his favour, as shown by *Nettleship* v *Weston (1971)* where it was held that a learner is judged against the standard of a reasonably competent driver. The defendant's inexperience as a driver who had only just passed her driving test could *not* excuse the fact that her driving was below the standard of a reasonably competent driver.

### *cc) Other elements to consider*

geeignet/angemessen
weit hergeholt

What is appropriate will depend on the circumstances of each particular case. What may seem far-fetched to one judge may seem natural and probable to another, as stated by Lord Macmillan in *Glasgow Corporation* v *Muir (1943)*.

Vorkehrungen

A duty of care is owed to each person individually and, consequently, a breach of duty and the extent of the need to take the precautions to avoid the risk of doing harm to another person will differ from case to case.

The following examples illustrate how the court goes about assessing each case.

feststellen/bewerten/beurteilen

*Example – Paris v Stepney Council (1951)*

The Council employed Mr Paris as a low-grade mechanic in one of their garages, and knew that he was blind in one eye. He was working in conditions which involved some risk of eye injury but the likelihood of this injury was not sufficient to call upon the Council to provide goggles to a normal two-eyed workman. Mr Paris was hammering on a rear axle when a chip of metal came flew off and into his good eye. He became blind in that eye, too.

***Held:*** that the duty of employers was owed to each particular employee. The Council, as employer, were negligent in failing to provide goggles to this particular employee. In this case, the risk to a two-eyed workman was the loss of one eye but this employee risked the much greater injury of total blindness.

niedrig qualifiziert/unausgebildet

Wahrscheinlichkeit – veranlassen

Schutzbrille

Hinterachse

This decision shows that the obligations of a potential defendant may increase where the risk to a particular claimant is greater than normal.

steigen/zunehmen

*Example – Kirkham v Greater Manchester Police (1990)*

Mr Kirkham, while suffering from clinical depression, had been arrested and charged with an offence. His wife told the police that her husband was a suicide risk but, after he had been remanded in custody, the police failed to follow the procedure for notifying the prison authorities that he had suicidal tendencies. At the remand centre, Mr Kirkham was treated like a normal prisoner and he committed suicide there. His wife claimed damages for *negligence*.

***Held:*** that her claim would be successful as the police, by failing to pass on relevant information, had been in **breach of their duty of care**. The defence of *volenti non fit injuria** failed because, in the light of the deceased's mental condition, his suicide had not been a truly voluntary act. Also the defence of *ex turpi causa non oritur actio* did not apply as suicide is no longer an affront to the public conscience.

klinische Depression

zu einer Strafe verurteilen

selbstmordgefährdet sein – in Gewahrsam nehmen – verständigen

Untersuchungsgefängnis

weiterleiten/-geben

freiwillige Handlung

* Remember: The voluntary assumption of risk constitutes a complete defence.

*hier:* Übernahme/Eingehung

The maxim *ex turpi causa non oritur actio* mentioned above – also known as the *illegality defence* – means that no action can be brought where the parties are guilty of illegal or immoral conduct. The law will not allow a claim based on something illegal.

*lat*: „die Sache spricht für sich selbst"

#### *dd) Res ipsa loquitur*[8]

Beweis – liefern/erbringen
nachweisen – wahrscheinlich

In general, the *claimant* has to prove that the defendant has breached his duty of care. The proof is furnished if the claimant demonstrates that it was more likely than not that the damage was caused by the defendant's negligence.

offensichtlich

There are, however, some situations when it is obvious that a person has been negligent. These situations are expressed by the maxim *res ipsa loquitur*, as they would not have happened without someone having been negligent. The *res ipsa loquitur* rule has been applied, for instance, where

Sack – oberes Stockwerk – treffen
wahrscheinlich sein
Wattebausch/Tupfer

- bags of sugar fell from an upper floor of warehouse, hitting a person passing below. As sugar bags do not normally fall from the sky, the defendant was likely to have been negligent – *Scott v London & St Katherine's Dock Co (1865)*;
- swabs were left in a patient's body after an operation – *Mahone v Osborne* (*1939*).

Beweislast
übergehen/sich verlagern auf

In situations such as these, therefore, the burden of proof moves to the *defendant*. It is for him to show that he had *not* acted negligently in order to avoid being held liable for having breached his duty of care.

Sachzusammenhang, *hier*: haftungsbegründende Kausalität

### c) Factual causation

We have seen at the beginning of this section that the court must first decide that the defendant *owed a duty of care* to the claimant. Secondly, the claimant must prove *that the duty was breached*. Finally in order to establish his claim, the claimant must show that he or his property has suffered *damage*.

ohne; *hier*: condictio sine qua non/ Äquivalenzkausalität

#### *aa) The "but for" test*

Kausalkette

The claimant must prove that the *damage was caused by the negligent act* of the defendant. This is often referred to as the **chain of causation**.

8 In Latin: "the thing speaks for itself".

The breach of the duty must be the factual cause, or the factual material cause, of the damage.

tatsächlich – Ursache
maßgebliche Ursache/Hauptursache

The general test used by the courts to determine **factual causation** is known as the **"*but for*" test.** As Lord Denning underlined in *Cork* v *Kirby MacLean Ltd (1952):* "If the damage would not have happened but for a particular fault, then that fault is the cause of the damage. If it would have happened just the same, fault or no fault, the fault is not the cause of the damage".

wenn nicht/ohne

*Example – Barnett* v *Chelsea & Kensington Hospital Management Committee (1968)*

Mr Barnett drank tea which had, unknown to him, been contaminated with arsenic. He attended at the casualty department of a hospital saying that he had been vomiting for some three hours after drinking the tea. The casualty doctor failed to examine him but sent a message that he should report to his own doctor. Some five hours later Mr Barnett died and his widow claimed for damages.
***Held:*** that the hospital authority owed a *duty of care* and that the doctor was negligent in failing to examine and admit Mr Barnett to the hospital. Accordingly there had been *a breach of that duty*. However, on the facts the deceased's condition was such that he would have died despite any medical attention which the hospital could have given, so **causation** was not established and the widow's claim failed.

aufsuchen/sich anmelden
Notfall-/Unfallaufnahme
vorstellig werden
aufnehmen
demzufolge

*Example – Ogwo* v *Taylor (1988)*

Mr Ogwo, a fireman, called to put out a fire which Mr Taylor had negligently caused in the loft of his house by using a blowlamp to remove paint from the fascia board behind the guttering of his terraced house. The fireman had to go into the roof space in order to put out the fire, which he did with water. Whilst he was spraying the water onto the fire, heat of the fire caused some of the water to turn to steam and scalded the fireman underneath his protective clothing.
***Held:*** Mr Taylor was liable as his negligence had created a foreseeable risk that a fireman would come to put out the fire, and there had been no break in the **chain of causation.**

Dachboden/Speicher – Lötlampe
Simsbrett/Traufbrett – Dachrinne
verbrühen
Unterbrechung der Kausalkette

Although the *"but for"* test might seem straightforward, there are situations in which proving **factual causation** can be quite difficult.

klar/einfach

Ursachenvielfalt/mehrfache Ursachen

### *bb) Multiple causes of damage*

verschiedene Ansichten einnehmen

Where there is more than one possible cause of harm to the claimant (problem of **multiple causation**), the courts have taken different views.

If, for instance, A and B shoot C *at the same time* and the combined effect of the double injury results in C's death, the "*but for*" test leads to the result that neither A's nor B's shot is the material cause of C's death.

angesehen werden als

Where, however, two *independent events* cause the damage, and the second defendant's act produces the same damage as that caused by the first defendant, the first event is treated as the cause.

Where there is *more than one or two causes*, the defendant's conduct must be the material cause of damage.

zu früh geboren
Säuglingsstation – übermäßig
Netzhaut
unheilbarer Zustand der Netzhaut
Frühchen
medizinische Beweisführung
ergebnislos
Augenlicht

> *Example – Wilsher v Essex Area Health Authority (1988)*
>
> A baby was born prematurely and needed extra oxygen to survive. In the baby unit of the hospital he was given excess oxygen which caused damage to the retina (part of the eye) and consequent blindness.
> *Inter alia*, it was later discovered that the baby had an incurable condition of the retina. This condition could have been caused by excess oxygen, but it was a condition which also occurred in premature babies suffering from the same illnesses as this particular baby. The medical evidence at the trial was inconclusive as to the true cause of the condition of the retina.
> ***Held:*** that it had not been proven that the negligence in giving excess oxygen was *the material cause* of the damage to the baby's eyesight. As there were five possible causes of the baby's blindness and none of the potential causes was more likely to have happened than any of the others, the actual material cause could not be determined.

*lat.*: „neu eintretende Handlung"; *etwa*: Unterbrechung des Kausalzusammenhanges durch ein dazwischen tretendes Ereignis

### *cc) Novus actus interveniens*

This Latin phrase means "a new act intervenes", i.e. a fresh act of someone other than the defendant which occurs between the happening of the alleged wrong and the damage in question being suffered. The intervening act may be an act of a third party, an act of the claimant himself or an act of nature.

*Example – Baker v Willoughby (1970)*

In a road accident caused by the defendant's negligence, the claimant suffered an injury to his left leg. Before the trial of his negligence action, the claimant was the victim of an armed robbery at his place of work. He suffered gunshot wounds to his left leg and, as a result of his injuries, his leg had to be amputated. The defendant admitted negligence but argued that his responsibility ended when the claimant was shot and, therefore, all losses from the date of the shooting flowed from the robbery.
***Held:*** that the defendant's argument was to be rejected on the ground that it produced a manifest injustice and that he remained liable for the full extent of the claimant's damage. Thus, the second event was not considered by the court as a *novus actus interveniens.*

bewaffneter Überfall
Schussverletzung
herrühren von
zurückweisen

In a later case, however, it was held that if the second event had occurred naturally and had been unconnected with the first event, it may be unfair to make the defendant also responsible for that second event.

passieren/geschehen – ohne Zusammenhang

*Example – Jobling v Associated Dairies Ltd (1981)*

In 1973, in the course of his employment and as a result of his employer's negligence, a man suffered a slipped disc; his earning capacity was reduced by 50 %. Nearly four years later he was found to be suffering from a spinal disease, unrelated to his accident, and by the time (1979) that his claim came to trial, this disease had rendered him totally incapable of any work.
***Held:*** that the employer's liability was limited to loss of earnings up to the time when the disease resulted in total incapacity.

bei Verrichtung seiner Arbeit
Arbeitgeber – Bandscheibenvorfall
Rückenleiden – ohne Bezug zu
Verdienstausfall

*Example – Sayers v Harlow Urban District Council (1958)*

The Council owned and operated a public lavatory. Mrs Sayers paid for admission and entered a cubicle. Finding that there was no handle on the inside of the door and no means of opening the cubicle, she tried for some 10 to 15 minutes to attract attention. Having failed to do so, and wishing to catch a bus to London in the next few minutes, she tried to see if there was a way of climbing out. She placed one foot on the seat of the lavatory and rested her other foot on the toilet roll fixture, holding the pipe from the cistern with one hand and resting the other hand on the top of the door. She then realised it would be impossible to climb out and she proceeded to come down, but as she was

betreiben – öffentliche Toilette
Kabine
Griff
auf sich aufmerksam machen
herausklettern
Rohrleitung
Spülkasten
sich anschicken

sich drehen
ausrutschen

in diesem Fall – *hier*: sich einlassen auf
die Konsequenzen tragen

Zwangslage

vermindern
Anteil

doing so, the toilet roll rotated owing to her weight on it and she slipped and injured herself. She sued the Council for negligence. In the county court, the Council was found to have been negligent in maintaining the door of the cubicle. However, she was in no danger on that account, and as she chose to embark on a dangerous act, she must bear the consequences.

***Held*** *(by the Court of Appeal):* that her act was not a *novus actus interveniens*, and the damage was not too remote as a consequence of the Council's negligence. She was 36 years of age, and in her predicament, her act was not unreasonable, though if she had been an old lady it might have been. However, the damages recoverable by Mrs Sayers would be reduced by one-quarter in respect of her share of the responsibility for the damage.

Entferntheit/Abgelegenheit – *hier*: haftungsausfüllende Kausalität

## d) Remoteness – legal causation

A defendant is only liable for damage which a reasonable man could have foreseen. Otherwise the damage is considered *too remote*, and so the breach of the duty of care is not considered *in law* to have caused the damage (the principle of **legal causation or causation in law**).

The last question in the context of negligence is for how much of the claimant's loss should the defendant be responsible?

unabhängig davon, ob

überdenken/überprüfen

Until comparatively recently, the court applied the principle that the defendants were liable for *all* damages resulting from the breach of the duty, regardless of whether or not that damage was foreseeable by the defendant *(Re Polemis and Furniss, Withy & Co Ltd (1921))*. This was criticised for its unfairness and reviewed in various cases including the following:

*Example – "The Wagon Mound"; Overseas Tankship (UK) Ltd v Morts Dock & Engineering Co Ltd (1961)*

Unachtsamkeit
Heizöl – auslaufen
Wind und Gezeiten/Tide – Werft
Schweissarbeiten – durch-/ausführen
Auskünfte einholen

loderndes Feuer

Owing to the carelessness of the defendant, a large quantity of fuel oil was discharged from their ship into Sydney Harbour. The oil was carried by wind and tide onto a wharf about 600 feet away, where welding on another ship was being carried out. After making enquiries, the wharf owners were advised that it was safe to continue with the welding operations on their wharf. Two days later, the oil caught fire and the wharf and the ships being repaired were damaged in the blaze. The oil also

congealed on the slipways and interfered with the use of the slips. The wharf owners claimed in negligence against the person who had discharged the oil into the water.
***Held:*** the damage by the oil to the slipways was foreseeable. However, the defendant was not liable for the fire damage, because the oil would have had to be heated to a very high temperature in order to catch fire, and it was not reasonably foreseeable that that would happen. The **correct test for remoteness of damage** was whether the **kind or type of damage** sustained was **reasonably foreseeable**.

gerinnen – Helling* – stören
Helling/Aufschleppe (*Hafen*)

Entfernung des (Folge-)Schadens
erleiden

* „Helling" ist eine Vorrichtung im Hafen, um Schiffe vom Stapel laufen zu lassen.

This leading case establishes the **test of remoteness** for liability in negligence and is based, *inter alia*, on the **reasonable foreseeability of the damage** happening as a result of the negligent act. As the then Lord Chancellor Viscount Simmonds put it, "after the event even a fool is wise. But it is not the hindsight of a fool; it is the foresight of the reasonable man which alone determines responsibility".

damalig
Narr/Dummkopf – klug/weise
nachträgliche Einsicht – Voraussicht/ Weitblick – bestimmen

*"The Wagon Mound"* was heard in the *Privy Council.* Therefore – following "the doctrine of precedent" according to which decisions of the Judicial Committee of the Privy Council are not binding on English courts – the case is of persuasive authority only and could not overrule *Re Polemis* in the Court of Appeal. However, it has been followed in important cases, for instance by the House of Lords in *Hughes* v *Lord Advocate* (1963) and by the Court of Appeal in the following case:

verhandeln
Lehre des Präzedenzfalles

einschlägige (nicht bindende) Vorentscheidung

*Example – Doughty* v *Turner Manufacturing Co Ltd (1964)*

Mr Doughty was employed by the Turner Manufacturing. A fellow employee let an asbestos cement cover slip into a cauldron of molten metal. At that time, it was unknown that asbestos cement coming into contact with the molten metal would cause an explosion. An explosion resulted and Mr Doughty was injured. No similar accident had been known to occur previously.
***Held:*** that the accident, although it was a direct result of the action of an employee of the defendant company, it was not *reasonably foreseeable*. Therefore, the employer was not liable.

Asbestzementplatte – gleiten
großer Kessel – geschmolzenes Metall

Today, *"The Wagon Mound"* is accepted by the courts as the relevant test to analyse the question of remoteness.

Mitverschulden – *etwa*: Verteidigungsmittel, das die Haftung begrenzt

## 3. Contributory negligence as a partial defence

Besides the general *complete* defences such as consent (*volenti non fit injuria*) and illegality (*ex turpi causa non oritur actio*), there is a defence which is *partial* only.

In these cases, the defendant's liability for damages (i.e. the level of damages payable to the claimant) will be reduced if the defendant can show that the claimant did not, in his own interest, take reasonable care of himself and therefore contributed to his own injury.

Betrag
halten für – Anteil

Under the *Law Reform (Contributory Negligence) Act 1945,* the amount recoverable is reduced "to such an extent as the court thinks just and equitable having regard to the claimant's share in the responsibility for the damage."

zusprechen
*hier*: Schadensersatzsumme – Prozentsatz – halten für
gefangen

In practice, the court usually awards damages and then reduces the award by the percentage for which the claimant is held to be responsible. As we have seen above (cf. above, p. 49 f.) in *Sayers* v *Harlow Urban District Council (1958),* the woman who was trapped in a toilet was held to be contributory negligent by stepping on a toilet-roll holder when trying to escape.

*Contributory negligence* often arises in road traffic accidents:

Schutzhelm
nicht geschlossen

| *Example – Capps* v *Miller (1989)* |
|---|
| The claimant, a motor-cyclist, suffered head injuries as a result of the defendant's negligent driving. The claimant's crash helmet, which was unfastened, fell off before his head hit the road.<br>***Held:*** that although the sole responsibility for the accident lay with the defendant, the claimant's failure to secure his helmet had *contributed* to the injury. |

einen Unterschied machen
Schuld
verantwortlich
tragen

In this context, it is important to note that a distinction is drawn, in law, between blame *for an accident itself* and blame *for the injuries* that result from that accident. In this case, Miller was 100% to blame for the collision between his car and Capps' moped, but was held to be only 90% to blame for the injuries sustained by Capps. The court further considered that the reduction would have been greater if a helmet had not been worn at all.

A child is generally not found guilty of contributory negligence.

## 4. The *Occupiers' Liability Acts*

Grundstückshaftung/*dt. Recht:* Haftung wegen Verkehrsicherungspflicht

Readers will note that almost the whole of the law of negligence is based on case law – there are very few statutes. However, the issue of the liability of an occupier of premises, to persons who injure themselves or damage their property while on the occupier's premises, is **statutory law** governed by the *Occupiers' Liability Acts 1957 and 1984*. These *Acts* were passed after some rather difficult decisions in the courts led to a call for the law to be clarified.

*hier*: Besitzer/Betreiber/Eigentümer von Grundstücken, Räumlichkeiten, Firmengeländen etc.

Occupiers' liability is an important topic which is worth mentioning at the end of our chapter on negligence. We are all confronted with situations of everyday life when entering land or premises belonging to others: shops, university, pubs, the gym and even friends' houses.

Under *Occupiers' Liability Act 1957 s.2(1)* the **occupier of premises** owes a **common duty of care** to see that all **lawful visitors** will **be reasonably safe** when using the premises.

rechtmäßig

Let us take a short look at these preconditions:

(1) The **occupier of premises** is the person who controls them, or the landlord if he is responsible for repairs to the premises.
(2) The **common duty of care** means that the occupier owes a general and personal duty to take reasonable care to keep the visitor reasonably safe.
(3) **Lawful visitors** are all people with express or implied permission to enter the property, for example a guest, the postman or a contractor who is undertaking work on the building. Thus, lawful visitors are *neighbours* in the sense of the "neighbour principle" stated by Lord Atkin in *Donoghue* v *Stevenson* (see p. 29).

ausdrücklich – stillschweigend

**Unlawful visitors** are persons on the premises without the occupier's consent. They can be burglars or trespassers, and also people who wandered into the premises by mistake because they became lost. An occupier still owes some *duty of care* to such persons, but the *Occupiers' Liability Act 1984* provides that it is *at a lower level*. In order to be liable to an *unlawful visitor*, the occupier must:

Einbrecher – Besitzstörer

- be aware of the danger or have reasonable grounds to believe that it exists – for example, cellars or pools on derelict land which cannot be seen because the land has become overgrown;

verlassen/aufgegeben

überwachsen/überwuchern

Nähe/Umgebung/Nachbarschaft

- know or have reasonable grounds to believe that there are others in the vicinity of the danger, or who may come into the vicinity, and
- the risk is such that he may reasonably be expected to offer the other persons some protection.

*hier*: entfallen – Warnschilder

The duty that he then owes is to take such care as is reasonable in all the circumstances of the case to see that the person concerned does not suffer injury on the premises by reason of the danger concerned. This duty maybe discharged by putting up warning signs, but that by itself may not be sufficient – for example, if young children are likely to be involved.

darüber hinaus/obendrein

Moreover the general defence to negligence *volenti non fit iniuria* (see p. 35) is also included in the *1984 Act*.

**Diagram 40**

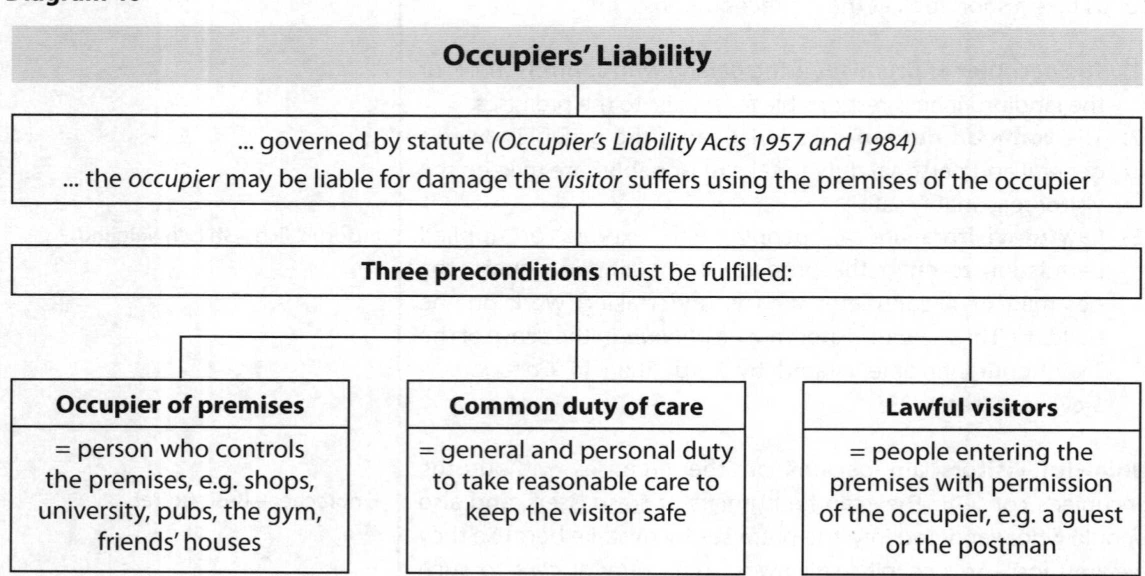

Diagram 41

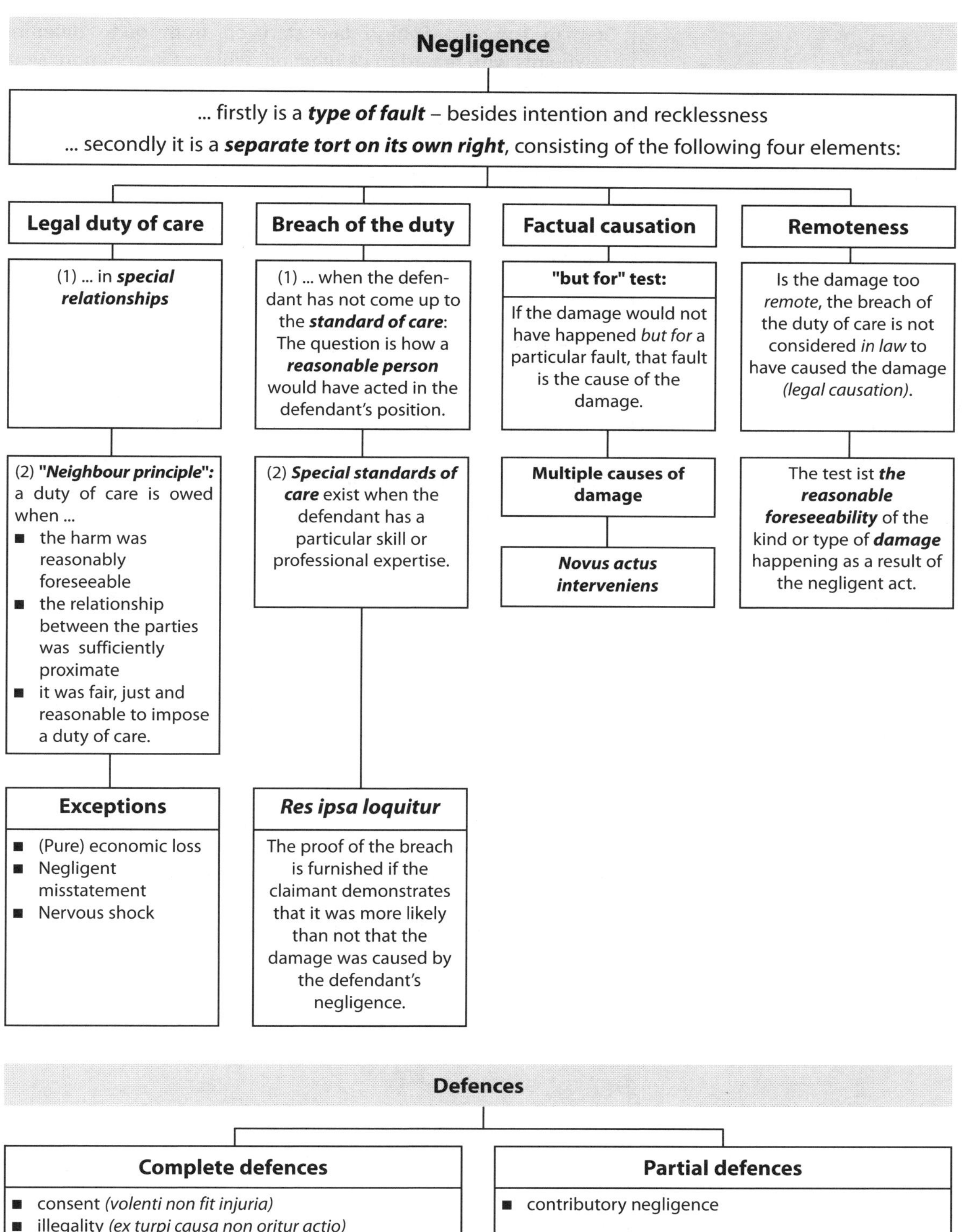
Negligence
... firstly is a type of fault – besides intention and recklessness
... secondly it is a separate tort on its own right, consisting of the following four elements:
Legal duty of care
(1) ... in special relationships
(2) "Neighbour principle": a duty of care is owed when ...
the harm was reasonably foreseeable
the relationship between the parties was sufficiently proximate
it was fair, just and reasonable to impose a duty of care.
Exceptions
(Pure) economic loss
Negligent misstatement
Nervous shock
Breach of the duty
(1) ... when the defendant has not come up to the standard of care: The question is how a reasonable person would have acted in the defendant's position.
(2) Special standards of care exist when the defendant has a particular skill or professional expertise.
Res ipsa loquitur
The proof of the breach is furnished if the claimant demonstrates that it was more likely than not that the damage was caused by the defendant's negligence.
Factual causation
"but for" test:
If the damage would not have happened but for a particular fault, that fault is the cause of the damage.
Multiple causes of damage
Novus actus interveniens
Remoteness
Is the damage too remote, the breach of the duty of care is not considered in law to have caused the damage (legal causation).
The test ist the reasonable foreseeability of the kind or type of damage happening as a result of the negligent act.
Defences
Complete defences
consent (volenti non fit injuria)
illegality (ex turpi causa non oritur actio)
Partial defences
contributory negligence

Ehrverletzung (Oberbegriff)/Verleumdung/üble Nachrede

## V. Defamation

Standpunkt
ausschlaggebend/entscheidend

Schmerzensgeld

German law and English law start off from quite different viewpoints with regard to *defamation*. Whereas in common law a right of action for damages has been a crucial legal instrument for centuries in protecting oneself against defamation, courts in Germany, by comparison, have only started to award compensation for immaterial damage comparatively recently. The reason behind the latter was that it had long been regarded as quite disgraceful to accept financial compensation for a situation in which one's reputation had been damaged in society.[9]

### 1. Definition and meaning

Veröffentlichung – ein schlechtes Licht werfen auf – Ruf – herabsetzen – Achtung – rechtschaffen denkend
Redefreiheit

*Defamation* is the publication of a statement which reflects badly on a person's reputation and tends to lower him in the estimation of right-thinking members of society generally. Although one of the fundamental human rights is freedom of speech, the tort of defamation protects an individual's private interest in his reputation.

Voraussetzung

In order to establish the *tort of defamation*, **three preconditions** are necessary:

ehrrührig/beleidigend/diffamierend

(1) There must be a **defamatory statement**.
(2) The statement must be **published to a third party**, (as necessary for the German crime of „Beleidigung" *§ 185 StGB*).

sich beziehen auf

(3) The defamatory statement must **refer to the claimant**.

### a) Defamatory statement

"Would the words tend to lower the plaintiff in the estimation of right-thinking members of society generally?" This was the question put by Lord Atkin in the following case:

9 Vgl. allgemeines Persönlichkeitsrecht als sonstiges absolutes Recht i.S.v. § 823 Abs. 1 BGB.

| *Example – Sim v Stretch (1936)* |
|---|
| When Edith Saville, a maid who had left the Mr Stretch's employment, went to work for Mr Sim, Mr Sim sent a telegram to Mr Stretch saying: "Edith has resumed service with us today. Please send her possessions and the money you borrowed also her wages to Old Barton. Sim." Mr Sim alleged that the telegram suggested that he was short of money and had had to borrow money from his housemaid. ***Held:*** that the words in question were not reasonably capable of a *defamatory* meaning. |

Dienstmädchen

neu aufnehmen – Beschäftigung/ Dienstverhältnis – ausleihen/ausborgen – Lohn

knapp bei Kasse

The test of what "right-thinking" members of society think appears to be determined by what they *should* think rather than what in fact they *do* think.

eher als

| *Example – Byrne v Deane (1937)* |
|---|
| A golf club had some gambling machines unlawfully kept in the club house. These were removed after somebody had informed the police about this. Soon afterwards, someone wrote an anonymous poem and put it on the notice board of the club. The poem ended with the lines: "But he who gave the game away, may he byrne* in hell and rue the day." Mr Byrne was a member of the golf club, and claimed that the poem was defamatory because it suggested that he was guilty of underhand disloyalty to his fellow members. ***Held:*** that the claim failed. It could not be *defamatory* to "allege of a man ... that he has reported certain acts, wrongful in law, to the police ...". |

Glücksspielautomat

schwarzes Brett

Zeilen

in der Hölle schmoren – den Tag bereuen

heimlich – Untreue/Illoyalität – Vereinsgenossen

* The English pronunciation of the name Byrne is the same as the verb "to burn", which means „schmoren/brennen".

So Byrne's action was dismissed because *right-thinking* members of society would have approved of a person informing the police of an illegal practice.

Klage abweisen

billigen/gutheißen

### b) Innuendo

versteckte Andeutung/Anspielung/ beleidigende Unterstellung

It is possible that words are not defamatory *at first sight* and only appear as such when the surrounding circumstances have been considered. Thus, the statement may be **defamatory by implication**. It is sufficient if the statement was understood by others to have a defamatory meaning. In such a case, the claimant must show that the words contain an *innuendo* or *hidden meaning*

auf den ersten Blick

stillschweigend

versteckte Bedeutung

and that a reasonable person could, and in fact would, interpret the words used in a defamatory sense.

| *Example – Cassidy* v *Daily Mirror Newspapers Ltd (1929)* |
|---|
| The *Daily Mirror* published a photograph of Mr Cassidy with a woman, below which was an announcement of their engagement. The information on which the newspaper based its statement came from Mr Cassidy alone and the newspaper had made no effort to verify it from any other source. Mr Cassidy was already married, although he lived apart from his wife. However, he did occasionally stay with his wife at her flat. She brought an *action for libel** claiming that readers who knew her as Mr Cassidy's wife would assume that she had been lying about being married to him, and instead had been engaged in immoral cohabitation. ***Held:*** that the newspaper was liable. The story would be understood by others as referring to Mrs Cassidy and the newspaper's complete ignorance of the circumstances could not prevent the statement from having a *defamatory meaning*. |

Verlobung – engagement
bestätigen lassen – to verify
gelegentlich/bisweilen – occasionally
Beleidigungsklage – action for libel
vermuten/annehmen – assume
*damals*: unmoralische Lebensgemeinschaft – immoral cohabitation
völlige Unkenntnis – complete ignorance

* See below section 2, libel and slander.

Furthermore, it is defamation if the claimant relies on an *innuendo* where the words are not defamatory in their natural and ordinary meaning but may be **defamatory when combined with extrinsic facts known to others about the situation**.

sich auf etw. stützen/berufen – relies on
äußerlich – extrinsic

| *Example – Tolley* v *J.S. Fry & Sons Ltd (1931)* |
|---|
| Mr Tolley was a leading amateur golfer. Without his knowledge or consent, a chocolate manufacturer issued an advertisement showing Mr Tolley playing golf with a packet of their chocolate protruding from his pocket. A caddy was depicted as saying in a limerick* that the chocolate advertised was as excellent as Mr Tolley's drive. Mr Tolley brought an *action for libel* and alleged that the advertisement meant that he accepted money for the publication of this advertisement, and thereby prostituted his reputation as an amateur golf player. ***Held:*** the advertisement was defamatory as it was capable of bearing the meaning alleged in the *innuendo*. |

führend/maßgeblich – leading
Werbung/Anzeige – advertisement
herausragen – Caddie *(Golf)* – darstellen – Limerick – protruding – caddy – depicted – limerick
Treibschlag *(Golf)* – drive
preisgeben/verkaufen – prostituted
stützen – bearing

* Limerick ist ein „typisch britischer" fünfzeiliger Vers mit dem Reimschema „aa bb a" sowie „lang, lang, kurz, kurz, lang". Er sollte kurz und lustig sein. Example:

*There was an old lawyer called Rainer,*
*who thought English law could be finer.*
*So he soon undertook*
*to write this new book,*
*although a lawyer is not a rhymer!*

### c) Publication of the statement

This means that there is no defamation if the statement is published only to the claimant. It is defamation, however, if a third party hears the defamatory words, even by accident. Postcards can easily be read by other people. Thus, they are deemed to be published, even if the postman (or someone other than the recipient) has not actually read them.

zufällig
als veröffentlicht gelten
Empfänger

### d) Reference to the claimant

Bezug zum Kläger

Pertaining to the third element of defamation, the defendant's statement must be shown to be referring to the person claiming he has been defamed, but need not be a specific reference e.g. by name. The test is to ask whether ordinary sensible observers would believe that it was this person who was being referred to.

betreffend
beleidigen/diffamieren/verleumden

| *Example– Morgan v Odhams Press Ltd (1971)* |
|---|
| The newspaper, *The Sun*, alleged that a girl had been kidnapped by a dog doping gang because she was threatening to inform the police of their activities. At the relevant time the girl had been staying at Mr Morgan's flat. Mr Morgan produced six witnesses who swore that they understood from the article that he was connected with the gang. ***Held:*** that the story was capable of a defamatory meaning. There was no rule that the article should contain some kind of key to indicate the claimant himself, the question was whether readers who knew of the circumstances would reasonably have understood the article as referring to that person. |

Bande, die Rennhunde dopt (Hunderennen: typisch brit. Wettspiel) – drohen – *hier:* herbeischaffen
Zeugen
*etwa*: Aufschluss geben über den Kläger

The tort of defamation does **not require an intention** of the defendant to refer to the claimant with his statement.

| *Example – Hulton & Co v Jones (1910)* |
|---|
| The *Sunday Chronicle*, which was owned by Hulton, published an article in which appeared statements defamatory of a person described as 'Artemus* Jones', a churchwarden at Peckham, a district of London. The writer of the article and the editor of the newspaper both believed 'Artemus Jones' to be a purely fictious person. In fact, there was a real person named Artemus Jones, although he was not a churchwarden and did not live in Peckham. |

Kirchenvorsteher
fiktiv/erfunden

*brit.*: plädierender Anwalt bei höheren Gerichten

einräumen/zugeben

früher

behaupten/geltend machen

unabsichtlich

Vorname/Rufname

He was in fact a barrister** who, 7 years earlier, had written articles for that newspaper under his own name.
Mr Jones conceded that neither the author, the editor nor the owner of the newspaper intended to defame him, and accepted that they had in fact been unaware of his previous articles, but succeeded in showing that some of his friends thought that he was the subject of the article.
***Held:*** that the article was defamatory of the real Artemus Jones, because it was no defence for the author to contend that the defamation was unintentional.

* Artemus is a very rare first name in England.

** We have learned the role of a barrister in vol. 1, chapter 3, p. 58 ff.

Cases like this may today make use of the **defence of innocent publication** (see below). The defendant will not be liable under *s.1 of the Defamation Act 1996* if he can show 3 things: firstly, that he was neither the author, editor nor publisher of the statement; secondly, that he took reasonable care in relation to its publication; and lastly, that he did not know nor had any reason to believe that what he did caused or contributed to the publication of a defamatory statement.

Verleumdung und üble Nachrede

## 2. Libel and slander

The *tort of defamation* is divided into two categories, **libel** and **slander**. They differ in two ways, (1) the manner in which the statement is publicised, and (2) the consequences that are required before damages are paid.

Beleidigung/Verleumdung, und zwar schriftlich/gedruckt/dauerhaft

### a) Libel

senden

Karikatur

im Verlauf von – Theateraufführung

A libel is a defamatory statement which is **published in some permanent form**. The usual form is writing or printing. It also can be broadcasted on radio or television (*s.1, Defamation Act 1952*); it could be in painting or as a cartoon, on record or as an audio tape, CD or on the Internet *(see Godfrey v Demon Internet Ltd (1999))*. Equally, the publication of words in the course of performance of a play shall be treated as libel under the *Theatres Act 1968*.

Vermögens-/ finanzieller Schaden

Libel is **actionable *per se***, which means that it is the conduct which is wrong, irrespective of whether or not any harm is caused to the claimant as a result. Thus, he does **not have to prove special damage** (i.e. pecuniary loss).

Furthermore, libel also may be a *crime* as well as a *tort* if it tends to provoke a breach of the peace.

Störung der öffentlichen Sicherheit und Ordnung

### b) Slander

Beleidigung/Verleumdung in mündl. o. in anderer nicht dauerhafter Form

Slander is the publication of a defamatory statement in a transient, **non-permanent form**, usually by spoken words (but not if they are broadcasted as that falls within libel), gestures and facial mimicry.

vorübergehend/vergänglich – Geste – Mimik

Slander is **not actionable *per se***. Slander **requires special damage**. Thus, the claimant must establish some loss or harm that is quantifiable in financial terms, such as loss of a job or damage to business interests.

beweisen/Nachweis erbringen

There are **four exceptions** to the requirement for special damage to be shown. Slander is **actionable *per se*** if the following serious allegations are involved:

Behauptung – beteiligt/*hier*: darin vorkommen

(1) the claimant has committed a serious criminal offence,
(2) a girl or a woman is unchaste (*Slander of Women Act 1891*),
(3) the claimant is suffering from an infectious disease that prevents others from associating with him, or
(4) the claimant is unfit, dishonest or incompetent in relation to his trade, profession or business.

unkeusch – ansteckend – Umgang pflegen mit – ungeeignet – unehrlich – unfähig

In all these exceptions it is presumed that the claimant has suffered damage; thus slander is *actionable per se*.

## 3. Defences

There is a range of defences – besides the self-evident defence of **consent** of the claimant – that may defeat a claim for defamation even if the claimant has established all elements of the tort.

Reihe – selbstverständlich
Beleidigungsklage abschmettern

### a) Justification

Wahrheitsbeweis *(bei der Beleidigungsklage)*

The defence of justification, or truth, is a complete defence. The onus is on the defendant to prove that the allegations are true in substance and defamatory in character. Peripheral inaccuracies are tolerated (*s.5, Defamation Act 1952*).

*etwa:* Rechtfertigungsgrund, der zur völligen Haftungsbefreiung führt – die Beweislast liegt bei – nebensächlich – Ungenauigkeit

Privileg/Sonderrecht/*hier:* Immunität/Indemnität

### b) Privilege

sich durchsetzen gegenüber

Böswilligkeit

There are situations in which freedom of expression of facts or opinions prevail over private interests of an individual. The privilege can be *absolute* – such a statement is never actionable – or *qualified*, when privilege may be defeated by proof of the defendant's malice.

vollen Schutz genießen

The following statements carry complete protection from actions in defamation (**absolute privilege**):

- statements made in Parliament and official reports of parliamentary proceedings,
- statements made in judicial proceedings,
- information provided to the police *(Buckley v Dalziel (2007))*,
- communication between solicitors or barristers in the course of legal proceedings.

handeln aus Böswilligkeit – aus Boshaftigkeit

Certain other statements are also protected from actions for defamation (**qualified privilege**), however, only *as long as* the maker of the statement did not act out of malice, or out of spite, or knowing that the statement was untrue, or being reckless as to whether the statement was true or not:

- fair and accurate reports of parliamentary proceedings, e.g. in a newspaper,
- fair and accurate reports of public judicial proceedings,
- statements made to protect one's private interests,
- professional confidential communication between solicitor and client on legal advice,
- statements in testimonials or references to prospective employers,
- statements in a petition to Parliament,
- fair and accurate newspaper reports on various public matters of public interest and importance; *s.15 Defamation Act 1996 schedule 1* comprises a long list of publications that carry the protection of the qualified privilege.

Arbeitszeugnis – Empfehlung – zukünftig

Anhang

Tatsachenbezug/sachbezogene Natur

In the following case, the *defences of justification* (see above) and *fair comment* (see below) were unavailable because of the factual nature of a newspaper article. Therefore, the House of Lords had to decide if the *defence of qualified privilege* should be extended to cover mass media.

*Example – Reynolds v Times Newspapers (1999)*

*The Sunday Times* had published an article in Ireland stating that Reynolds, the former Irish Prime Minister, had deliberately and dishonestly misled the Irish Parliament. The article was subsequently published in the UK but did not include the explanation that Reynolds had given for the events, which had been printed in the original article. Reynolds brought a *libel action.*

***Held:*** that the defence that the article was subject to qualified privilege by reason of being political information was rejected. The court provided a non- exhaustive list of 10 criteria which the court should take into account in connection with the acceptance of the **defence of qualified privilege** when put forward by newspapers and other media. For example, the seriousness of the allegation, the nature of the information and the extent to which the subject-matter was a matter of public concern, the source and status of the information, the urgency of the matter, the tone of the article and other similar factors.

vorsätzlich
in die Irre führen
danach/anschließend
Erläuterung/Erklärung
Beleidigungsklage einreichen
erschöpfend/abschließend

Since then the court has recognised that there are occasions when the public interest requires that publication to the world at large should be privileged. The jurisdiction has been upheld in later decisions.

bestätigen/aufrecht erhalten

In *Jameel* v *Wall Street Journal Europe (2006)* the House of Lords has liberalised the *Reynolds* guidance, paving the way for British investigative journalism.

Richtlinien – den Weg bereiten für Enthüllungsjournalismus

*Example – Jameel v Wall Street Journal Europe (2006)*

*The Wall Street Journal Europe* published a story saying that bank accounts associated with a number of prominent Saudi citizens, including Mr Jameel's family, had been monitored by the Saudi government at the request of the US authorities to ensure that no money was provided intentionally or knowingly to support terrorist.

***Held:*** that the journal's appeal was successful. What the journal had published was clearly in the public interest. In doing so the House of Lords liberalised the "**public interest test**".

assoziieren mit/in Verbindung bringen mit – überwacht

## c) Innocent publication

arglos/schuldlos

weiterleiten/-geben

voraussetzen/erfordern

Veröffentlichung im Internet ermöglichen

There is a *defence* for those who merely pass on a defamatory statement without having taken an active part in creating it. Thus it is not defamation for a person, who is not the author, editor or publisher of the material, to *reproduce* material that they did not believe contained defamatory comment. That presupposes, however, that they took reasonable care in publishing the statement (*s.1 Defamation Act 1996*). In *Bunt* v *Tilley (2007)* it was held that an Internet service provider which performed no more than *a passive role* in facilitating postings on the Internet could not be considered to be publisher either.

## d) Fair comment

Beifall bekommen

People in public life, such as politicians, sport or film stars, etc. receive praise and must accept criticism. Provided that (1) the comments concern their **public activities**, (2) are based upon **true facts** and (3) are not made out of malice (i.e. they must be **fair**), they are not actionable in defamation. It is important to note, however, that this *defence of fair comment* only relates to statements of opinion on matters of **public interest**, e.g. government.

**Diagram 42**

## Defamation

... is the publication of a statement which reflects badly on a person's reputation and tends to lower him in the estimation of right-thinking members of society generally.

**Three preconditions:**

- **Publication of the statement**
- **Defamatory statement**
- **Reference to the claimant**

### Innuendo

... is a statement which is *defamatory by implication*. It is sufficient if the statement was understood by others to have a defamatory meaning.

### Libel

... is a defamatory statement published in some *permanent form*; e.g. writing, printing, broadcasting on radio or TV.

... is actionable *per se* and requires no proof of special damage.

### Slander

... is a defamatory statement published in a *transient, non-permanent form*; usually by spoken words, gestures or facial mimicry.

... is generally not actionable *per se*. The claimant must prove special damage.

## Defences

- **Justification**
- **Privilege**
  - absolute
  - qualified
- **Innocent publication**
- **Fair comment**

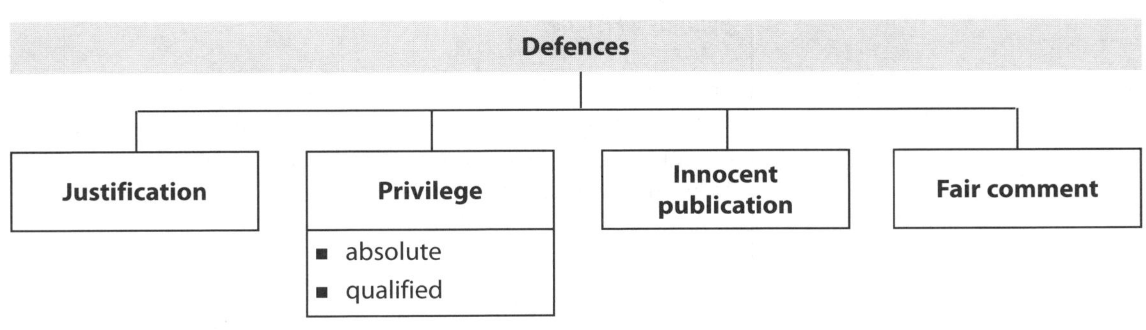

verschuldensunabhängige Haftung/ Gefährdungshaftung

## VI. Strict liability

### 1. General rule of liability in tort

schuldig sein (für)

A person is generally liable in tort when his act is done *intentionally, recklessly or negligently* – in German we would say „schuldhaft" (to be at fault for), see above p. 27.

In some cases, however, a person may be liable for his act merely for having done it, whether or not he acted intentionally, recklessly or negligently. This is called *strict liability*.[10]

Hersteller

*Strict liability* can be imposed by duties created by statute. For example under the *Consumer Protection Act 1987*, the manufacturer of consumer products is liable for any harm which the product causes, whether he was at fault or not. This liability for defective products is also strict and will be dealt with below (cf. section 4).

Beispiel/Umstand/Vorgang

A common law instance of *strict liability*, which is more than a hundred years older, is generally known as the rule in *Rylands* v *Fletcher (1868)*.

### 2. The rule in *Rylands* v *Fletcher*

Sparte/Bereich

This branch of the law of tort derives from the case of *Rylands* v *Fletcher*, a case which went to the House of Lords in 1868. It has not been given any other name in English law books except "the rule in *Rylands* v *Fletcher*".

Austritt

The situation which this rule addresses is the *escape* of something. In the case itself, it was an escape of water – *from land* occupied by one person (the defendant), which causes *damage* to the *property* of another person (the claimant).

10 Dieses englische Rechtskonzept war das Vorbild für das deutsche Produkthaftungsgesetz.

## a) The facts of the case

Sachverhalt des Falles

*Example – Rylands v Fletcher (1868)*

A mill operator constructed a reservoir on land he was renting to supply water to his steam-powered textile mill. The adjoining land was used for mining. Both activities were lawful uses of the respective lands, which were in Lancashire, in an area known for its mines, in the northwest of England. The mill operator engaged competent independent contractors and engineers to do the work of building the reservoir, which was completed in December 1860. While excavating the construction site, the contractors came across some disused mine shafts which had been loosely filled with marl and soil. No attempt was made to seal these shafts. The shafts actually led, via a series of interconnected shafts and tunnels, into the adjoining mines. Water from the new reservoir flooded into the adjoining mines on 11 December 1860, just days after completion of the reservoir and after it had been partially filled. There had been no excessive rains or local floods. There was a claim, against the mill operator by the owner of the adjoining mine, for damage to his mines and land caused by the flooding. ***Held:*** that the mill operator had *not been negligent*, but the claim would nevertheless succeed. The principle decided was that if **a person** (the defendant) **deliberately brings something onto his land** which, **if it escapes, would cause damage** ("any thing likely to do *mischief* if it escapes") **to the land of his neighbour** (the claimant), he is **liable if it does escape**, for all the natural consequences of its escape, whether or not he was at fault for the escape. The reasoning is that the claimant should not have to suffer on his land from what the defendant chose to do on his (the defendant's) land, because that is something outside his control.

Fabrikbetreiber – (Wasser-)Sammel-/Speicherbecken – dampfgetrieben

angrenzend/benachbart – Bergbau/Abbaubetrieb

selbstständiger Vertragsnehmer/Unternehmer

ausbaggern/ausschachten

Baustelle – stillgelegt

Schacht (Bergbau) – locker/lose – Mergel und Erde – abdichten

überfluten/-schwemmen

Fertigstellung

To give examples from the judgment of the type of situation which the court had in mind (in the 1860s), a claim under the rule in *Rylands* v *Fletcher* can be brought by "the person whose grass or corn is eaten down by the escaping cattle of his neighbour, or whose mine is flooded by the water from his neighbour's reservoir, or whose cellar is invaded by the filth of his neighbour's privy, or whose habitation is made unhealthy by the fumes and noisome vapours of his neighbour's alkali works ... ."

Dreck/Schmutz – Abtritt/Plumsklo

schädlich

Richtlinie/Leitfaden

## b) Guidelines

Instances when the rule in *Rylands* v *Fletcher* can apply are not particularly common, but cases do arise from time to time – indeed one also reached the House of Lords in 2004 (see below). From these cases, we can establish a few guidelines:

(1) **Collecting and keeping:** Something is artificially brought onto land by the defendant and is *collected and kept* on the land. Liability cannot be established if something that occurs naturally on the land escapes and causes harm. A person is not liable for permitting a spontaneous accumulation of water on his land because that occurs naturally.[11]

erhöht – geringer oder üblicher häuslicher Gebrauch

Mietshaus

häusliche Feuerstelle/Herd

(2) **Non-natural use of land:** The defendant has to be using his land for a *non-natural purpose*. That means that the things collected on the land by the defendant for his own purposes are used in a special – not *ordinary* – way which brings with it an increased danger to others. Minor or common domestic uses of water or fire have some potential for danger, but they are considered an ordinary use of land, so there is no claim under *Rylands* v *Fletcher* for water entering a flat in a block of flats where the water comes from the flat above, or for a fire which escapes from a domestic grate. The requirement of an non-natural use of land today must be considered by *contemporary circumstances*, which is illustrated by the following case:

(Rohr-)Leitung – *hier*: verlieren wegen Undichtheit

örtliche Gemeinde

Bahndamm/Böschung – aufdecken/freilegen – unvorhergesehene Ausbesserungsarbeiten

Wasserversorgung

Risiko/Gefahr/Wagnis

| *Example – Transco plc v Stockport Metropolitan Borough Council (2004)* |
|---|
| A pipe supplying a block of flats leaked water for a long time undiscovered. Thus, there was an escape of water from this pipe owned by the local authority (the defendant) caused an embankment to collapse, which exposed a gas pipe, thus necessitating expensive emergency remedial work by the claimant.<br>***Held:*** that the claimant did not succeed under the rule *Rylands* v *Fletcher*. The supply of water through pipes was normal and routine and not something that presented a particular hazard. The **risk** presented by any particular activity **has to be considered by contemporary circumstances**. As the pipe carried no more risk of fracture |

11 Note that a person could, however, be liable for the tort of nuisance, if he does not abate a nuisance which arises naturally on his land.

leading to the escape of water than any other pipe, it could not be considered a *non-natural use of land*. It was noted by the court that damage to property caused by leaking water was a risk against which insurance was available, so this situation did not meet the high threshold of exceptional risk arising from *non-natural use* that is required under *Rylands* v *Fletcher*.

Schwelle/Grenze

(3) **"Likely to do mischief if it escapes":** It is necessary to have a *dangerous thing* or – and this is also sufficient – a thing which is likely to cause harm if it escapes. There will be obviously dangerous things, such as gas, oil, chemicals, or blasting which, if they escape, will cause damage. There are things which are less obviously dangerous, such as water, but which can be used in a particular way so as to become dangerous. Having a glass of water on one's land will not cause mischief if the water escapes, but having millions of gallons in a reservoir would do.

Unheil anrichten

wahrscheinlich

Sprengarbeit/Sprengung

Gallone (Hohlmaß: 4, 54 l)

(4) **Escapes and causes harm:** The thing must escape and cause harm to the claimant's *property* or *interests in property*. Claims for recovery of personal injury should be brought under negligence and not under the rule *Rylands* v *Fletcher*.

Schadensersatzklage wegen Personenschaden/Körperverletzung

(5) **Foreseeability:** The potential for harm needs to be *foreseeable*. It has to be having been reasonably foreseeable that damage of the relevant type would occur as a result of the escape. This precondition cannot be found in the original case and has been added in more recent times.

Voraussehbarkeit – Möglichkeit

*Example – Cambridge Water Co v Eastern Counties Leather plc (1994)*

An old established leather manufacturer used PCE, a chemical solvent in their tanning process. PCE evaporates quickly in the air but is not readily soluble in water. In the course of the process, before a change of method in 1976, continual small spillages had gradually built up a pool of PCE under the factory. The solvent seeped into the soil below and contaminated the aquifer from which Cambridge Water Co drew their water to provide the public water supply in the area.

***Held:*** there was no liability under *Rylands* v *Fletcher* because the factory operator had not known, and could not **reasonably** have **foreseen**, that the spilled chemical would get into the aquifer or, even if it did, that it would be found in

Lösungsmittel – Gerbungsprozess

leicht wasserlöslich

kleine Pfütze

durchsickern/tropfen

grundwasserführende Schicht

öffentliche Wasserversorgung

nachweisbar – stromabwärts

detectable quantities downstream where the water was drawn.

selbstständiger Unternehmer
heruntergekommen/verfallen
Funken

*Example – Emanuel Ltd v Greater London Council (1971)*

The government arranged for an independent contractor to remove two derelict bungalows and all materials and rubbish from a site owned by the defendant Council. The contractors started a fire to burn unwanted materials. Sparks blew onto the neighbouring property and the resulting fire caused damage.
***Held:*** that the Council, as occupier, was *strictly liable* under the rule in *Rylands* v *Fletcher* for the escape of fire caused by the negligence of anyone other than a stranger. The contractors were on the land with the Council's permission, and although the contractors were forbidden by the terms of their contract from starting fires on the land, the Council could **reasonably** have **anticipated** that they might start a fire.

Verteidigungsmittel/Einwendung/Einrede/Klageerwiderung

## c) Defences

There are certain defences to a claim under *Rylands* v *Fletcher*:

- the claimant had **consented** to the collecting and keeping of the dangerous thing that escaped, and the defendant had not been negligent;
- the escape was due to the **act of a stranger**;
- the event was an **act of God**, which could not have been foreseen or prevented; (höhere Gewalt)
- the defendant's actions were **authorised by statute** (statutory authority), in which case he will not be liable, provided that he has acted in line with the statutory requirements and he had not been negligent in carrying out his duty; (im Rahmen der/in Übereinstimmung mit)
- if the claimant was partly to blame for the damage to his property, e.g. by failing to take proper precautions against the sort of harm, which occurred, any award of damages may be reduced to reflect this: **contributory negligence**. (zum Teil – schuld sein; etw. versäumen; Mitverschulden)

### d) The role of *Rylands* v *Fletcher* in modern tort law

It must be noted that this area of law greatly overlaps with *negligence, private nuisance* and *trespass to land*. This has evoked much criticism from the judiciary and academic commentators who suggest that *Rylands* should be integrated into the principle of ordinary negligence (as in Australian jurisdictions). The House of Lords (in *Transco plc* v *Stockport Metropolitan Borough Council (2004)*, see above) quite firmly refused to do this. Once more, it underlined its view that the *Rylands* rule was an particular aspect of the law of private nuisance for the following reasons:

- the case established the principle of strict liability which has been applied for many years (since the 1860s); abandoning this principle would therefore create a new legal situation;
- it was feared that the interpretation of statutes which create strict liability might require proof of negligence from thereof;
- finally, the court justified its position of adhering to the principle of strict liability by emphasising its proximity to continental law in Europe (e.g. Germany and France).

For the time being, strict liability as established in *Rylands* v *Fletcher* is not likely to disappear from the map of English tort law.

sich überschneiden mit
hervorrufen
Justiz/rechtsprechende Gewalt
festhalten an
bis auf Weiteres/fürs Erste

### 3. The *Consumer Protection Act 1987*

In addition to the common law rules under cases such as *Donoghue* v *Stevenson*, the *Consumer Protection Act 1987* provides a further route to compensation for loss or damage. Rather unusually for tort law, the *Act* provides a regime of **strict liability**, that is, liability without proof of fault – in this case concerning liability for defective products.

Verschuldensnachweis

The *Act* provides that **producers** (including manufacturers, importers and suppliers) will **owe a duty** to the victim of the loss where it can be shown that the **product** was **defective**.

The word *defective* is defined by the *Act* as not providing the level of safety which persons are generally entitled to expect. The claimant under the *Act* can make a claim for death, personal injury or property damage. It may again be noted that, unusually for tort law, there is no need to prove that the defendant producer was at fault in any way.

Diagram 43

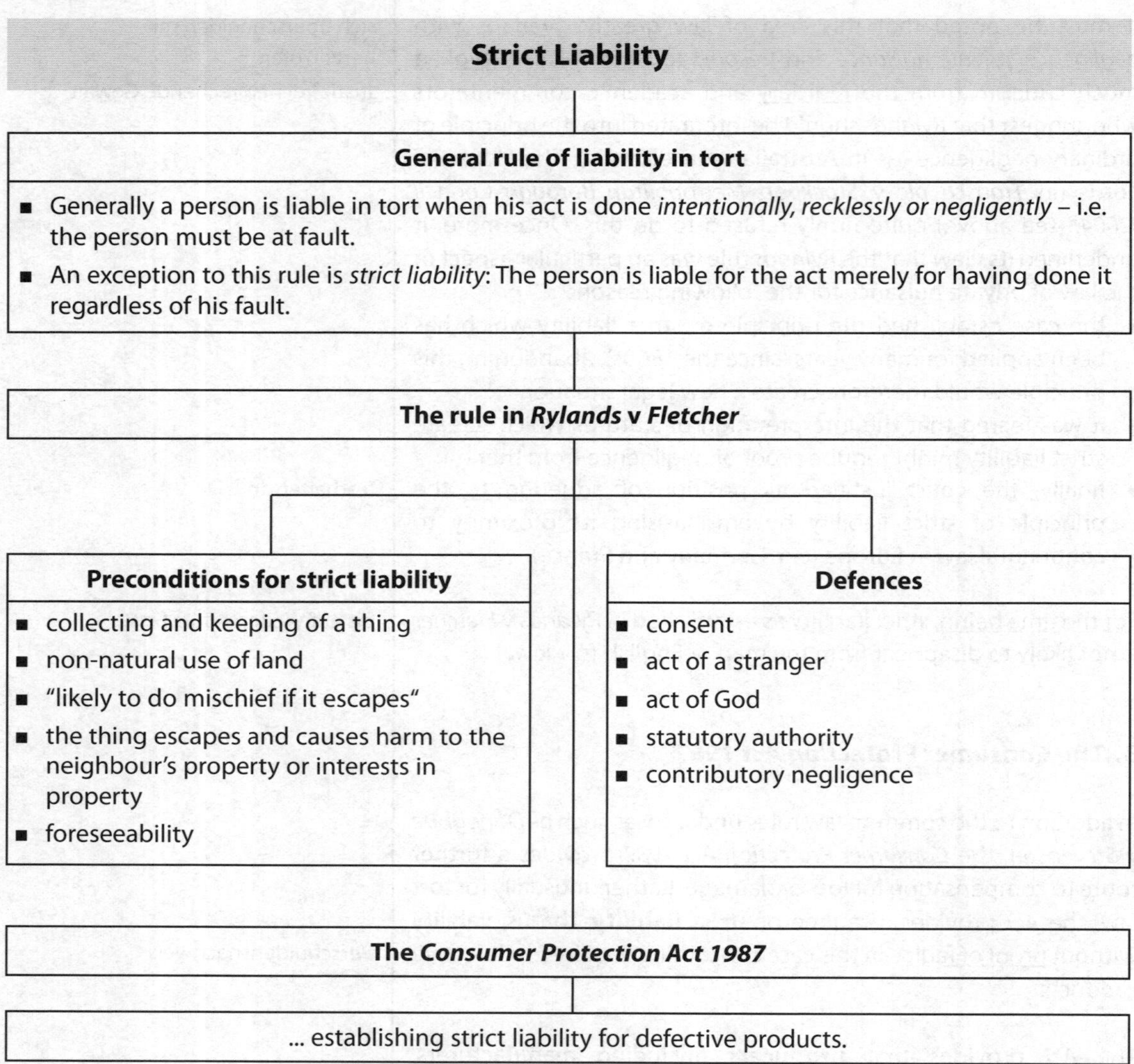
Strict Liability
General rule of liability in tort
Generally a person is liable in tort when his act is done *intentionally, recklessly or negligently* – i.e. the person must be at fault.
An exception to this rule is *strict liability*: The person is liable for the act merely for having done it regardless of his fault.
The rule in *Rylands* v *Fletcher*
Preconditions for strict liability
collecting and keeping of a thing
non-natural use of land
"likely to do mischief if it escapes"
the thing escapes and causes harm to the neighbour's property or interests in property
foreseeability
Defences
consent
act of a stranger
act of God
statutory authority
contributory negligence
The *Consumer Protection Act 1987*
... establishing strict liability for defective products.

## VII. Vicarious liability

Haftung für (zurechenbares) Drittverschulden/fremdes Verschulden

### 1. Introduction

*Vicarious liability* is the liability of one person for torts committed by *another* person (comparable with the liability of *§ 831 BGB* in German law). In such a case both are liable as joint tortfeasors.

Gesamtschuldner

Situations of where and when this can occur are best illustrated by way of an example. A is driving his company's lorry, and negligently collides with B's car. B can sue A in negligence. As A was driving on company business, and the company employs A as its employee, the principle of vicarious liability makes A's employer equally liable to B for the negligence which was committed by A in the course of A's employment.

im Zuge/im Rahmen von

**Employment** is the most common situation where *vicarious liability* arises as a result of the relationship between the person who commits the tort (the *employee* or servant)[12] and a third party (*employer* or master). There are certain other instances, because the principle applies whenever the common law holds that there is a particular legal relationship between the person who actually committed the tort, and the person whom the law also holds liable for it. Such relationships have been established *inter alia* between principal and agent, business partners or vehicle owners and delegated drivers.

*i. dt. Recht:* Verrichtungsgehilfe
*i.dt. Recht:* Geschäftsherr
Rechtsbeziehung
Fahrzeughalter
Fahrzeugführer

In the case of *employer* and *employee*, **three preconditions** must be fulfilled for vicarious liability:

(1) The person committing the tort has **to be an employee** as opposed to an independent contractor.
(2) The employee must have **committed a tort**.
(3) The tort must have been committed **in the course of employment**.

selbstständiger Vertragsnehmer/Unternehmer
in Ausübung der Tätigkeit (für den Geschäftsherrn)

These three essential components are also general principles for *vicarious liability* and are not limited to the relationship between *employer* and *employee* only.

12 The terms „master" and „servant" are traditional, but also used in recent cases, e.g. *Dubai Aluminium Co Ltd* v *Salaam (2003).*

## 2. Who is an employee?

beschäftigen

zentrales Charakteristikum

The person who engages an *independent contractor* is not vicariously liable if the contractor commits a tort. Therefore, the **distinction between employee and independent contractor** is very important. The central feature for this distinction is *not the type of work* that they do *but the way* in which the work is done.

unzweifelhaft
Verkäufer – Auszubildender/Lehrling

Schreiner/Tischler
selbstständig – ausgebildet/qualifiziert

Many working relationships fall undoubtedly into the relationship of *employer/employee*, for instance, sales assistants, apprentices, solicitors and university lecturers. Others are clearly *independent contractors* who provide their services to a range of people, for instance, electricians, carpenters, dressmakers or landscape gardeners. These are self-employed skilled workers.

abfassen/entwerfen

The courts have formulated a number of different tests that help distinguish between *employee* and *independent contractor*.

In 1880, the court established in *Yewen* v *Noakes* what is known as the **"control test"**, by asking whether the employer had a right to control the nature of the work done, and most importantly, how it must be done. It was held that an *employee* is: "… a person who works for another on terms that he is to be subject to the control of that other as to the manner in which he does his work". The "control test" has its origins in the "master and servant" nature of employment. Nowadays, it is an inadequate way of distinguishing *employees* and *independent contractors*. So, the management of a hospital cannot control in detail the way that one of their surgeons carries out an operation, but the hospital is liable to the patient if the surgeon is negligent.

Chirurg
durchführen

Arbeits-/Dienstvertrag *(§ 611 BGB)*
Werkvertrag *(§ 631 BGB)*

In *Stevenson, Jordan and Harrison Ltd* v *Mc Donnell and Evans (1952)* the **"organisation (or integration) test"** was put forward to distinguish between a *contract of service (or of employment)* and a *contract for services.* By the former, a person is part of the business and his work is done as an integral part, by the latter, the work is not integrated into the business but is only accessory to it.

Since both tests mentioned above do not cover all situations in which it is necessary to determine whether someone is an *employee* or an *independent contractor*, the courts developed the **"economic reality test"**.

grundsätzliche Entscheidung/Präjudiz

The following **three preconditions** for an employee were established in the leading case below:

(1) the employee must provide work or skill in return for payment of a wage or some other remuneration;
(2) the employee agrees, expressly or impliedly, that he will work under the control of the employer;
(3) all other circumstances (e.g. method of payment, tax and national insurance, working hours, equipment, level of independence) are consistent with the situation being characterised as a contract of service/employment.

entsprechen/im Einklang stehen mit

*Example – Ready Mixed Concrete Ltd* v *Minister of Pensions and National Insurance (1968)*

The drivers were hired by the claimant organisation to deliver concrete, using vehicles owned by the drivers which they purchased from the claimant and which had to be painted the company colours and carry the company logo. The drivers were responsible for the maintenance of the vehicles and had flexible hours of work.
***Held:*** that the drivers were not *employees*, but rather *independent contractors* because on occasion they could substitute another driver to do their work provided they obtained the consent of the company which used their services. Also the claimant was not liable for their national insurance contributions.

Beton – unter Verwendung
Sozialversicherungsbeiträge

In this context, it is worthwhile mentioning that the express intentions of the parties as to the classification of their working relationship may be an important factor but this is not conclusive.

lohnenswert
betreffend/was … betrifft
abschließend/zwingend

*Example – Ferguson* v *John Dawson & Partners (Contractors) Ltd (1976)*

The claimant, a building worker, was injured when he fell off a roof at the defendant's construction site. Contrary to regulations, there was no guard railing on the roof. If he had been an *independent contractor* he would have been responsible for his own safety and unable to sue the company. At the time of hiring, the claimant was expressed to be a "labour only sub-contractor", although he was an unskilled labourer and subject to the control of the site agent.
***Held:*** that the employers were liable. Despite the label that the parties had given to the employment relationship, in other respects the claimant was treated as an *employee* working under a contract of service.

Bauarbeiter
Dach – Baustelle
Schutzgeländer
einstellen – nur als Subunternehmer
arbeiten – ungelernter Arbeiter
Bauleiter
Bezeichnung
ansonsten

## 3. Has a tort been committed?

übersehen

This second requirement is often overlooked. It is essential because there cannot be a vicarious (*secondary*) liability without a direct (*primary*) liability of the employee.

jdm. zur Verfügung stehen

Vicarious liability can apply to any tort, often it will be negligence. Before holding the employer liable, it must be established that the employee had actually committed the tort in question, by applying all the relevant law relating to that tort, including whether any particular defences are open to the employee.

## 4. In the course of employment

Of course an employer cannot be made liable for every tort which his employees commit. The tort must have been committed whilst the employee *was in the course of* carrying out the employer's business.

Ausmaß

einfach/unkompliziert

The extent of what falls within the *course of employment* is fairly wide: if a bus driver negligently injures someone while driving a bus, his employer will be vicariously liable. Not all situations are so straightforward, however.

entfernt/abseitig

*etwa:* Privatvergnügen

Umweg

If what the employee was doing was something sufficiently remote from what he was employed to do, he can be considered to have been engaging in what is termed a "**frolic of his own**" *(Joel v Morrison (1834)).* The employer will not be liable as the tort will not then have been committed during the *course of the employee's employment*. Such conduct falls outside the course of employment because it is something that the employee has done within working time but unrelated to his work and therefore undertaken on his own account. A good example is the deviation a delivery driver takes from his authorised route to visit a friend in a hospital or to go shopping.

Of course, an employer can be liable if the employee commits a tort by an act authorised by the former. It is less straightforward if the employee is acting contrary to instructions or is performing an authorised task in a negligent manner.

| *Example – Limpus v London General Omnibus Co (1862)* |
|---|
| London General's instructions to its drivers were that they "must not on any account race with or obstruct another omnibus, or hinder or annoy the driver or conductor thereof". One of their drivers did in fact drive his bus in such a way as to obstruct a bus operated by Limpus and prevent it passing. His action caused injury to one of Limpus' horses and severe damage to the bus itself.<br>***Held:*** that despite the instruction, London General as employer were liable, as their driver's conduct had occurred within the course of his employment. |

obstruct: behindern
annoy: ärgern/stören
passing: vorbeifahren
severe damage: schwerer Schaden

## 5. Employer's indemnity

indemnity: Haftungsfreistellung/Entschädigung/Schadloshaltung

As mentioned above, the employee and the employer are **joint tortfeasors**. The employer who has been held vicariously liable for an employee's tort may be able to recover from the employee the damages which he has had to pay, under the principle of vicarious liability, to the person who has suffered the injury or damage. The employer is entitled to seek such an indemnity from the employee.

recover: wiederbekommen
entitled: berechtigt/befugt

There are two kinds of indemnity: (1) under *s.1(1) Civil Liability (Contribution) Act 1978* and (2) the common law indemnity.

(1) The *1978 Act* allows a defendant who has paid damages to a claimant, to recover a contribution from any other defendant who is responsible for the harm or loss caused, whether liability is joint or several.

(2) The full cost could be recovered if the harm or loss had been caused by the employee's breach of contract.

| *Example – Lister v Romford Ice & Cold Storage Co (1957)* |
|---|
| Mr Lister was a lorry driver employed by Romford Ice and, while he was backing his lorry into the yard of a slaughterhouse, to which he had been sent to collect waste, he negligently ran into and injured his father, who was also working on the same job. The father obtained judgement for damages against Romford Ice, on the ground that they were vicariously liable for the negligent driving of the son, their employee. Romford Ice claimed reimbursement of those damages from their employee, the son. |

lorry driver: Lastwagenfahrer
backing – yard: zurücksetzen – Hof
judgement: Urteil/Entscheidung
reimbursement: Rückerstattung

Sorgfaltspflicht verletzen

***Held:*** that the son had <u>been in breach of his duty to take care</u> in the way that he carried out his work. The employer was therefore entitled to recover from the son the money which the employer had been ordered to pay to the father.

## 6. Liability for independent contractors

There can be circumstances in which a person may be liable for torts of an *independent contractor* employed by him.

zugrunde liegend

Although these are not *cases of vicarious liability*, it is worth introducing them here, as the underlying idea is that the employer himself is in breach of a primary duty which he owes the claimant.

ausdrücklich – „anheuern"/anwerben/einstellen

auferlegen

Thus, a person who engages an independent contractor **can be liable for the tort of this independent contractor** if:

- the latter was expressly hired to undertake the act which amounted to a tort;
- the work necessarily created a dangerous situation;
- the work obstructed the highway, thereby creating a public nuisance or
- the former who engaged the contractor was delegating a duty imposed on him by statute or common law.

*Note*: Where liability is strict (independent of negligence), as is the case under the rule in *Rylands* v *Fletcher* (see above, section VI.2, p. 66–71), a person who engages an independent contractor will also be liable for acts of that contractor.

**Diagram 44**

## Vicarious Liability

- ... means to be liable for torts committed by *another* person, i.e. a third person.
- The person who is vicariously liable is called the *master* (mostly an employer), and the person who committed the tort is called the *servant* (mostly an employee).

**Three preconditions:**

| The person acting must be a servant **(employee)**, as apposed to an independent contractor. | This person must have **committed a tort**. | The tort must have been committed **in the course of employment**. |
|---|---|---|
| The *economic reality test:*<br>■ work or skill in return for payment of a wage or some other remuneration<br>■ works voluntarily under the control of the employer<br>■ other circumstances are consistent with the situation being characterised as a contract of service, e.g. method of payment, tax and national insurance, working hours, equipment etc. | ■ Any tort is possible.<br>■ However, all elements of the respective tort need to be fulfilled,<br>■ and there must not be a defence open to the employee. | ■ The extent of the course of employment is fairly wide.<br>■ The conduct of the employee must not be "a frolic of his own". |

## VIII. Further reading & references[13]

*Adams*, Law for Business Students; *Barker & Padfield*, Law Made Simple; *Bermingham*, Tort (Nutcases and Nutshells); *Boucher & Corns*, GCSE Law Casebook; *Cooke*, Law of Tort; *Cracknell*, Torts; *Deakin, Johnston & Markesinis*, Markesinis and Deakin's Tort Law; *Denham*, Law: a modern introduction; *Finch & Fafinski*, Tort Law; *Geldart*, Introduction to English Law; *Giliker & Beckwith*, Tort; *Harpwood*, Modern Tort Law; *Harris*, An Introduction to Law; *Harvey & Marston*, Cases and Commentary on Tort; *Hedley*, Tort; *Heuston & Buckely*, Salmond & Heuston on the Law of Torts; *Jones,* Textbook on Torts; *Kidner*, Casebook on Torts; *Lunney & Oliphant*, Tort Law – Text and Materials; *Lyall*, An Introduction to British Law; *Matthews, O'Cinneide & Morgan,* Hepple and Matthews' Tort – Cases & Materials; *Rogers*, Winfield and Jolowicz on Tort; *Rose (Ed.)*, Blackstone's Statutes on Contract, Tort & Restitution; *Shears & Stephenson,* James' Introduction to English Law; *Stapelton*, Product Liability; *Tayfoor*, Law Cartoons: Tort; *Templeman & Pitchfork*, Obligations: The Law of Tort (Casebook, Revision Work Book, Textbook); *van Gerven, Lever & Larouche*, Tort Law; *Weir*, A Casebook on Tort; *Wild & Weinstein,* Smith & Keenan's English Law; *Wilman*, Brown: GCSE Law.

13 Edition, publisher, place and year of publication are quoted in the bibliography.

# Chapter Eight

## Property Law

Sachenrecht *(i.dt.Sinne)*

## I. Nature and concept of property

Geldart wrote in his "Introduction to English Law" that "there is perhaps nothing more difficult than to give a precise and consistent meaning to the word property". There are many different translations of this word into German.

feststehend

In Dietl/Lorenz's Dictionary of Legal Commercial and Political Terms, for example, you can find: „Eigentum, Eigentumsrecht; Vermögen, Vermögensgegenstand, Vermögenswert(e); (bebautes oder unbebautes) Grundstück; Grundbesitz, Grund und Boden, Landbesitz; (charakteristische) Eigenschaft". The equally distinguished, but not so comprehensive dictionary by Romain suggests: „Eigentum, eigentumsähnliches Recht, absolutes Recht; Vermögen, Vermögensgegenstand; Grundstück; Sache ...".

umfassend/umfangreich

Why are there so many different translations and meanings of the expression *property*? This is because in English law there are different aspects to the concept of property. For example, property means „Eigentum" in the sense of *ownership*, defined as "the entirety of the powers of use and disposal allowed by the law" (see the legal historian Pollock in his "First Book of Jurisprudence"). Property as ownership is therefore comparable with the German notion of „Eigentum" in *§ 903 BGB*, where it means the legal domination over a thing. In this sense, ownership is to be distinguished from *possession*, which means the domination in fact over a thing.

Eigentum(srecht)
Gesamtheit der Gebrauchs- und Verfügungsbefugnisse – Rechtshistoriker
Begriff/ Vorstellung
rechtliche Herrschaft
Besitz – tatsächliche Herrschaft

In general, property is used to refer to things which can be owned, possessed, bought and sold etc. and this chapter will set out the different categories of property under English law.

sich beziehen/verweisen auf
darlegen

This chapter covers also *land law*, which, confusingly, English lawyers often refer to as the law of property. Note, however, that in English law (as in German law, see *§ 94 BGB*), *land* also includes any buildings on it. The buildings are considered to be part of the land, so when lawyers talk of land being bought, sold, conveyed, etc., they are also including everything which is on the land itself – houses, factories, offices and so on, – as well as just the ground which they stand on. That is why this area of law is called *land law* by academics.

„Immobilienrecht" – verwirrender Weise – etwas bezeichnen/von etwas sprechen – Grundstück/Grund und Boden
übereignen/abtreten
Grund/Boden

Immobilien/unbewegliches Vermögen – *hier*: bewegliches Vermögen

## II. Real property and personal property

### 1. Historical background to real property

English law divides property into *real property* and *personal property*, which is similar, but not entirely identical to the distinction made in German law between „Eigentum an unbeweglichen" and „Eigentum an beweglichen Sachen".

unbeschränktes Grundeigentum
umfassen – Eigentumsrecht

*Real property* refers to **freehold estates in land**[14], and *personal property* comprises all other proprietory rights, whether in land or any other type of property.

bewegliche u. unbewegliche Sachen
Lehnsrecht – „Aktionensystem" (*vgl. röm. Recht*)

Moveables and immoveables are not terms generally used in English law. The medieval law of lease and the old system of forms of actions[15] is responsible for determining what, strictly, may be termed *real property* and *personal property*. This classification, whilst technically still part of English law, does not reflect the way the law of property is approached nowadays.

gängiger Ansatz

For centuries, the established approach has been to consider, first, *land* – whether freehold or leasehold – and to call that one category *real property*.

The other category is called *personal property*, a substantial part of which is made up of objects (chattels); personal property also includes rights (choses in action) such as patents, and indeed anything else which is not land.

Anspruch erheben auf – tatsächliche Herausgabe – Gegenstand – Klagegrund – dingliche Klage

The reason that English law has a technical distinction between *real property* and *personal property* is because, historically, it was only possible to bring a claim for the actual return of an item of property, if that property was land. The cause of action was an **action *in rem*** (cf. vol. 1, chapter 2, p. 35), because the court would order the return of the thing (in Latin: *res*) itself. Therefore, the type of property for which this action was available came to be called *real property*.

Schadensersatz

All other types of property are called *personal property*, because the medieval courts would only allow a claim against the person (in Latin: *persona*) who took the property (**action *in personam***). That person could choose to pay compensation (damages) for the loss

14 And – in order to be technically correct – certain freehold interests in land such as easements and profits; also various other ancient rights now of historical interest only.

15 Cf. vol. 1, chapter 2, p. 27 ff.

of use of the property in question, or instead, to return the thing itself, but the choice was his. The court could not order the return of the thing itself.

The medieval courts did not regard a **lease** as an arrangement which created any form of ownership of land. Instead, it was a personal arrangement – a purely contractual relationship – between the landlord and the tenant for payment for the use of land for a period of time. Therefore a tenant, although he held land under a lease, held only *personal* property, not *real* property because the contract (i.e. the lease) created rights *in personam* (personal rights) between the parties and not rights *in rem* (proprietory rights) against the land.

Pacht/Miete – Vereinbarung
Grundeigentum/-besitz
*hier*: schuldrechtlich
Verpächter/-mieter – Pächter/Mieter

Forderung/schuldrechtlicher Anspruch – dingliches Recht

However, a lease of land is in practice much more than just a simple contract, and over the course of history many of the principles of land law have come to be applied to leases as well. Therefore, the term **chattels real** evolved as a way of referring to land held on lease. *Chattel* basically means something that can be physically possessed, such as a watch, a bicycle or a pencil. *Chattels real* are to be distinguished from *chattels personal*, as to which see below.

im Laufe der Geschichte
anwendbar sein auf
*etwa*: beschränkt dingliches Grundstücksrecht – sich entwickeln – bewegliche Sache
Eigentum oder andere dingliche Rechte an beweglichen Sachen

Over the course of legal development, and especially following the land law reforms of 1925 (mainly the *Law of Property Act 1925*), the distinction between *real property* and *chattels real* as a part of personal property has lost much of its significance. Nowadays chattels real have equality of status very close to real property. In particular, they entitle the claimant to an action *in rem*, and not only to an action *in personam* as in former times; today, they constitute *proprietory rights*.

berechtigen

This chapter follows the approach of English textbooks. *Real property* refers to all land whether freehold or leasehold – i.e. including chattels real. *Personal property* refers to all other types of property, as below.

Herangehensweise/Ansatz

## 2. Personal property – **pure personalty**

bewegliches Vermögen

We have seen above the way that, technically, *personal property* can be divided into (1) **chattels real** (in particular land held on a lease) and (2) all other types of personal property – the expression used for the second category is **pure personalty** which is dealt with in this section.

beschränkt dingliches Grundstücksrecht

There are two types of *pure personalty* – **choses in possession** and **choses in action**. *Chose* here means "thing" – i.e. an item of pure personalty.

besitzgebundenes Recht
Forderung/Recht/Anspruch

A *chose in possession* is primarily a tangible asset. However, although land is also tangible, it is immoveable. Therefore, a chose in possession is a moveable object such as a watch, bicycle or pencil, which can be physically possessed and thus enjoyed. Another name for this category of pure personalty is **chattels personal**.

körperlicher Vermögenswert
ausüben

A *chose in action* is where there is nothing physically to possess which constitutes the property, although the benefits of the property can be enjoyed. For example, shares in a company – the shareholder owns a part of the company, and dividends are paid to the owner of the shares when the company makes a profit; or a patent – royalties are paid to the owner of the patent, when someone manufactures products using the idea protected by the patent. Those benefits are regarded by the law as property, but the owner cannot demonstrate ownership by means of possession of the actual thing itself (a share certificate or the letters patent are documents of title, but not the thing itself). In order to enforce the owner's ownership, the owner has to bring an *action* (in other words, bring a claim) in the courts to protect his rights as an owner – for example, if the dividends are not paid, or if the patent is being infringed. Other examples of *choses in action* are debts, negotiable instruments, and other intellectual property rights such as copyrights and trade marks.

Vorteil/Nutzen/Begünstigung
Gesellschaftsanteil/Aktie
Aktionär/Anteilseigner

Patentrecht – Lizenzgebühren
herstellen

durch Besitz der Sache selbst
Aktienzertifikat/Anteilsschein – Patenturkunde – Urkunde über Rechtsanspruch – Klage erheben/einreichen
Forderung erheben/Anspruch geltend machen

verletzen – *hier*: Außenstände
umlauffähiges Wertpapier – geistiges Eigentum – Urheberrecht – Warenzeichen

We can conclude at this stage, that by approaching the concepts of *land* and *personal property* as suggested above, we are not far removed from the distinction in German law between „unbewegliche Sachen" and „bewegliche Sachen".

nicht weit entfernt

Diagram 45

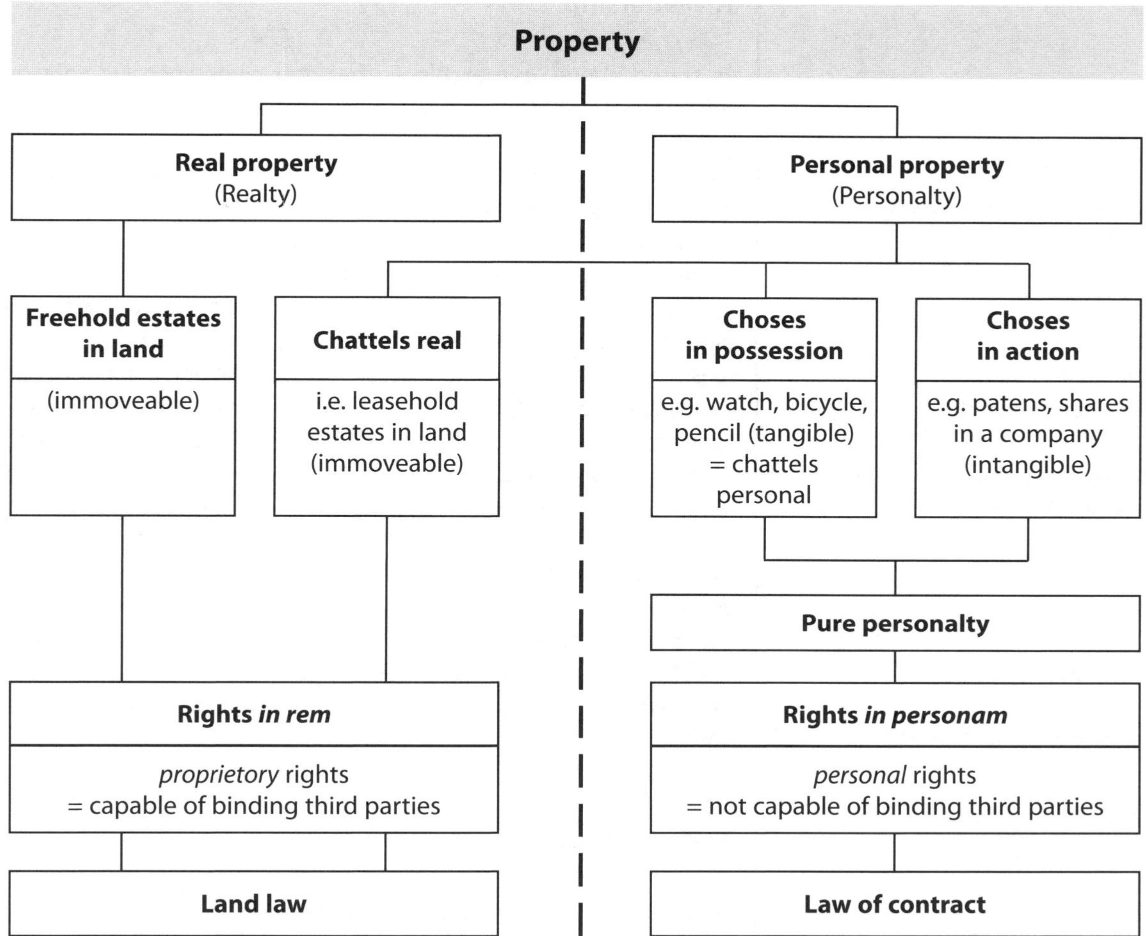
Property
Real property
(Realty)
Personal property
(Personalty)
Freehold estates in land
(immoveable)
Chattels real
i.e. leasehold estates in land (immoveable)
Choses in possession
e.g. watch, bicycle, pencil (tangible) = chattels personal
Choses in action
e.g. patens, shares in a company (intangible)
Pure personalty
Rights in rem
proprietory rights = capable of binding third parties
Rights in personam
personal rights = not capable of binding third parties
Land law
Law of contract

Eigentum – Besitz

## III. Ownership and possession

### 1. Ownership

As stated above, **ownership** is the *most comprehensive right* or collection of rights which a person can have over a thing.

Gebrauch – Nutzen – Verfügung – Zerstörung

aufhören

Fußweg – auch nicht

Zugang – Nachbargrundstück
Instandhaltungsarbeiten

The owner of a thing is the person who has the greatest rights of use and enjoyment, disposition and destruction of the thing. These rights, of course, are limited by the general rules of law which protect the rights of others. The rights of others may have been granted by agreement in the past, perhaps by an earlier owner, or may be rights which apply by statute. The owner of a field does not cease to be the owner simply because the public or a neighbour has the right to use a footpath across it. Nor is ownership infringed by the *Access to Neighbouring Land Act 1992*, which allows a person a right of access to neighbouring land in order to carry out certain types of repair and maintenance work to or on his own land.

von Rechts wegen

bekommen/erwerben

zunächst/einstweilen/fürs Erste

*Ownership* is to be distinguished from *possession*. Ownership is a *de iure* (i.e. legal) relationship; there is no need to possess the thing. If a bicycle is stolen by a thief, the owner's rights as owner remain intact, because the thief acquires no right to the bicycle against the true owner. The true owner is, however, not able to exercise his right of possession for the time being.

### 2. Possession

*jur.*: tatsächlich – faktische/tatsächliche Beziehung

Whereas ownership is a right or a collection of rights over a thing, **possession** is *de facto* (i.e. *factual* relationship between a person and the thing possessed).

rechtswidrig
unrechtmäßig – rechtmäßig

Possession may be either *unlawful*, as we saw in the case of the thief who has wrongful possession, or *lawfully* acquired without, however, being connected to ownership.

vermieten
das Gleiche gilt für

Verwahrung – verpfänden – Leihe/Kredit

An owner who hires a bicycle to another gives him the possession of it but he does not cease to be the owner. The same is true of a person who takes the bicycle to another for repair, or entrusts it to him for storage, or pawns it to him as security for a loan.

*jur.*: Besitzmittlungsverhältnis

Such transfers of possession *with the consent* of the owner are called **bailments**. As to the source of the expression bailment, it derives from the adoption by English law of an old French word to describe the handing over of goods without passing the title and property, i.e. "bailler" (to deliver). In such instances the right of ownership is not infringed by the object being in the possession of another (the **bailee**), but the contract between the parties creates rights in favour of the person who has possession. These rights limit the owner (the **bailor**) from exercising his rights of ownership for the duration of the contract.

Fall/Beispiel/Umstand

Verwahrer/*allg.*: (unmittelbarer) Fremdbesitzer

Hinterleger/*allg.*: mittelbarer Besitzer

In a bailment *for a fixed term*, for example, the person who has possession can have possession to the exclusion of the owner, and, is, therefore, the only person who could sue a third party for wrongful interference. This is different from German law, where the owner as the indirect possessor has the same rights against a third party as the actual possessor himself (see *§ 869 BGB*). However, when the bailment is *revocable at will*, the bailor also can bring an action for wrongful interference, because he, too, has an interest worth protecting.

bestimmte Zeit

verklagen

verbotene Eigenmacht/Besitzstörung

mittelbarer Besitzer

tatsächlicher/unmittelbarer Besitzer

frei widerruflich

A person in possession under a bailment can sue a third party in tort for loss or damage to the thing, even though he may not be liable to the owner for the loss or damage.

wegen unerlaubter Handlung – selbst wenn – jmd. ggü. haften

*Example – The Winkfield (1902)*

The ship *The Mexican* was hit at sea by the ship *The Winkfield*. *The Mexican* sank, carrying a quantity of mail, which was therefore lost. Some of the senders of the mail could be identified, but some could not. The Postmaster General claimed compensation, to be paid to him on behalf of those senders who could not be identified, and he would pay the money out if they could in due course be identified. The owners of *The Winkfield* defended the claim on the ground that, as a representative of the Crown and under the rules which applied at the time governing the sending of items by post, the Postmaster General was not himself liable to the senders if their mail was lost.
***Held:*** the Postmaster General did have a claim, because he had possession under a bailment; therefore, someone who disturbed that right of possession by causing the goods to be lost, would be liable for damages for that loss.

Post/Postsendung

Absender/Versender

*hist.*: Postminister

im Namen von/für

in Bälde/zu gegebener Zeit

abwehren – Anspruch

haftbar/verantwortlich gegenüber

schadensersatzpflichtig

Awarding damages for interference with possession forms part of the **law of tort** as wrongful interference with property is a wrongful interference with goods (see above, chapter 7, section II. 2).

*etwa*: Besitzstörung

Whilst we have seen that the person who has possession is not necessarily the owner, the person who claims to have possession must be the person who has **control** of the object. There are two elements to control:

tatsächliche/gegenwärtige Verfügungsgewalt

Absicht/Wille – aufrechterhalten – auf Seiten von

- the **actual power of control** over the thing possessed (physical control), e.g. the person riding a bicycle or holding a pen.
- an **intention to maintain that control** on the part of the possessor and to exclude others.

Besitzer

Arbeitnehmer – Arbeitgeber

nicht gelten als

Besitzdiener

The person who has both elements of control is the *possessor*. Thus, a servant who receives a thing from his master for the master's use (e.g. a chauffeur) is deemed not to be the possessor. He is (as in German law) only a *possessory servant*.

verbunden sein

Although ownership is the most comprehensive right over a thing, possession is a fact which has great legal significance, and to which rights are attached.

Eigentumsvermutung

Eintragung/Registrierung/Anmeldung

As in German law (cf. *§ 1006 BGB*), actual possession in English law gives a **presumption of ownership**. It can be difficult to prove one's own ownership if the thing is in the possession of another, except in cases where ownership is determined by registration. There are not many examples of ownership by registration in English law, but they include where land is registered at the land registry, patents and trade marks, and shares in companies.

Eigentumsnachweis

vorbehaltlich

Rechtsschutz

Moreover, possession is not merely evidence of ownership, but – subject to the rights of the true owner – is itself entitled to legal protection. The finder of a thing, as the person in possession, is entitled to possession of it against all persons other than the true owner.

*Example – Hannah* v *Peel (1945)*

zufällig – Brosche – Mauerspalte

gefunden werden

A soldier was stationed in a house which had never been actually occupied by the owner. During his stay, the soldier by chance discovered a valuable brooch in a wall crevice in an upstairs room. The real owner of the brooch could not be traced. The soldier wanted to keep it, but the owner of the house claimed that he should have it as the house belonged to him.
***Held:*** the soldier was entitled to the brooch because the owner had never been in physical possession of the house, and had no knowledge of the existence of the brooch until it was found by the soldier.

reifen/erwachsen

vorherig – wiedererlangen

Verjährung

Finally, we may note that even wrongful possession, if continued for a sufficient length of time, can mature into lawful ownership. Wrongful possession of a moveable thing for 6 years, or of land for 12 years, destroys the previous owner's right to recover the thing or the land by legal action, because the true owner is not permitted under the *Limitation Acts* to bring a claim after that time.

**Diagram 46**

**Ownership and Possession**

| Ownership | Possession |
| --- | --- |
| ... is the most comprehensive right or collection of rights which a person can have over a thing (= *legal* relationship) | ... is where a person has the actual control of a thing and the intention to maintain that control (= *factual* relationship) |

## IV. Acquisition of personal property: chattels personal

Eigentumserwerb an beweglichen Sachen (ohne Forderungen)

### 1. Introduction

In contrast to German law, English law does not have a „Trennungs- und Abstraktionsprinzip“[16].

Ownership of chattels personal can be transferred simply by *delivery of possession*, so long as there is an *intention* to transfer ownership by doing so – for example, a gift at Christmas. In such a case, no contract is involved.

Besitzübergabe
Geschenk
beteiligt

However, where an item of personal property is bought and sold, a contract will exist, even if it is not one which is in writing. It is the terms of that contract, rather than the law of property, which define when ownership passes, irrespective of when actual delivery takes place.

übergehen – unabhängig davon

The general rule, as set out in *s.18 Sale of Goods Act 1979*, is that – unless the contract provides otherwise – ownership will pass at the time the contract is made. That principle will apply even if the buyer is given a period of credit, so the buyer would acquire ownership before he has paid for the goods. The seller may therefore stipulate in the contract that ownership will not pass until the buyer has paid for the goods at the end of his period of credit. This is called *retention of title.*

ausführen/festlegen
vorbehaltlich/es sei denn/wenn nicht
Anwendung finden
Zahlungsfrist
festlegen
Eigentumsvorbehalt

16 The principle that rights *in rem* over objects are separated from any rights against a person in terms of any related contract.

gutgläubiger Erwerb

## 2. Problems with acquiring ownership – acquisition in good faith

rechtmäßiger Eigentümer

### a) Principle: acquisition only from the true owner

im Laufe der Zeit

angebliche/r

hat keine Auswirkung auf das Eigentum des wahren Eigentümers

„Niemand kann geben, was er nicht hat."

Unfortunately, many people have, in the course of time, paid for goods and taken possession of them, only to find out afterwards that they have not been dealing with the true owner. The purported seller might, for example, have been a thief. The starting point of English law is that such a sale can be of no effect with regard to the ownership of the true owner. This principle is expressed in the Latin rule **"Nemo dat quod non habet"** (no-one can give what he does not have), and is set out in the first part of *s.21(1) Sale of Goods Act 1979*. The seller (thief) in the example just given, did not have ownership himself, and so could not transfer it to the buyer.

### b) Exceptions to the *nemo dat* rule

gutgläubiger Erwerber

teilweise

There are a number of exceptions to this principle in order to protect a buyer who buys in good faith (a bona fide purchaser – buyer and purchaser have the same meaning) from someone who looks as if he is the owner because he has possession of the goods (see above: presumption of ownership). These exceptions, however, are, in part, different from the rules of acquisition of ownership in good faith found under German law. The main ones in English law are as follows:

Bargeld – umlauffähiges Wertpapier – auf den Inhaber ausgestellt

Empfänger – Veräußerer

- **Cash and negotiable instruments made out to bearer**. As in German law (c.f. *§ 935 II BGB*), so long as these are taken in good faith, the recipient will become the owner even if the transferor did not own the money or the instrument.

Handelsvertreter

Verkaufskommissionär

im Auftrag von

erwerben

kraft/gemäß

ungeachtet dessen

ermächtigt

- **Sales by a mercantile agent**. A mercantile agent, also called a factor, is a person who, in the course of business, sells goods on behalf of the owner of them, but without the buyer being aware that he is not buying from the actual owner. If (1) the mercantile agent has possession of the goods for sale with the consent of the owner, and (2) the buyer purchases in good faith and with no knowledge of any lack of authority by the agent who made the sale, the buyer can obtain ownership by virtue of *s.2 Factors Act 1889* notwithstanding that the agent was not in fact authorised to make that particular sale.
- **Where the seller remains in possession of the goods notwithstanding the sale.** If (1) the buyer does not collect the goods straight away, and before he does so (2) the seller sells

the goods to someone else who buys in good faith with no knowledge of the first sale, and (3) the goods are delivered to that other person (i.e. to the second buyer), that other person can obtain ownership of the goods by virtue of *s.24 Sale of Goods Act 1979*.

- **Where the buyer obtains possession of the goods even though he has not yet acquired ownership.** This deals with the situation where, for example, the contract with the seller provides that ownership will not pass until the buyer has paid for the goods (i.e. *retention of title*). The buyer in such a case has possession of the goods with the consent of the seller. If (1) the buyer sells the goods to someone else who buys in good faith with no knowledge of the fact that the buyer did not in fact own the goods, and (2) the goods are delivered to that other person (i.e. to the second buyer), that other person can obtain ownership of the goods by virtue of *s.25 Sale of Goods Act 1979*.

deals with – *hier*: betreffen
provides – vorsehen

This last situation is an example of someone having possession of goods, and thus looking as if he is the owner, without in fact being the owner. Over the years, banks and finance companies have established various ways of allowing individuals and businesses to buy goods and have possession of them at the outset, whilst making payment by instalments. The bank or finance company will want to hold onto ownership until all the instalments have been paid, but it can be seen that *s.25 Sale of Goods Act 1979* may in fact enable the customer to sell the goods to an innocent person and disappear with the money.

at the outset – anfangs/von vorneherein
instalments – Rate

One of the ways to stop this happening is to structure the arrangement in such a way that the customer is not technically buying the goods as such. An example of this is *hire-purchase*. Although the customer may think that all he is doing is agreeing to buy the goods and to pay for them by instalments, the legal structure is that the customer agrees to hire the goods from the owner (bank or finance company) until he has paid all the agreed instalments. When he has, he can, if he wishes, actually buy the goods and pay only a nominal sum, usually £1 as the price for the actual purchase. As the customer is not obliged to buy the goods after paying all the instalments, he is not a *buyer*, and so *s.25 Sale of Goods Act 1979* will not apply. Note that there is a statutory exception to this in the case of a car which is bought by an innocent private purchaser – *s.25 Sale of Goods Act 1979* will apply in that case, even though a hire-purchase agreement has been used – *Hire Purchase Act 1964*.

hire-purchase – Mietkauf
obliged – verpflichtet
Note – Kenntnis nehmen/beachten
statutory – gesetzlich festgelegt

betreffend

sich widerspiegeln – Lehrbuch

ergänzen

***Note:*** The majority of issues pertaining to the acquisition of ownership of moveable things, that arise under the English property law (= „Sachenrecht“, in the sense of the German civil law), can be found in the *law of contract*, with which we have dealt in vol. 1, chapter 6. The reason for this is that English law does not distinguish between the acquisition of personal property on one hand and the contract, on the other (in German terms: „Verfügungsgeschäft“ und „Verpflichtungsgeschäft“). The English law of property, as reflected in numerous textbooks, is mainly a law of *real property* or *land law*, supplemented by a special *law of trusts* (the latter forms our next chapter 9).

**Diagram 47**

## Acquisition of Personal Property (Chattels Personal)

### 1. Principle

*Note:* English law does not have the German concept of „Abstraktionsprinzip".

**Transfer of ownership by delivery of possession**

*e.g. gift*

**Transfer of ownership according to terms of contract**

e.g. contract for sale of goods

**General rule (no contractual provisions)**

Ownership passes at the time the contract ist made

**Alternatives can be agreed in the contract (contractual provisions)**

e.g. ownership passes when the goods are paid for

### 2. Acquisition in good faith

*Note:* the rules on acquisition of ownership over moveable things in good faith are part of the *law of contract* rather than the *law of property*.

**Principle**

Acquisition must be from the true owner: "Nemo dat quod non habet".

**Exceptions**

- cash and negotiable instruments made out to bearer
- sales by a mercantile agent
- seller remains in possession of the goods notwithstanding the sale
- buyer obtains possession of the goods before ownership has passed to him

Grundstücksrecht

## V. Land law[17]

### 1. Introduction – the meaning of land

English land law starts from the principle that all land is owned and can only be owned by the Crown. This rule dates from the Norman Conquest in 1066 (cf. vol. 1, chapter 2, p. 24). When William the Conqueror became King of England, he considered himself owner of all land in England. However, he granted to his loyal followers the right to occupy various parts of the country, in reward for their support for his invasion. That way, they became his tenants. Those rights were granted on various terms, such as being obliged to provide a number of soldiers to form an army if a military campaign was to take place, or to sing mass every Friday, or to give a certain sum of money to the poor – this called the feudal system. It is beyond the scope of this book to discuss the development of the feudal system of land holding, but the same basic structure underlies English land law even today, and much of the archaic terminology derives from this feudal system. There is often no equivalent in German law to these terms.

jmd. etwas einräumen
als Lohn für
*hist.:* Lehnsmann/Vassall
Bedingung
Lehnswesen/Feudalsystem
Grundbesitz
veraltet

Therefore, although the Crown still *owns* every piece of land throughout the country, when its subjects talk of *owning* land, what they have is the right to hold that land from the Crown, to occupy it in perpetuity and to be entitled to pass on that right to someone else – e.g. by sale or on death. That right is not in reality any different from *owning* the land as such, but it means that English lawyers talk of persons *holding* land rather than *owning* it. In fact, as we will see later, they talk of persons holding not the land itself, but an *estate in land*. This matter is purely traditional and theoretical since the Crown has no rights over an estate held by a private person.

auf Dauer/auf ewig
*etwa:* Grundvermögen/Grundbesitz

**What is land?** Let us take a look at the relevant legislation in this field. In 1925, a thorough updating of land law was undertaken by the following statutes: *the Law of Property Act, the Settled Land Act, the Trustee Act (now 2000), the Administration of Estates Act, the Land Charges Act (now 1972) and the Land Registration Act (now 2002).*

gründlich/vollständig – Aktualisierung/Fortscheibung

*S.205(1)(ix) Law of Property Act 1925* states as follows: "Land includes land of any tenure, and mines and minerals, whether or not held apart from the surface, buildings or parts of buildings (whether the division is horizontal, vertical or made in any other way) and other

17 Land Law, in contrast to real property, also includes leasehold.

corporeal hereditaments; also a manor, an advowson, and a rent and other incorporeal hereditaments, and an easement, right, privilege, or benefit in, over, or derived from land; but not …"

This, however, is a description, rather than a definition of the term *land*, so we need to look a little more closely at the cases, and so another question which arises is **how far does land extend**? Land is not just the actual surface. Otherwise it would be impossible for the landowner to dig down and lay foundations for any building. English law follows the principle of Roman law, that "Cuius est solum eius est usque ad caelum et ad inferos." (= Whoever owns the soil also owns everything above it as far as the heaven and everything below as far as to the depths of the earth. Or in short: *up to heaven and down to hell*), but that principle has been restricted by modern law.

| *Example – Anchor Brewhouse* v *Berkley House (1987)* |
|---|
| A builder was using tower cranes to carry out a property development. As the cranes turned to and fro, their jibs passed over land owned by neighbouring owners, and they objected to this. ***Held:*** that the neighbouring owners owned the airspace above their land, and therefore had the right to an injunction to prevent the builder's cranes entering his property. On the other hand, if the intrusion was at a great height, such as in *Bernstein of Leigh (Lord)* v *Skyviews & General (1978),* where an aircraft was used to fly over Lord Bernstein's country house in order to photograph it, that would not amount to entering his property as his ownership would not extend that far. |

So the landowner owns the *airspace* only to the extent necessary for the reasonable enjoyment of his land.

Our next case concerns the *depth of the earth*:

| *Example – Duchy of Lancaster* v *Overton Farms Ltd (1982)* |
|---|
| A large hoard of Roman coins was found buried in a field belonging to a farmer. The original owner of the coins was not known. ***Held:*** that the farmer's land included things which were buried in it, even if the farmer did not know about them. The coins therefore belonged to the farmer rather than to the person who found them. |

vererbbare Vermögensgegenstände – Herrensitz/Landgut – Pfründenbesetzungsrecht

tatsächlich/vorhanden

römisch

„Wem das Land gehört, dem gehört alles bis zum Himmel und bis in die Tiefe der Erde."

einschränken

hin und her – Ausleger

beanstanden/Einwand erheben

gerichtliche Verfügung

Besitzstörung/Eingriff

auf etw. hinauslaufen

Umfang/Ausmaß/Grad

Schatz

etwa: Grundvermögen/Grundbesitz

## 2. Estates in land

Berechtigung/Rechtsanspruch

(förmliche) Urkunde

As mentioned above, strictly all land in England can be *owned* only by the Crown. The greatest entitlement to land that any other person can have is an *estate in the land*. Estates in land must be created by deed except in the case of certain leases for up to three years (*s.54(2) Law of Property Act 1925*; see below).

entscheidend/wichtigste

bestimmen/festsetzen/vorsehen

The key statutory provision concerning *estates in land* is *s.1(1) Law of Property Act 1925*. This provides that there are two legal estates in land – one **freehold** and one **leasehold**. The freehold legal estate in land is the *fee simple absolute in possession*. The leasehold legal estate in land is the *term of years absolute*.

unbeschränktes Grundeigentum

### a) The freehold estate in land

Volleigentum

wie oben erwähnt

The best equivalent to absolute ownership of land in English law is the right to enjoy the land **in perpetuity** and to be entitled to pass that right onto someone else, as mentioned above. That right is the *freehold legal estate* in land. Technically it is called the **fee simple absolute in possession**. This name derives from the feudal system referred to earlier:

Erbschaft – im Gegensatz zu

Erbe

- **fee** means it is an estate capable of being passed on by inheritance, as opposed to an estate which ends on death
- **simple** means that it can be passed on to anyone on death, and is not restricted to heirs of a particular class (e.g. only the male heirs)
- **absolute** means that it lasts in perpetuity, rather than ending on the happening of a certain event (e.g. on marriage)
- **in possession** means that it entitles the person to possession of the land immediately rather than at some later date (e.g. on reaching 21 years). Possession in this context includes the right to rent the land out and receive the income from it.

Land verpachten

Inhaber

We can conclude from this that the *holder of an estate of fee simple absolute in possession* is in the same position as an absolute owner, and his ownership corresponds to ownership under German law.

etwa: gemeinsames (Wohn-)Eigentum

### b) Commonhold

der Vollständigkeit halber

For completeness, we will mention that there is also a variation of freehold ownership, called *commonhold*[18], which was introduced by the *Commonhold and Leasehold Reform Act 2002.* This is a system

18 Teile des Geländes werden von den Inhabern der Wohnungen gemeinsam benutzt und als *commonhold* besessen, obwohl die Wohnungen in Form des *freehold* besessen werden.

designed to help with legal and practical problems which arise on estates which have shared common parts, such as blocks of flats and shopping centres. In German law this idea can best be found in the concept of „Wohnungseigentum"[19].

gemeinsame Einrichtung (z.B. Treppenhaus) teilen

However, it is beyond the scope of this book to expand on this system, which at the time of writing is hardly being used anymore. Out of a total of almost 23 million titles registered at the land registry in 2010, less than 20 are commonhold titles.

vordringen in etw./etw. weiter ausführen – kaum
Grundbuchamt/Grundstücksregisterbehörde

## c) The leasehold estate in land

zeitlich beschränktes Eigentum an einem Grundstück

We have seen that freehold is the nearest that English law has to the German concept of absolute ownership of land. The other legal estate in land is the *leasehold legal estate* or **the term of years absolute**. As opposed to the freehold estate which lasts in perpetuity, the leasehold estate lasts **for a definite time**.

auf ewig/unendlich

The owner (holder) of the freehold estate may grant another person the right to occupy it, for a period of time (long or short), usually in return for a rent. This arrangement often, but not always, creates a **lease** from the person who owns the freehold – i.e. the **landlord**, in favour of the occupier – i.e. the **tenant**.

gewähren/einräumen
Land„pacht"
Verpächter/Vermieter – Pächter/Mieter

We shall deal with leases and leasehold tenure below, but first there is an important distinction to note.

### *aa) Distinction between leases and licences*

*allg.*: Benutzungsrecht

We have seen in section II.1 how it took time for the legal system to come to grips with the concept that the grant of a right by a landowner to someone to occupy his land was something more than a simple contract between them. Whilst every lease is a contract as well, not every contract to occupy land or a building creates a lease; it could create a licence only. Herein lies the distinction between a *lease* and a *licence*, and it is convenient to deal with this at this stage.

mit etw. zurechtkommen – Einräumung – bewohnen/in Anspruch nehmen
angebracht/praktisch
behandeln

The basic principle is that a **lease** creates an *estate in land* for the duration of the lease. The parties are called **landlord** and **tenant** (or **lessor** and **lessee**, although these terms are slightly outdated). The tenant pays a form of consideration called **rent.** A **lease** will

leicht/etwas
Gegenleistung – Pacht-/Mietzins

19 Geregelt im *WEG* = Wohnungseigentumsgesetz.

continue to exist even if the freehold estate of the landlord comes into the hands of someone else – for example, on sale or on death. Therefore, the tenant can assert his rights against the land itself – i.e. with an action *in rem*. The lease gives him a **proprietory right**, capable of binding third parties, e.g. the purchaser of the freehold. This is in contrast to the early days of English law as mentioned above, when a lease did not have this status.

*seine Rechte behaupten/durchsetzen*
*Rang/Stellung*

A **licence**, on the other hand, is intended only to be **a short-term personal contractual arrangement** between the parties, who are called **licensor** and **licensee**. It comes to an end when the contract says that it does, or when the freehold estate is transferred to someone else. As it is a **personal right** only, not capable of binding third parties, the licensee can assert his rights not against the land itself, but only against the licensor – i.e. *in personam*.

*kurzzeitig/kurzfristig*
*schuldrechtlich*
*Nutzungsgeber – Nutzer*

A **lease** would be found where a tenant *rents* a flat from a landlord, or for a shop in a shopping centre. In each case, the tenant pays a rent. However, it is also generally the case in England that, when a flat is *owned*, the *owner* has a lease of that flat which was granted for a term of say 99 or 999 years. The rent payable may be only a nominal sum of say £100 per year, or even no rent at all. Where no rent is payable, the lease often refers to a symbolic rent of a peppercorn per year. There are practical reasons concerning repair obligations which prevent flats being sold freehold. The lease of a flat, however, can be readily bought and sold. When a flat is sold, the lease which the seller holds is transferred, for the agreed price for the flat, to the new owner. The new owner thereby acquires the benefit of the remaining years of the lease.

*hier: unbedeutend*
*symbolische/nur der Form halber gezahlte/nominelle Pacht oder Miete*
*leicht/ohne Weiteres*

A **licence,** in contrast to a lease, is the basis upon which a hotel guest occupies his room, a business occupies its stand at a trade fair and representatives of e.g. a particular perfume seller occupy a sales area (called a concession) in the cosmetics section of a department store.

*Handelsmesse*
*Kaufhaus*

It would be possible to create either **a lease or a licence** in any of these situations. However, because there are differences in effect between a lease and a licence, the courts have been at pains to ensure that one party (usually the tenant) is not taken advantage of by the superior negotiating position of the other.

*sich bemühen, etw. zu tun*
*von jmd. ausgenutzt werden*
*überlegene Verhandlungsposition*

We have seen above that a licence comes to an end when the owner of the freehold (the licensor) sells the property, whereas a lease binds the new owner. Another difference is that the tenant of business premises has the right to renew his lease when it runs out,

*Mieter eines Geschäftslokals/-hauses/ gewerblicher Mieter*

unless certain exceptions apply (*Landlord and Tenant Act 1954*). In the past, the tenant of residential premises had the benefit of limits imposed by the *Rent Acts* on what rent his landlord can charge, and the right to continue to occupy the premises even after the lease has ended (but note that the *Rent Acts* do not apply today). Both these Acts of Parliament apply only to *leases*, and not to *licences*.

Mieter von Wohnraum – in den Genuss der Mietobergrenzen kommen

It would be too easy to avoid these rules and other restrictions of landlord and tenant law, by the parties signing a document which calls itself a licence rather than a lease. Therefore, the test is *what arrangement* it is that the parties have in fact established between them, and *not* the name which they have used for it. If the arrangement establishes in reality (1) *exclusive possession of the property*, (2) *for a definite period* and (3) *payment* is being made, it is likely to be a lease. Thus, for example, a guest in a hotel room who does not have exclusive possession because the hotel proprietor retains general control over the room, has arranged for a licence not a lease.

umgehen/unterlaufen

wahrscheinlich

bestellen/planen/vereinbaren

The following case shows the **three characteristics of a lease**:

| *Example – Street* v *Mountford (1985)* |
|---|
| Mr Street owned a house with several rooms which were occupied by different persons. Mrs Mountford occupied one under an agreement which was called a licence agreement. Mr Street reserved in the agreement a right to go into the room to read the meters and check for any damage, but otherwise Mrs Mountford had exclusive possession of the room. The agreement was called a licence, because if it were a lease, Mrs Mountford would have had the right under the *Rent Act 1977* to have the rent reduced. Mrs Mountford signed several clauses in the licence agreement by which she confirmed that she understood that she was not being given a lease, only a licence. ***Held:*** by the House of Lords that the arrangement was in reality a lease rather than a licence, as the tenant had (1) **exclusive possession** of the room, (2) for the **agreed period** and (3) at the **agreed rent**. The other provisions of the document were an attempt to disguise the true position |

Versuch – verschleiern

The parties cannot alter the legal effect of the agreement merely by insisting that they intended to create only a licence.

abändern/modifizieren

### *bb) Different types of lease*

Leases (which can also be called *tenancies)* fall into various categories, classified by the length of time they last:

festgesetzte Dauer

- A lease can be granted *for a fixed term*, which can be as short (e.g. 1 day) or as long (e.g. 999 years) as the parties wish. It comes automatically to an end when the fixed term runs out[20]. This is called a **fixed-term tenancy**.

wiederkehrend

- A lease can be granted for a *recurring period*, e.g. from week to week, month to month or year to year. The tenancy will automatically be renewed at the end of each period unless it is brought to an end by sufficient notice, e.g. 6 months' notice for a tenancy from year to year. This is called a **periodic tenancy**.

Ankündigung/Vorlauf/*hier:* Frist

(regelm.) wiederkehrend/periodisch

jederzeit kündbares Miet- oder Pachtverhältnis – jederzeit – fristlos

Haus zum Verkauf inserieren

Baugenehmigung

- A **tenancy at will** is a lease which can be ended by either party at any time without prior notice. Such a tenancy is used in situations where this is expressly the type of relationship which the parties wish to create. For example, a house owner is advertising his house for sale; he is not using his garage, so he allows his neighbour to store things in it temporarily. When the house is sold and the house owner moves out, the neighbour must remove his things from the garage. Another example: The landlord wished to demolish his building and rebuild. He required the usual planning permission for this. There was a shop within the building which he let as a tenancy at will until the planning permission was granted *(see Manfield v Botchin (1970))*.

Dulden/Duldung

- A **tenancy at sufferance** describes the situation where a tenant stays on at the property after his lease has ended. Technically, he is not a tenant at all, as his lease has expired. He pays the former landlord compensation for his occupation at the same rate as the previous rent. The relationship can be terminated by either party at any time.

*etwa:* Gewährung einer Miete/Recht an der Miete

When a flat is sold in England for the first time, the flat is sold on the basis that the purchaser buys the grant of a lease for a term of 99 years or 125 years, or even 999 years (see above for the reason why flats are not sold on the basis of freehold title). That lease is, in the above categorisation, a *fixed-term tenancy*. In Germany, this form of ownership corresponds either to *shared freehold* or to *freehold* of land with property on it, and is often compared to the German concept of „Erbpacht"[21].

---

20 This is the position at common law. There are statutes which change this result in certain cases, for example tenants of business premises *(Landlord and Tenant Act 1954)*.

21 Umgangsprachliche Bezeichnung für das Erbbaurecht an Baugrundstücken, wonach man gegen Zahlung eines regelmäßigen Entgelts auf einem fremden Grundstück ein Bauwerk errichten/unterhalten darf: beschränkt dingliches Recht. Erbpacht im Sinne der dauerhaften Trennung von Eigentums- und Nutzungsrecht gibt es in Deutschland heute nicht mehr.

### *cc) Creating a lease*

A lease is capable of being a *legal estate* under *s.1(1)(b) Law of Property Act 1925* provided that it is a *term of years absolute* and is created in the correct manner. Under *s.52(1) Law of Property Act 1925*, in order to create a lease at common law, the lease must be entered into in writing by means of a **deed** (see vol. 1, chapter 6, p. 113). There is, however, an exception in *s.54(2)* for a lease for a term of 3 years or less under which the tenant is entitled to take up occupation straight away, and the lease is at the best rent reasonably obtainable: such a lease can be entered into by an ordinary contract in writing or verbally.

deed: (förmliche) Urkunde

A lease which complies with these rules establishes a **leasehold legal estate** in land. The technical name for this is **a term of years absolute**. The words *term of years* refer to the fixed and certain duration of the lease, and cover both a lease granted for a *fixed term* and *a periodic tenancy*. A periodic tenancy is included because, strictly, it is in fact granted at any stage for a fixed period, even though that period becomes extended. The word *absolute* in the expression *term of years absolute* has no significance.

complies with: einhalten/beachten

However, if the above formalities have not been observed, in many cases it will be found that the arrangement, whilst it does not establish a lease *at law* (in other words, a legal estate), will nevertheless create a lease *in equity*:[22] giving it the status of an equitable interest. This is an example of the way that equity operates in a situation where it would be unconscionable for either party to claim that he had not intended to enter into a lease. Therefore, if the tenant is in occupation and paying a rent, and the parties have signed a written agreement not signed by deed, that agreement will be regarded *in equity* as a lease. This is because of the maxim "Equity looks upon that as done, which ought to be done". Either party has the right, in these circumstances, to require the other to enter into a deed in order formally to grant the lease which they have agreed. That right can be enforced through the courts in equity by a **decree of specific performance**. Equity considers that the deed has in fact been entered into, and that there *is* in existence a lease on the terms of the written agreement. Since this is a different conclusion to the situation at common law, which would not enforce the terms of the agreement because it was not entered into as a deed, the answer in equity prevails over the answer at common law.

at law / in equity: *typ. engl. Gegensatzpaar:* „gesetzlich" (i.S.d. common law) und „nach Billigkeit" (i.S.d. equity law)

unconscionable: unzumutbar/unverschämt

either – to enter into – occupation: eine von beiden/beide – schließen (einen Vertrag)/Verpflichtung eingehen – Besitz/Inbesitznahme

Equity looks upon that as done, which ought to be done: „Equity betrachtet das als getan, was getan werden soll."

to enter into a deed: urkundlichen Vertrag schließen

formally: in förmlicher Weise

decree of specific performance: gerichtliche Anordnung der (tatsächlichen) Vertragserfüllung

conclusion: Ergebnis/Folgerung

enforce – terms of the agreement: durchsetzen – Vertragsbedingungen

prevails over: siegen über/sich durchsetzen gegen

22 See vol. 1 chapter 2 section III for the historical difference between rules of English law which derive from the *common law* and those which derive from the courts of *equity*.

| Example – *Walsh* v *Lonsdale (1882)* |
|---|
| The owner of a mill (landlord) signed an agreement to let the mill to the tenant for a term of 7 years. The agreement (contract) was in writing but had not been signed as a deed. The agreement stated that the tenant was to pay his rent yearly in advance, if the landlord demanded it. Otherwise, he was to pay the rent quarterly in arrears. The landlord, some time after the agreement had been entered into, did demand one year's rent in advance, half way through the year.<br>When the tenant did not pay, he claimed the right of a landlord under a lease to exercise distress – i.e. to take away and sell property of a tenant who has not paid his rent. The tenant argued that the landlord was not entitled to exercise distress, because the lease had not been formally granted.<br>***Held:*** The position at common law was that the tenant was a tenant from year to year, with rent payable in arrears, and so the landlord could not have a right of distress because the rent was not yet due. However, the court was entitled, applying the maxim that "Equity looks on that as done which ought to be done", to consider that the parties had in fact entered into their arrangement by deed. Therefore, the rent was payable in advance as set out in the contract, and so the landlord did have the right to exercise distress when the rent had not been paid. |

Laufzeit/Dauer/Frist

vierteljährlich/quartalsweise – rückständig/nachschüssig

nach einem halben Jahr

Pfändung/Beschlagnahme (distress sale = Notverkauf)

#### *dd) The relationship between landlord and tenant*

*(1) Express covenants*

ausdrückliche Vereinbarung/ausdrücklich festgelegte Bedingung

When a lease is in writing, it will usually contain detailed obligations and other provisions which apply to each party. Where the lease has been signed as a deed, such obligations are called *covenants*, and that expression is used in practice even if the lease has not been signed as a deed, for example, if it is a verbal agreement. A lease in writing will contain the obligations which the parties have agreed. Common examples are the *payment of the rent,* which is to be *responsible for the repair* of the property, and whether the tenant is *permitted to transfer* the lease to someone else.

Verpflichtung

Bestimmung

*(2) Implied covenants*

stillschweigende Vereinbarung

There are also obligations which the law will imply into the lease. This can happen either when the lease does not deal specifically with that point, or because the implied obligation by statute applies even if the lease itself states something different.

implizieren/voraussetzen/unterstellen

kraft Gesetzes/von Gesetzes wegen

The main **implied obligations** of the **landlord** are:

- The landlord must ensure that the tenant receives **quiet enjoyment of the property.** This does not mean that there will be no noise, but rather that the landlord will ensure that no third party will lawfully disturb the tenant's use of the property. This obligation may be reduced by the terms of the lease, but not excluded entirely. *etwa*: ungestörter Besitz
- **Not to derogate from his grant**, i.e. the landlord must not take steps, or grant rights to another party, which render the premises unfit or unsuitable for the purpose for which they were let. The principle is, however, limited: it does not offer protection for uses not contemplated by the landlord when he granted the lease, or from actions of the landlord which have an economic effect on the tenant, but no physical effect on its use of the let premises, e.g. the landlord may let a neighbouring building to a competitor of his tenant. beeinträchtigen/schmälern/vermindern; in Erwägung ziehen; überlassen/vermieten; Konkurrent/Wettbewerber
- In a lease of residential accommodation for a term of 7 years or less, the landlord must be **responsible for repairs to the structure and exterior, and for the heating and utilities such as water etc.** This obligation will apply even if the lease purports to make the tenant responsible for these items. Wohnung; vorgeben/behaupten

The main **implied obligations** of the **tenant** are:

- **To pay a rent.** If no specific rent is agreed, the obligation is to pay a reasonable rent. angemessen
- **To pay the rates** on the property. Grundsteuer
- **Not to commit waste**, which means that the property must not be deliberately or negligently damaged. *hier*: Wertminderung (Gebäude); absichtlich

## 3. Interests in land

Rechtsanspruch/Vorteil

The relationship of landlord and tenant that we have been describing, shows how more than one person can be involved in the same piece of land. The landlord *owns it* (i.e. holds the freehold estate in the land), and the tenant has the *right to occupy it*. bewohnen/in Anspruch nehmen

There are a great many other situations where one person has a right over the land of another. For example, A needs to cross B's land in order to get to the public highway. B therefore grants A right of way across his (B's) land. A's right over B's land is an *interest* which A holds over B's land.

Therefore, an **interest** is the general expression used to describe a **right** which one person has over the land of another, which does not carry with it the right to possession. Examples of interests in land are:

dt. Recht: (Grund)Dienstbarkeit
Wegerecht
jemands Wasserleitungsrecht

gegenüberliegen – Nutzungsrecht an „Luft und Licht"
Abfangungsrecht
Nutzungs-/Entnahmerecht
Heu, Holz, Torf ernten
Weiderecht
Belastung mit einem Grundpfandrecht/Hypothek

- **Easements**: These are rights over one property for the benefit of another, such as the *right of way* mentioned above. Other examples are the *right of A to use a drain passing* under B's land, the right for A to receive light to windows in his building which face onto B's land (*right to light*) and, in a row of terraced houses, the right of each house owner to have his house supported by the other houses (*right to support*).
- **Profits-à-prendre:** These are rights to take things off the land of another, e.g. the right to cut grass, timber and peat, the right to fish or the right of grazing.
- **Charges by way of mortgage**: These are the right of a lender to enforce a charge (or mortgage) over the land which the lender has taken as security from the borrower (as to mortgages, see more detail in this chapter, section VII).

Dienstbarkeiten (*i.S.d. dt. Rechts*)

Easements and profits correspond to the German concept of „Dienstbarkeiten" (*servitudes*).

There are further situations which also create an *interest* rather than an *estate* in land - in other words, a right in favour of A over the land of B. Two examples may suffice to illustrate this. They contain the *right to possession*, using the word "interest" in a slightly different way:

hinauslaufen auf

- **Estates created informally:** Where a lease has been entered into which does not amount to a leasehold legal estate, such as the lease in *Walsh* v *Lonsdale* (see above in this chapter, section V. 2, p. 103). The lease could not have been a lease at law, because it was not granted by a deed. It amounted to a lease in equity, and therefore counts as an equitable interest: *equitable* – because it was not a *legal* estate, *interest* – because it was not a legal *estate*.

Begünstigter

- **Interests of beneficiaries under a trust:** Where A is the beneficiary under a trust, so that B (the trustee) holds the property of the land on trust for A. B holds the *legal estate* and A has an *equitable interest*. (Trusts are dealt with in chapter 9.)

**Diagram 48**

## Land Law

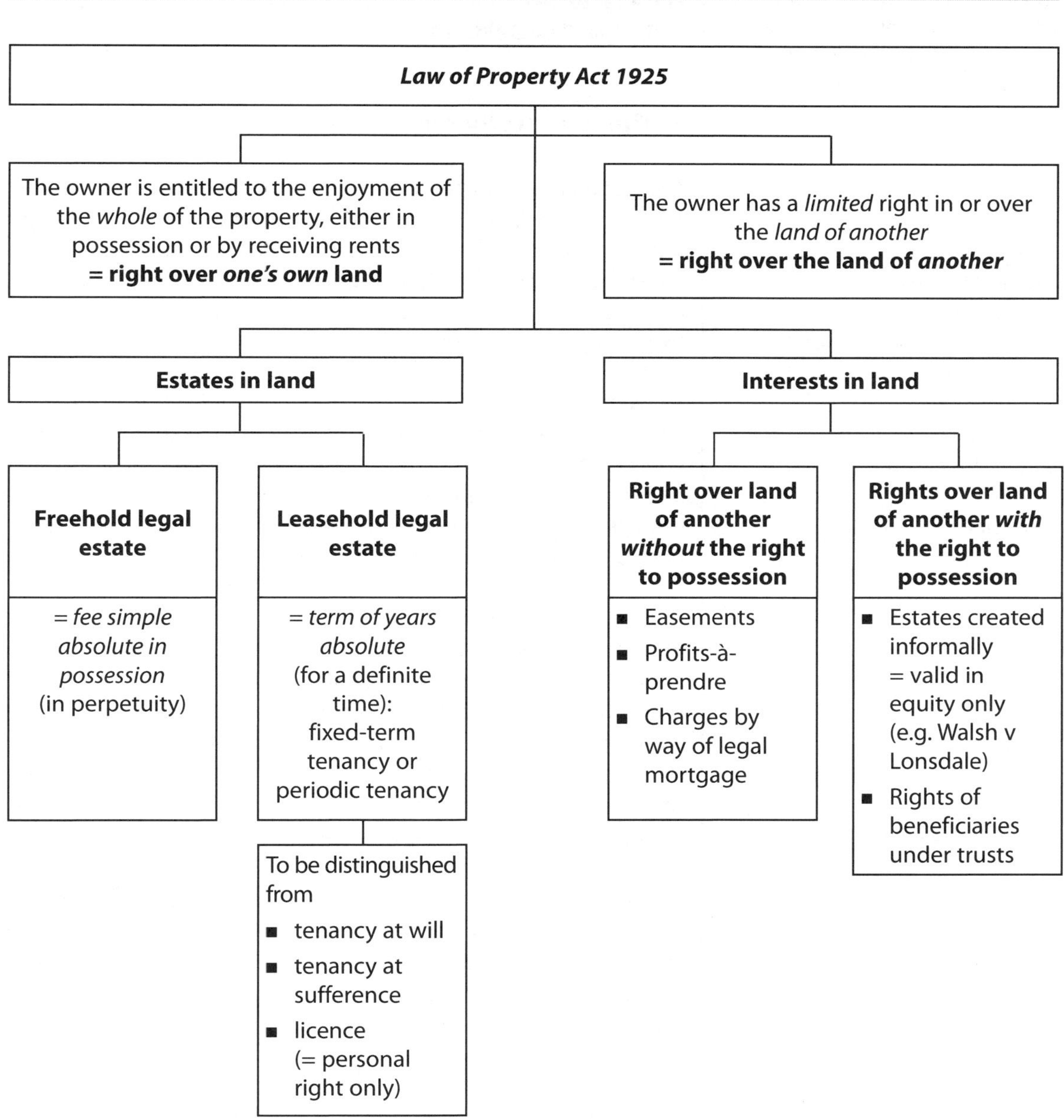

Grundstücksübertragung

## VI. The transfer of land

Übertragung eines Rechtstitels
Grundstückskaufvertrag – Übertragung – Eigentums-/Rechtsübertragung – (Vertrags-)Erfüllung/Vollendung

In English law, the procedure for the acquisition of land is called *conveyancing*, and usually involves two stages: (1) the **contract for sale**, and (2) the delivery of the land by transfer of title to it – called **completion**.

### 1. The contract for sale of land

Geschäftsfähigkeit
einen Termin festlegen
erfüllen/abschließen/beenden

The general rules of the law of contract apply to a contract for the sale of land. For example, the price and any other relevant terms must be agreed upon, and both parties must have contractual capacity. There must be the usual offer and acceptance, and the contract will set out a date on which the sale is to be completed – see below.

Voraussetzung
gültig/rechtswirksam
unwirksam

As we have seen in the chapter on the law of contract (see vol. 1, chapter 6, p. 111 ff.), there is also an additional requirement for a contract for the sale of land to be valid. *The Law of Property (Miscellaneous Provisions) Act 1989* provides that a contract for the dispositions of land is invalid unless it is in **writing**. This rule dates back originally to the *Statute of Frauds 1677*.

abgeschlossen werden (Vertrag)
sich etw. verschreiben/festlegen auf
Treuhänder – Eigentum als Treuhänder verwalten
Bedingung
in Anspruch nehmen/nutzen

The buyer of land is therefore in a different position to the purchaser of goods. Although, there is no „Abstraktionsprinzip" in English law as we have seen in section IV. 1 of this chapter, the buyer of land does not acquire ownership at the time the contract is entered into. The seller (also known as the vendor) and the buyer (also known as the purchaser) are committed to the sale because they have entered into a binding contract. This results in the seller being in the position of a trustee, **holding the property on trust** for the buyer until the date for completion (as to trusts, see chapter 9). This means that the buyer has an *equitable interest* in the property with the rights of a beneficiary under a trust, until he acquires the *legal estate* on completion. However, the terms of this particular trust are that the buyer is not permitted to occupy the property until completion.

im Wert steigen
umgekehrt
den Verlust tragen

As there is a binding contract in place between seller and buyer, if the land increases in value after the date of the contract, the buyer gains the benefit of that. Conversely, if the value of the land goes down, the buyer bears the loss and must still pay the agreed price. Interestingly, the law regards the risk of accidental damage (e.g. fire) to the land as passing to buyer at the time of the contract, so the buyer should insure the property from that time. This principle can, however, be changed by the terms of the contract.

Before the seller and buyer enter into the contract, neither of them is committed to the sale and either may withdraw from the transaction for any reason and without incurring any liability.[23] In England, the ability to withdraw without liability can be used tactically to re-negotiate the terms of the sale, for example the price. In a rising market, the seller may threaten to withdraw from a sale agreed to one buyer, before the contract is entered into, in order to sell to another at a higher price. The first buyer may therefore have to increase his price if he wishes to proceed with his purchase.[24]

sich zurückziehen
Verpflichtung eingehen/übernehmen
bei anziehenden Preisen

## 2. Completion of the sale – conveyance

*hier:* Auflassung/Umschreibung

The **conveyance** is the document, signed as a *deed* (see vol. 1, chapter 6, p. 113), which transfers legal ownership of a freehold estate to the buyer. This document is handed over, by the seller's solicitors to the buyer's solicitors, on the completion date, in return for payment of the price. If the estate is leasehold, the document is an **assignment**.

Auflassungsurkunde
gegen Zahlung
*hier:* Abtretungsurkunde

*Conveyance* (and *assignment*) is the traditional words. Today, most land is registered under the *Land Registration Acts,* so the document which transfers title is called a *transfer* (which covers both freehold and leasehold). For many years conveyances[25] and transfers could only be prepared by solicitors and barristers (e.g. *Solicitors Act 1974* and statutes before it) or, in theory, by the buyer himself. Since *Administration of Justice Act 1985* persons who have obtained the qualification of a licensed conveyancer, may also prepare conveyances[26] and transfers. The current legislation regulating this is the *Legal Services Act 2007* which grants authority to prepare these documents to all appropriately qualified persons.

Rechtstitel/Anrecht/Eigentum – Übertragungsurkunde
Spezialist für Immobilienrecht/Grundstücksübertragungen *(aber kein solicitor)*

## 3. Procedure for the sale of land

The reason for having this **two-stage process**, first **contract** and then **completion**, is both practical and historical. The time between entering into the contract and completion can be as long

Vertragsabschluss

23 There is no English concept comparable to the German „vorvertragliche Haftung" (in Latin: „culpa in contrahendo); *§ 311 BGB.*

24 This is called gazumping *(slang).*

25 Including assignments.

26 Including assignments.

umziehen

or as short as the parties wish (but up to a maximum of 21 years); traditionally it is 4 weeks. For people who are moving house, it gives them the certainty of moving on a particular date, and time to plan their arrangements.

Eigentumserwerbsurkunde/*heute auch*: Grundbuch(blatt)

At common law, the interval between entering into the contract and completion was when the seller produced his title deeds to demonstrate his ownership of the land, and the buyer checked that that was the case. Until the *Land Registration Acts* were passed (see below), ownership of land was an entirely private matter. There were no registries such as the German „Grundbuchämter". Landowners were only required to prove their ownership to someone who had signed a contract to buy their land.

Unlike in Germany, notaries are not involved in the sale of land in England. The procedure has similarities with bringing a case to court. The seller and the buyer each instruct their own solicitor (or licensed conveyancer etc., see above). The two solicitors negotiate the contract. The seller's solicitor produces the title deeds to the buyer's solicitor for checking. The two solicitors negotiate the conveyance, and together they arrange for the sale to be completed.

eingetragen

## 4. Registered land

For centuries it has been sufficient for ownership of land to be proved by means of private title deeds, but the system is not appropriate for the modern world. The common law system relies on title deeds being checked each time the land is sold, which takes time and is expensive (but good work for solicitors). There is also the possibility of mistakes being made which are not realised until the land comes to be sold next time, and then it may be too late to find the people involved to put the problems right.

angemessen/geeignet

The advantage of registered land is that the state guarantees ownership (in the sense of holding the legal estate in the land) once and for all.

ein für allemal

In the late 19$^{th}$ century, experiments were carried out, in a very small way, in creating a system of registering ownership of land in a central registry. In 1925, legislation was passed *(Land Registration Act)*, setting the framework for a system of land registration to cover the whole country. It has, however, taken many years for the system to be brought into force. Unlike Mary and Joseph being required by the Romans to travel to Bethlehem to be registered, it

Rahmen/Grundstruktur – amtliche Eintragung

was not thought *right* to require everyone to register their ownership of land on date X. Instead, it is only necessary to register land when it changes hands or is otherwise dealt with (e.g. on inheritance). At present, it is estimated that about **75%** of the land in England and Wales has been registered, but if land is never sold – for example, the Tower of London – it will never become registered.

The authority which issues and records registered titles is the **land registry**. When the title to a piece of land has been registered at the land registry, it is then described as registered land. The current statute regulating registered land is *Land Registration Act 2002*.

ausfertigen/ausstellen – eintragen/erfassen – Grundstücksregisterbehörde/Grundbuchamt

**Diagram 49**

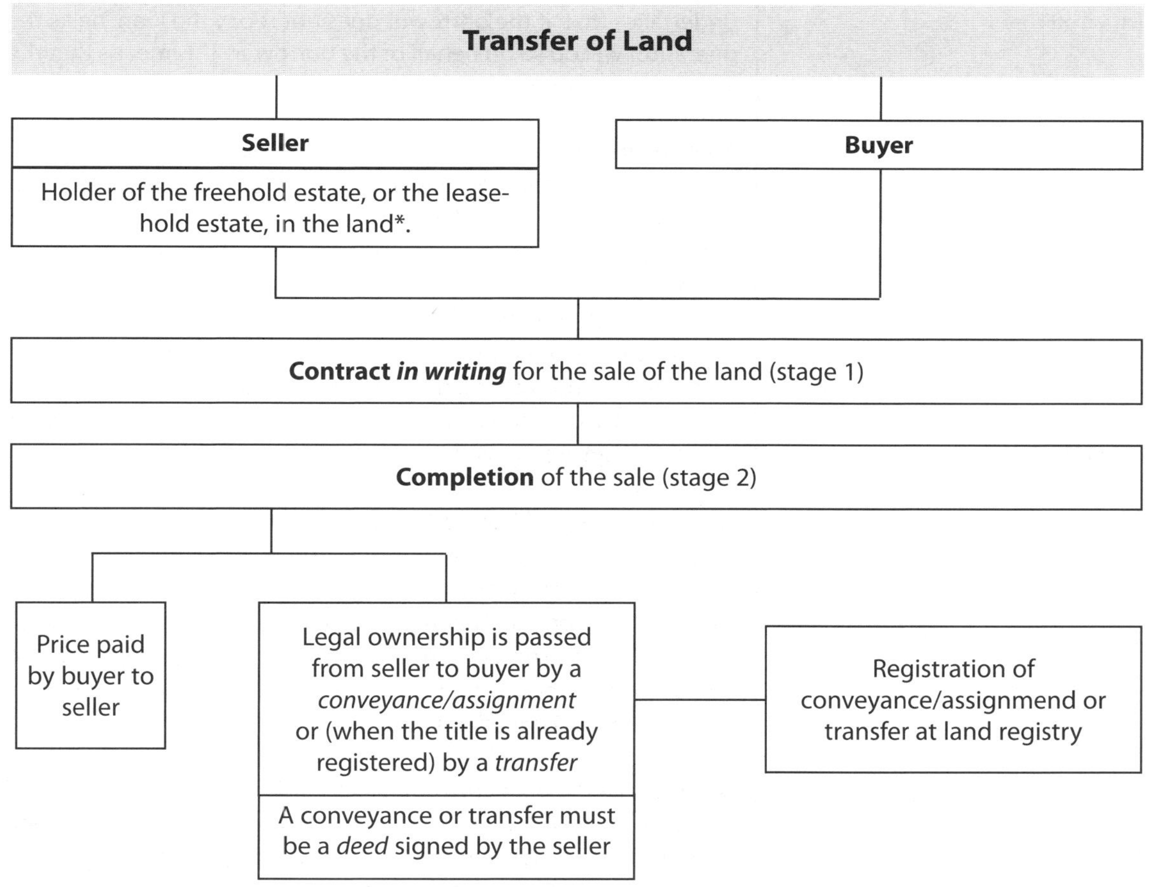


* The holder of any other interest in land (e.g. an equitable interest) is also legally able to sell it, but that situation is not addressed in this diagram.

## VII. Mortgages of land

Grundpfandrecht/Hypothek

### 1. Introduction

Geld leihen
Darlehens-/Kreditgeber/Hypothekengläubiger

When someone needs to borrow money, one of the important points for the **lender** will be – how can I be confident that I will get my money back?

Darlehen/Kredit
Darlehens-/Kreditnehmer/Hypothekenschuldner – Rechtsmittel/-behelf – verklagen

**Loans** can be either *secured* or *unsecured*. When a loan is unsecured, and the **borrower** does not repay the loan when he should, the lender's only remedy is to sue the borrower for the money. If the borrower has, for example, disappeared or become insolvent, the lender will have lost his money. The lender may therefore require **security** for the loan. Security can be either *personal* or *real*.

Sicherheit

persönliche Sicherheit – Bürge
sich verpflichten

**Personal security** means e.g. that another person, a guarantor, undertakes that, if the borrower does not repay the loan, he as the guarantor will do so on behalf of the borrower. This means that the lender has someone else that he can sue for the money he has lent.

Realsicherheit

**Real security** means that some form of property is provided to the lender so that, if the borrower does not repay the loan, the lender can sell that property and recover the money he has lent that way. The property provided as security can be either *real* property or *personal* property (for the difference, see the beginning of this chapter 8). An example of real security over *personal* property (referring here to *chattels personal*, see above section II.2) would be where the borrower has a gold watch, and he gives possession of it to the lender until the loan is repaid. This delivery of possession is called **pledge**. Possession is returned when the loan is repaid.

Verpfändung

*Land*, however, is likely to be more valuable than watches, even gold watches. If a large amount of money is involved, the lender may require security over land (and remember that land includes the buildings on it). This happens regularly in England (and in Germany) when someone buys a house. The buyer then borrows some of the money to buy the house, and the lender has security over the house for repayment of the loan.

„tote" Verpfändung

When the land is being provided as security, the deed which is used to create the security is called a **mortgage**. This word is derived from Norman French and means "dead pledge". When the concept of mortgages was first developed in medieval times, the land was transferred to and possessed by the lender (see the similarity with pledge of a chattel mentioned above). If the income from the land (e.g. the crops grown on the land) was used to repay the loan, it was a *live pledge*. If the lender kept the income himself, it was a *dead pledge*.

Ernte

The *Law of Property Act 1925* sets out two main ways for a mortgage to be created:

### a) Mortgage by demise for a term of years

Besitzübertragung/-verpachtung

This means that the borrower grants the lender a *lease* of the land for a very long period (usually 3000 years), with a provision that the lease will come to an end before the 3000 years have run out, when the loan is repaid. During the term of the lease the borrower is allowed to occupy the land. You will remember that a lease is a legal *estate* in land.

Vorbehalt/Bestimmung

This method of creating a mortgage is not very common, but you need to know about it because of the second alternative, which is:

### b) Charge by way of legal mortgage

Belastung mit einem Grundpfand-recht/Hypothek

This is the more common way. A *charge by way of legal mortgage* operates as if the borrower had granted a lease for 3000 years to the lender, but because no lease is actually granted, it is a simpler procedure. This method of security creates a legal *interest* in land rather than a legal *estate*.

einräumen/gewähren

## 2. Rights of the borrower

The borrower has the **right to occupy the land**, until the lender needs to enforce his security.

He also has the right to repay the loan and have the security cancelled. This is called **redeeming the mortgage.**

zurückzahlen (Hypothek)

## 3. Rights of the lender

If the borrower does not repay the loan when he should, the lender will want to enforce his rights, which are as follows:

durchsetzen

Forderung/Anspruch einklagen

## a) To sue for debt

Zahlungsversprechen
Hauptschuld und fällige Zinsen
Schuld/Verbindlichkeit – Beitreibung

The repayment covenant is a contractual obligation of the mortgage. The amount to be repaid is the loan and the interest due on it. Thus, the lender may *sue for the debt* (i.e. for the recovery of the loan and interest).

However, if the borrower has disappeared or does not have the money (for example, if he is insolvent), this right will not be effective, so a lender who has security will want to enforce his security.

A lender with security over land by way of a *mortgage by demise*, or a *charge by way of legal mortgage*, has the right to require the borrower to stop occupying the land, so that the lender can enforce his security by one of the following methods:

## b) To take possession

verpachten/vermieten – Ertrag/Einnahmen

jmd. etw. belegen/jmd. verantwortlich sein für – *hier*: ortsüblich
entlasten/gutschreiben

anwenden um zu

This means that the lender uses the land himself – either to occupy it himself, or to rent it out to someone else and receive an income from the land in order to repay the loan. However, because the borrower still actually owns the land, the lender is responsible for making sure that he accounts to the borrower for *the best rent reasonably obtainable* in the circumstances. This means that he must either credit the borrower himself with this amount, or ensure that the rent from any tenant to whom he lets the land is at least this amount and is applied towards reducing the debt.

The obligation to realise *the best rent reasonably obtainable* is one which the lender must be careful to observe, because the courts will enforce it strictly against him. Therefore, this right is not often used.

betreiben/verwalten
verpfänden/hypothekarisch belasten

Brauerei-/Vertragsgaststätte

*Example – White v City of London Brewery Co (1889)*

The borrower Mr White operated a public house and obtained a loan of £900 from City of London Brewery. He mortgaged the public house as security, and when he did not repay the loan, the brewery took possession. The brewery rented the pub to a tenant under a lease which obliged the tenant to buy his beer only from that brewery: the pub was therefore a "tied house". Under such a lease, the tenant pays a lower rent than if he was free to buy his beer from any supplier: that would have been a "free house".

> ***Held:*** that the brewery must reduce the loan by the additional amount of rent which the tenant would have paid if the lease had been on the terms of a free house, even though the brewery was only actually receiving rent on the basis of a tied house.

### c) To foreclose the mortgage

für verfallen erklären

Remember that, when the borrower gives security over land, he remains the owner of the land. An *order of foreclosure*, which must be applied for from the court, ends the borrower's right to repay the loan and free his property from the security interest. The effect of this is to vest the full legal estate in the land in the lender, so that the land becomes the lender's own property absolutely, to deal with as he wishes.

Vollstreckungs-/Verfallserklärung
beantragen
Folge
übertragen auf jmd.

This is a drastic remedy which is *rarely used* by lenders as there must be no realistic chance of the loan being repaid. Also, the court has power, in appropriate circumstances, to reverse an order of foreclosure if the borrower in fact manages to repay the loan and interest at some time in the future: the lender would be ordered to transfer the land back to the borrower.

einschneidend/tief greifend
rückgängig machen

### d) To sell the land

This is the *most common way* of enforcing security. The lender has the legal right, called a *power of sale*, to allow him to sell the land even though he does not own it. The lender will use the money to repay the loan due with interest, together with the expenses of the sale. If there is any money left over, this surplus must be paid to the borrower, because the land was previously his property.

Auslagen/Unkosten
Überschuss
früher

The lender may not buy the land himself (unless he obtains a court order allowing this). When selling it, he must use all reasonable care to obtain a proper price. This means that the land is sold either by auction or is extensively advertised.

Gerichtsbeschluss
angemessen
Versteigerung – inserieren/anpreisen

### e) To appoint a receiver

bestellen/einsetzen/festsetzen – *hier:* Zwangsverwalter

A receiver is a person, often an accountant, who is appointed by the lender to sell the property or rent it out and pay the rent to the lender. The advantage to the lender of using this method of enforcement of his security is that the lender is not responsible for the level of rent which the receiver obtains or the price at which the land is sold. This is because the receiver is, under *s.109(2) Law*

Wirtschaftsprüfer/Steuerberater
Höhe

Bevollmächtigter/Beauftragter für Rechnung/im Auftrag/im Interesse von

*of Property Act 1925*, acting as the agent of – and therefore on behalf of – the borrower, and not the lender.

## 4. Other forms of security

skizzieren/kurz darstellen

At the end of this chapter we would like to briefly outline other forms of security which are beyond the scope of our introduction.

Security by way of mortgage can be created over *choses in action* – such as shares in a company –, or over *chattels personal* if sufficiently valuable to make it worthwhile doing so – perhaps a large piece of machinery. The latter is called a *chattel mortgage*.

It is also possible to enter into a slightly different form of security to a mortgage, called a *charge*[27] and also to enter into a type of security which is an *equitable mortgage* or an *equitable charge* rather than a *charge by way of legal mortgage*.

**Diagram 50**

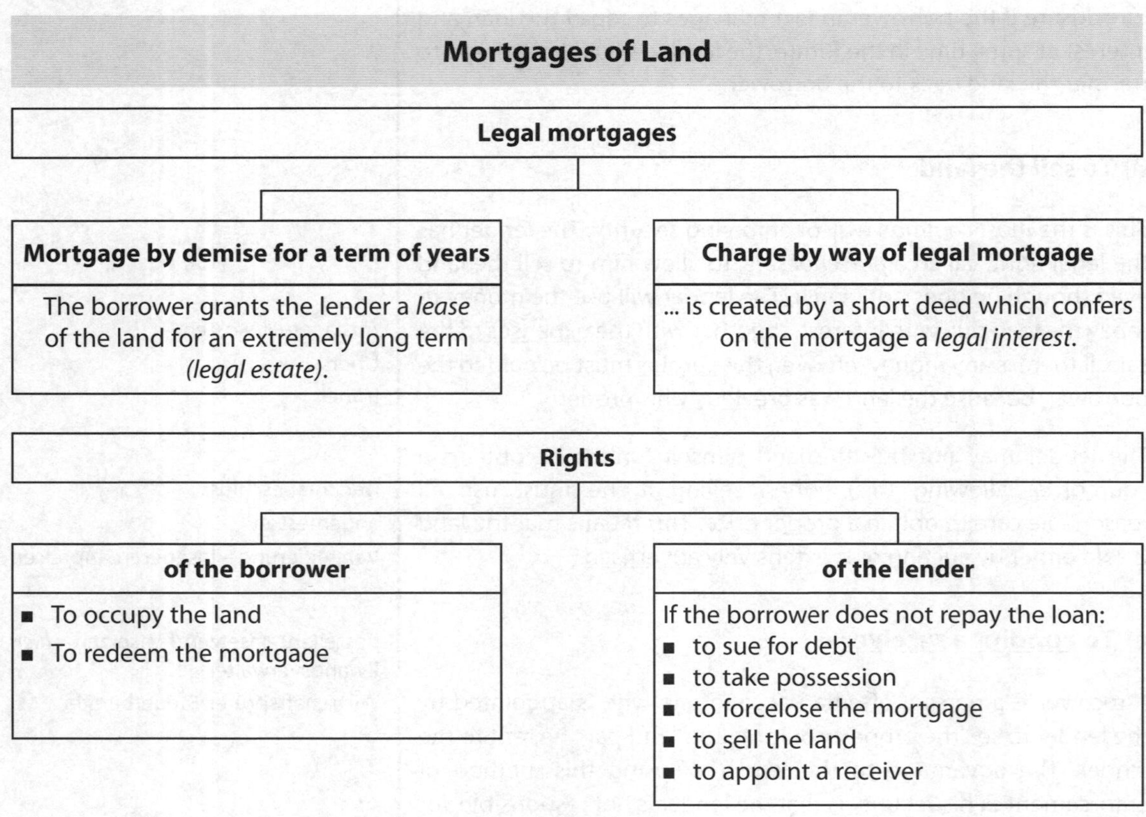


27 ***Note:*** This is a different concept to the *charge by way of legal mortgage* which is discussed above.

## VIII. Further reading & references[28]

*Adams*, Law for Business Students; *Barker & Padfield*, Law Made Simple; *Bell*, Real property; *Boucher & Corns*, GCSE Law Casebook; *Burn*, Cheshire and Burn's Modern Law of Real Property; *Chang*, Land Law; *Davey & Wicks*, Butterworths Property Law Handbook; *Dobson*, Sale of Goods and Consumer Credit; *Duddington*, Land Law; *Geldart*, Introduction to English Law; *Haley*, Land Law; *Harpum, Bridge & Dixon*, Megarry & Wade: The Law of Real Property; *Harris*, An Introduction to Law; *Lawson & Rudden*, The Law of Property; *Lyall*, An Introduction to British Law; *Riddall*, Land Law; *Shears & Stephenson*, James' Introduction to English Law; *Stevens, Pearce & Jackson*, Land law; *Templeman & Bell*, Land: The Law of Real Property (Casebook, Revision Work Book, Textbook); *Templeman & Burr*, Conveyancing (Casebook, Revision Work Book, Textbook); *Wild & Weinstein*, Smith & Keenan's English law; *Wilman*, Brown: GCSE Law.

28 Edition, publisher, place and year of publication are quoted in the bibliography.

# Chapter Nine

## Law of Trusts

Recht der Treuhandverhältnisse

## I. Introduction

auffällig/eigentümlich
Auffälligkeit/Besonderheit
Rechtsinstitut

*Trusts* are one of the most characteristic and peculiar institutions of English civil law.[29] The peculiarity of *trusts* becomes obvious when you consider that there is no corresponding legal institution, either in German law or in other continental legal systems, which plays the same role as *trusts* in England. Therefore, readers should approach the concept of a trust free of pre-conceptions of their own legal system.

Rechtswörterbuch

If you were to look for a translation of the word *trust* in dictionaries of legal terms, you could find for example the following:

Begriff

„1. Treuhandverhältnis; Treuhandvermögen: Ein *trust* ist eine auf *equity* beruhende Rechtsbeziehung zwischen dem Treuhänder (*trustee*) und dem Begünstigten (*beneficiary*, früher: *cestui que trust*) – auf beiden Seiten kann eine Mehrheit von Personen auftreten –, durch die das vom Besteller des *trust* (*settlor* oder *trustor*) auf den Treuhänder zugunsten des Begünstigten übertragene Vermögen von diesem verwaltet wird. Während der Begünstigte der *equitable owner* des Treuhandgutes ist, wird der Treuhänder der *legal owner* ..." - cf. Dietl/Lorenz, where this definition is followed by 2 ½ pages of notions combined with the word *trust*. Then follows: "2. Trust, Sonderform des Konzerns; ..." mentioned as the second possible translation.

The type of *trust* on we will focus in this chapter is the one pertaining to the first translation: „**Treuhandverhältnis**".

ungewohnt/nicht vertraut

Before giving a more detailed definition of *trust*, let us first consider its historical development – particularly we (in Germany) are rather unfamiliar with this concept of English law.

## II. Historical background

Rechtsverhältnis – bezeichnen
Ritter

Looking back at medieval England, you will note that legal relationships, which today are denoted as *trusts*, were already known in the 12th and 13th centuries. If, for example a knight

29 And in other common law countries such as USA.

intended to participate in a crusade, he needed someone to run his estate in his absence. Therefore, he transferred his land to a person enjoying his confidence, in order for that person to administer the land *for the benefit of* the family of the absent knight.

Kreuzzug – sich kümmern um

Person seines Vertrauens – verwalten/bewirtschaften – zugunsten von/zum Nutzen von

This arrangement was in medieval times called a ***use***, and nowadays is called a *trust*. The reason is a linguistic one: as well as *for the benefit of*, one can also say *to the use of*. The word *use* is said to derive from the Latin word "opus".

*hier*: Treuhand

entstammen/herrühren – *lat.*: Werk/Hilfe/Nutzen

The legal owner (the trusted person) held the land on trust for the person(s) whom the knight wished to benefit. The legal owner is called the **trustee** (in former times: the *feoffee to uses*), the persons for whom he holds the property are the **beneficiaries** (in former times: the *cestuis que trust* or *use*) of the trust. The person who sets up the trust – the knight in medieval times – is called the **settlor**.

treuhänderischer Erwerber von Grundvermögen – Begünstigter/Nutznießer/wirtschaftlicher Eigentümer *(bei Trusts)* – Treugeber/Trustgründer

The concept of the *use* was necessary because many of the remedies of the medieval common law were only available to the person who was actually holding the land. The arrangement of the *use* was convenient so long as the person to whom the land was transferred did not abuse the knight's confidence in him. This confidence could easily be abused, because the medieval common law did not recognise the rights of the family or the original owner. Thus, it happened, for example, that the property was not handed back to the knight upon his return.

Therefore, the rights of the knight or his family required protection. As the common law courts refused this protection because no writ[30] existed which provided an action against the **trustee**, there was no claim at law for the knight or his family.

Schutz bedürfen
gerichtlicher Klagebefehl/Klageschrift
bereitstellen/vorsehen
Rechtsanspruch

It was the concept of **equity**[31] which helped in such a case. The knight petitioned the King, who would refer the matter to his Lord Chancellor. In the 15th century, the Court of Chancery intervened. It is true that the court could not disturb the fact of legal ownership of the *feoffee to uses* but it forced him to administer the property for the benefit of the *cestui que use* according to the terms of the grant. Over the course of time, the *cestui que use* came to have a special interest in the property enforceable only in the Court of Chancery. Thus, this interest, protected by the Chancellor's equitable jurisdiction, became an **equitable interest.** This is the reason why *equity* and *trust* are inseparable in terms, and English law books are often entitled "Equity and Trusts", accordingly.

ersuchen/Eingabe machen bei – die Angelegenheit zur Entscheidung weiterleiten – zwar

*hier*: Treuabrede

einklagbar

dementsprechend/folglich

30 The system of writs was illustrated in vol. 1, chapter 2, p. 27 ff.

31 For more details see vol. 1, chapter 2, p. 30 ff.

## III. Definition of a trust

Versuch
zufriedenstellend
auslassen – Art/Sorte/Spielart

Many attempts have been made to define a trust, but no definition seems entirely satisfactory. The number of different types of trust which exist leads to definitions which omit some varieties, or can be rather vague and not particularly helpful.

*hier:* verstorben
Treuhänder/Verwalter
Treugeber/Treuhandbegünstigter

According to the late Sir Arthur Underhill's[32] definition, a trust is "an equitable obligation binding a person (who is called a trustee) to deal with property over which he has control (which is called trust property), for the benefit of persons (who are called beneficiaries or cestuis que trust), of whom he may himself be one, and anyone of whom may enforce the obligation."

allumfassend – denn
abdecken/erfassen – wohltätige/gemeinnützige Stiftung

This is certainly a good definition, but it shows that it is impossible to give a comprehensive definition of all kinds of trusts, for Underhill's definition does not cover the type of *charitable trusts*.

Hauptmerkmal
Dualität/Zweiheit
rechtliches Volleigentum
vorläufiges (wirtschaftl.) Eigentum
übertragen/erworben
vorkommen

Instead of searching for a definition of a trust, it is easier to give an explanation of *what a trust can be*. The main characteristic of the trust is the **duality of ownership** which can be achieved by the *legal* title (legal ownership) on the one hand, and the *equitable* interest (equitable ownership) on the other hand. As a matter of law, under trusts, the *legal* title will be vested in the *trustees* and the *equitable* interest in the *beneficiaries*. This might arise where S (the *settlor*) transfers land to T1 and T2 (the *trustees*) to hold the land on trust for the benefit of A, B and C (the *beneficiaries*).

The following diagram[33] may help to clarify this situation:

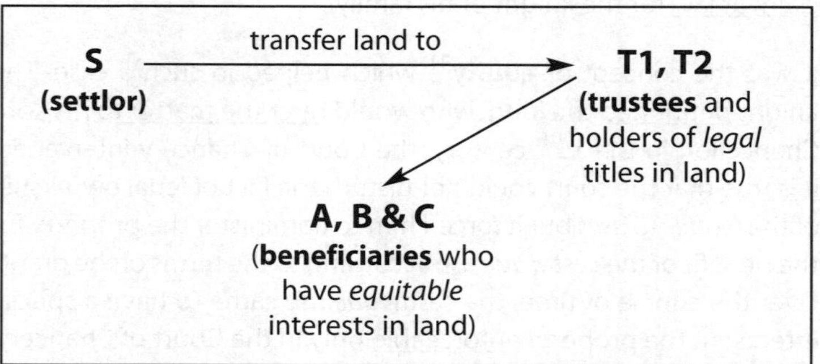


32 Whose definition, which he offered in Underhill & Hayton, Law of Trust and Trustees, is cited in other textbooks, such as *James'* Intodruction to English Law, p. 241 and *Oakley*, Parker and Mellows: The Modern Law of Trusts, p. 9.

33 Borrowed from *Templeman & Halliwell*, p. 1.

The trust does not interfere with the legal position of the title to the land; at law, the title rests with T1 and T2, since it was transferred to them by S. However, equity recognises that the title was not transferred to T1 and T2 for their own use, but *for the benefit of* A, B & C as the settlor S intended. The *trustees* are considered as having a *bare title* only and the benefits of the land will accrue to the *beneficiaries*. Through this device, the courts are able to uphold essential doctrines of common law and give effect to the true intention of the settlor.

etw. beeinträchtigen/stören/in Konflikt geraten mit – da

nackt/bloß

zuwachsen/anfallen – Kunstgriff/Erfindung – aufrechterhalten

Wirkung verschaffen/*hier*: umsetzen

To summarise, it can be said that a trust is a relationship whereby **property** is **managed** by one person **for the benefit of another**.

## IV. Classification of trusts

Trusts may be classified into **private trusts** and **charitable trusts (public trusts)**. They must be considered separately as there are important differences between them.

Trust zugunsten bestimmter Privatperson

### 1. Private trusts

A *private trust* is a trust for the benefit of either a named **individual** (e.g. "£10,000 to be held on trust for James") or a named class of **individuals** (e.g. "£10,000 to be held on trust for my children").

There is no such thing as a "private purpose trust". Private trusts cannot be used to benefit a particular purpose as public trusts do. The reason is that no person could enforce the trust (see the "beneficiary principle" explained in section 2 below). Thus, a trust promoting a non-charitable purpose is void.

fördern – Zweck

vorantreiben/begünstigen

*Private trusts* can be divided on the one hand into **express trusts**, and in **implied trusts**, on the other.

ausdrücklich erklärtes rechtsgeschäftliches Treuhandverhältnis (= T.) – *etwa:* unausgesprochenes T.

#### a) Express trusts

An express trust is a trust *expressly* created by the settlor, usually it is written, often it is set out in deed form, sometimes orally during life, or by will. An express trust will benefit one or more specified persons or a group of persons. The majority of trusts are created as express trusts.

unter Lebenden – Testament

Sicherheit/*hier*: Bestimmtheit (= B.)
B. des Vorhabens/des Ziels
B. des Gegenstandes/Inhalts
B. der Objekte (d.h. der Begünstigten)

The essential elements of an *express private trust* were laid down in *Knight* v *Knight (1840)* by Lord Langdale, who declared that "**three certainties**" are necessary for the creation of a trust:

- certainty of intention to create a trust
- certainty of subject matter and
- certainty of the objects of the trust (i.e. beneficiaries).

The third certainty does not apply, however, to *charitable trusts*. Where the purpose of the trust is charitable, there need not be necessarily a human beneficiary as the trust can be enforced by the Attorney General.

Generalstaatsanwalt/*brit.*: Kronanwalt

*Example – Knight v Knight (1840)*

falls er ausfällt

bestimmen – erben
bezeichnetes Vermögen – Testamentsvollstrecker – pflichtgemäß ausführen (to carry duly into execution)

Ungenauigkeit – Vorbehalt
verbinden mit
Erblasser/Testamentsverfasser
vermachen – Abkömmling – gerade männliche Linie

A man who died in 1824 left all his estates real and personal to his brother, Thomas Andrew Knight, and, failing him, to his nephew, Thomas Andrew Knight the younger. The will stated: "I do hereby constitute and appoint the person who shall inherit my said estates under this my will my sole executor and trustee, to carry the same and everything contained therein duly into execution; confiding in the approved honour and integrity of my family, to take no advantage of any technical inaccuracies, but to admit all the comparatively small reservations which I make out of so large a property ..."
The will stated that the testator's intention was that the estates should be settled on the next descendant in the direct male line of the testator's grandfather, Richard Knight of Downton. On the testator's death, Thomas Andrew Knight, the testator's brother, succeeded to the estates. In 1827, Thomas Andrew Knight the younger died childless, intestate, and the testator's brother immediately settled the estates upon persons who were not the next descendants in the direct male line of Richard Knight of Downton. The question arose whether the testator had imposed a binding trust on his brother.

kinderlos – testamentlos/ohne Testament – *hier*: aufteilen/regeln

zwingend

schenken/übertragen
Schenker – Verfügungsmacht
empfehlen – ersuchen

im Ganzen – auslegen

***Held:*** that the words which the testator had used in his will were not sufficiently imperative to create a trust which was binding. Lord Langdale M.R.:* "As a general rule, it has been laid down, that when property is given absolutely to any person, and the same person is, by the giver who has power to command, recommended or entreated, or wished, to dispose of that property in favour of another, the recommendation, entreaty, or wish shall be held to create a trust. **First**, if the words were so used, that upon the whole, they ought to be construed as imperative; **secondly**, if the subject of the recommendation or wish be certain; and **thirdly**, if the objects or persons intended

> to have the benefit of the recommendation or wish be also certain."

* M.R. = Master of the Rolls; Präsident des Berufungsgerichts in Zivilsachen (Court of Appeal), der früher die Aufgabe hatte, Staatsurkunden („Rollen") aufzubewahren; daher der Name.

Thus, the "**three certainties**" mean **first**, that the words used must show a clear intention (*certainty of intention*) that a trust shall arise. Mere precatory words such as request, hope and desire are insufficient to establish a trust. **Secondly**, the *certainty of subject matter* speaks for itself: if the subject matter to be held on trust is indeterminate (e.g. "the bulk of my estate"), the courts cannot enforce the trust. **Thirdly**, the *certainty of the objects* means that the persons whom the trust is intended to benefit must be clearly identifiable or at least ascertainable (if they are not, a *resulting trust* may arise, as explained below).

precatory: bittend/ersuchend
indeterminate – bulk: unbestimmt – Großteil
enforce: durchsetzen/Geltung verschaffen
identifiable – ascertainable – resulting trust: identifizierbar – bestimmbar/ermittelbar – gesetzlich vermuteter Trust

As to the *third certainty*, it is vital to distinguish between **fixed** and **discretionary trusts**: e.g. there is no room for any discretion in the phrasing of "to all my children in equal shares". Contrast this with a discretionary trust, where the trustees have discretion as to whether a person will be a beneficiary or not. In such trusts the test is to assess whether any given individual is or is not a member of the class in question. The test is, for example, not satisfied by "a gift to my old mates".

As to – vital – fixed – discretionary – phrasing: was ... betrifft – unerlässlich – feststehend/unveränderlich – im Ermessen stehend – Formulierung
to assess: bewerten/beurteilen/feststellen
mates: Kamerad/Gefährte

## b) Implied trusts

*Implied trusts* are trusts which are not expressly created by the settlor and which arise *by implication* or *by operation of law*. They include **resulting trusts, constructive trusts** and **trusts imposed by statute**.

by implication – by operation of law: stillschweigend – kraft Gesetzes
constructive: konstruiert/angenommen

### *aa) Resulting trusts*

The most common type of implied trust is the resulting trust which arises *by operation of law*. It does not need to be expressly created by a settlor nor does it require any formal aspects for its creation. The resulting trust takes its name from the fact that it operates to ensure that the beneficial title "results back" to the transferor – meaning that it re-vests in the transferor (i.e. the settlor).

results back – transferor: *hier:* zurückfallen an – Veräußerer

There are two main contexts in which a resulting trust arises:

- the **failed trust**, where has been an attempt to create a trust but some part of the beneficial interest has not been entirely dealt with (*automatic resulting trust*) or
- the **apparent gift**, where there is a voluntary transfer of property without an express indication as to how the equitable title is to be held (*presumed intention resulting trust*).

fehlgeschlagen/gescheitert; behandeln/bearbeiten/erledigen; „Scheingeschenk"; Angabe/Hinweis – was ... betrifft/bezüglich

Two examples may illustrate the two different contexts:

An *automatic resulting trust* would arise, e.g. if a settlor created a trust of £100,000 "for A for life". This does not indicate what is to happen to the money on A's death and, thus, *equity* helps in such a case: on A's death the money would revert to the settlor or his estate.

zurückfallen/heimfallen

The second example illustrates a *presumed intention resulting trust*:

| *Example – Re* Abbott Fund Trusts (1900)* |
|---|
| Dr Fawcett collected a sum of money, raising subscriptions from the public, to support two distressed ladies who were deaf and dumb and to enable them to live in lodgings in Cambridge. No provision was made as to the disposal of any surplus. On the death of the two ladies, a surplus remained.<br>***Held:*** that it was not the intention of the subscribers that the money should be an absolute gift and become the absolute property of the ladies and it followed that the trustees held the balance on a ***resulting trust*** for the subscribers. |

*hier*: Spende eintreiben; notleidend; Wohnung; Überschuss; Spender; das Guthaben behalten

* "Re" means "in that matter" (= in dieser Angelegenheit/in diesem Rechtsstreit); diese Zitierweise ist in Streitigkeiten üblich, in die mehr Personen als nur ein Kläger und Beklagter verwickelt sind.

### *bb) Constructive trusts*

Constructive trusts arise through *operation of law*, regardless of the intention of the parties. *Equity* will often find such a trust to exist to prevent unjust enrichment, or where it would be unconscionable to allow an owner to retain beneficial ownership of property. A constructive trust, for example, will be imposed on a trustee or other fiduciary who tries to make a secret profit from his fiduciary position; it is imposed whether or not he realises this.

ohne Rücksicht auf; unrechtmäßige Bereicherung; unzumutbar/sittenwidrig; Treuhänder; auferlegen/verhängen/aufbürden

| Example – Keech v Sandford (1726) |
|---|
| A trustee held a lease of Romford Market on trust for an infant beneficiary. The trustee attempted to renew the lease for the benefit of the infant but the lessor refused to grant a renewal to the infant. The lessor agreed, however, to renew the lease in favour of the trustee personally. The lease was accordingly made out to the trustee. **Held:** that the trustee held the new lease on ***constructive trust*** for the infant. |

Pacht
Begünstigter im Kindesalter
Verpächter
demzufolge/folglich/demgemäß

Another more modern case which illustrates the *constructive trust* is:

| Example – Agip (Africa) Ltd v Jackson (1991) |
|---|
| The claimant requested the defendant not to arrange for the transfer of money in its possession to a third party, as it had been obtained by fraud by one of the claimant's employees. The defendant ignored the request. **Held:** that the defendants were liable as ***constructive trustees***. |

ersuchen/verlangen
Betrug
Anliegen/Bitte

***cc) Statutory trusts***

Statutory trusts are imposed in certain specific circumstances, such as on bankruptcy, intestacy (see chapter 11, section III. 3, p. 177 f.) and on the conveyance of land to a minor. A specific form of statutory trusts also applies where land is vested in the name of more than one person.

Grundstücksübertragung/-umschreibung

## 2. Charitable trusts – public trusts

karitativ/gemeinnützig

*Charitable trusts* are public (purpose) trusts which are usually designed to promote a **purpose** that is **beneficial to society**. *Charitable* status brings with it a variety of fiscal and legal privileges. Note that a *charitable* organisation can exist not only as a trust, but also as a company or an unincorporated association.

ein Ziel/Zweck verfolgen – dienlich/förderlich/nützlich
(nicht eingetragener) Verein

### a) Definition of charity

Wohlfahrtsorganisation

For an institution to have *charitable* status it has to pass successfully the following **three basic tests**:

absolvieren/bestehen

(1) The activity must be **recognised by law as charitable**.
(2) It must be for a recognised **public benefit**.
(3) It must be **wholly and exclusively charitable**.

gänzlich – ausschließlich

The *charitable purposes* recognised by law are set out in *s.2(2) (a)–(m) of the Charities Act 2006*.

gemeinnütziger Zweck

## b) Charity in law – the 13 heads of charity

Oberbegriff/Überschrift

There are 13 charitable purposes known as **heads of charity** – set out in the *Charities Act 2006* – comprising 12 specific charitable purposes derived from existing case law, followed by a final general residual category. This last item enables the interpretation of charitable purposes to evolve according to the needs of contemporary society.

abgeleitet
Rest – ermöglichen
entwickeln

The **heads** under *s.2(2) Charities Act 2006* are as follows:

(a) prevention or relief of poverty
(b) advancement of education
(c) advancement of religion
(d) advancement of health or saving of lives
(e) advancement of citizenship or community development
(f) advancement of arts, culture, heritage or science
(g) advancement of amateur sport
(h) advancement of human rights, conflict resolution or reconciliation or promotion of religious or racial harmony or equality and diversity
(i) advancement of environmental protection or improvement
(j) relief of those in need, by reason of youth, age, ill health, disability, financial hardship or other disadvantage
(k) advancement of animal welfare
(l) promotion of efficiency of the armed forces of the Crown or efficiency of the police, fire and rescue services or ambulance services
(m) other purposes currently recognised as charitable and any new charitable purposes which are similar to another charitable purpose.

Verhinderung – Linderung
Förderung
Krankheit
Behinderung
Tierschutz

Note that trusts for *political* purposes are not charitable and will therefore fail. The reason is that - given the tax advantages which charities have - it is not for the courts to decide which political purposes are for the public benefit and which not.

### c) Benefit for the public

If the main intention of a trust is to benefit certain specified persons, no *charitable trust* arises. For example, a trust for the education of the lawful descendants of three named persons is not charitable.

ganz bestimmte(r)

gesetzlicher Erbe/ Abkömmling

| *Example – Re Compton (1945)* |
| --- |
| By her will, a testatrix left money on trust for the education of the children of C, P and M, who were under twenty-six years of age. There were twenty-eight descendants of these persons eligible. ***Held:*** that a class of persons determined by reference to a personal relationship was not a sufficient *section of the public* so as to the requirement that to be charitable a trust must be for the **public benefit**. The trust was therefore not charitable. |

Erblasserin

wählbar/geeignet

unter Bezug auf

*hier:* Ausschnitt/Teil

The trust must be of benefit to the *public at large* or a *sufficient section* thereof. Employees of a company do not form a section of the public for this purpose. Thus, a trust to educate children of the employees of a company has been held not to be charitable.

in diesem Sinne

| *Example – Oppenheim v Tobacco Securities Trust Co Ltd (1951)* |
| --- |
| The Tobacco Securities Trust Co Ltd held certain investments on trust to apply the income 'in providing for the ... education of children of employees or former employees' of British American Tobacco Co Ltd.<br>***Held:*** that a class of persons who are determined by applying a test of relationship with a given person or body, is not a *section of the public* for the purpose of satisfying the requirement that for a gift to be charitable, it must be for the **public benefit**. The trust was thus not charitable. |

Kapitalanlage

verwenden – Einkünfte

beschenkt

The main areas where charity operates continue to be **poverty**, **education** and **religion**. With the *Charities Act 2006,* the presumption of public benefit was abolished. Public benefit must be *proved* in all cases and it is *no longer assumed* that education and religion are, by themselves beneficial to the public. In addition, trusts for the relief of poverty will in future have to prove public benefit, although this test is not likely to be very demanding (the reason for it being that the relief of poverty is *per se* considered altruistic, thus charitable).

annehmen/vermuten/unterstellen

außerdem

anspruchsvoll/schwierig/streng

an sich/schlechthin

### d) Wholly and exclusively charitable

A charity cannot have some purposes that are charitable and some that are not *(s.1(1)(a) of the Charities Act 2006)*. The requirement that a charitable trust must be **wholly and exclusively charitable** is not satisfied if, under the terms of the trust, the property can be applied to non-charitable as well as to charitable purposes.

mildtätig/gütig
nichtig

verdienstvoll

Therefore, trusts for "charitable *or* benevolent purposes", for example, have been held void *(Chichester Diocesan Fund and Board of Finance Inc v Simpson (1944))*. The word "*or*" imports an alternative, so phrases such as "charitable *or* benevolent" and "charitable *or* deserving" have been held to lack the necessary exclusivity.

### e) The Cy-près Doctrine

The term **cy-près** means *as near as possible*. The doctrine determines what happens when trust property devoted to charitable purposes cannot be applied in the manner intended by the donor. A trust can fail for many reasons. In private trusts, this will give rise to a resulting trust in favour of the settlor or his estate.

With charitable trusts, this is not the same. The doctrine allows the court to apply the funds to similiar bodies or charitable purposes which, of course, differ to the original charitable purposes.

## 3. Non-charitable purpose trusts

The general rule is that *non-charitable purpose trusts* – also known as *private purpose trusts* – are **void**.

| *Example – Re Astor's Settlement Trusts (1952)* |
|---|
| A trust was established for various purposes including the maintenance of good relations between nations and the preservation of the independence of newspapers.<br>***Held:*** The trust was void. It was for **non-charitable purposes** (it was not even argued that they were charitable) and there was *no one* who could *enforce* the trust. |

Erhaltung/Aufrechterhaltung

For a private trust to be valid it must have generally a **human beneficiary** by whom the trust can be enforced *(Morice v Bishop of Durham (1804))*. This is known as the **beneficiary principle**.

*Private* trusts can be enforced by their beneficiaries, *charitable* trusts by the Attorney General, but non-charitable purpose trusts (private purpose trusts) have no one to enforce them. There are very limited exceptions to the rule that private purpose trusts are not permitted. The courts have held that trusts established to look after a testator's pets, or specific monuments for a specific period of time, may be upheld in appropriate circumstances.

## 4. Rules against perpetuities

*etwa*: Verbot von Zuwendungen auf ewige Zeit

According to English law, *private trusts* should have a lifespan, and it has indeed long prevented people from tying up their assets indefinitely, i.e. in perpetuity.

Laufzeit
binden
für alle Zeiten/ewig

**Two rules** have been developed to deal with this, both of which apply to *private trusts*.

### a) The rule against remoteness of future vesting

Ferne – Eigentumsübertragung

This rule deals with the maximum length of time. It provides that property must vest in the recipient within a certain period. The *common law perpetuity period* is "lives in being plus 21 years", i.e. the period expiring 21 years after the death of the last survivor of certain individuals who were alive when the trust was created.

Empfänger – Frist
Dauer
auslaufen/enden

Under English law, the **purpose of this rule** is to avoid the legal title and the equitable interest being separated for an unlimited period of time. This rule was laid down by the House of Lords in *Cadell* v *Palmer (1833)* and is now governed by the *Perpetuities and Accumulation Act 1964* and its amendments.

vermeiden

- Trusts that are subject to the *Perpetuities and Accumulation Act 2009* have a statutory fixed perpetuity period of 125 years.
- Trusts that are subject to the *Perpetuities and Accumulation Act 1964* have a fixed perpetuity period of 80 years.
- All trusts created before 16.07.1964 have the *common law perpetuity period* (see above).

The effect of this is that where property is held on trust, the beneficiaries must become absolutely entitled to the property within an acceptable perpetuity period.

vollberechtigt

in der Regel/grundsätzlich

*Charitable trusts* are generally subject to this rule. Whereas a gift to charity must vest within the perpetuity period, a gift from one charity to another can occur outside *(Christ's Hospital v Grainger (1849))*.

Unveräußerlichkeit

## b) The rule against inalienability

nichtig machen – Verfügung – binden

unendlich

This rule renders void any disposition that attempts to tie up property for a period longer than a "life in being plus 21 years". It prevents *non-charitable* trusts for purposes, rather than for individuals, from lasting indefinitely.

This rule does not apply to *charitable* trusts, which can therefore continue indefinitely. Accordingly, capital can be dedicated indefinitely to, for example, the relief of poverty or the advancement of religion.

**Diagram 51**

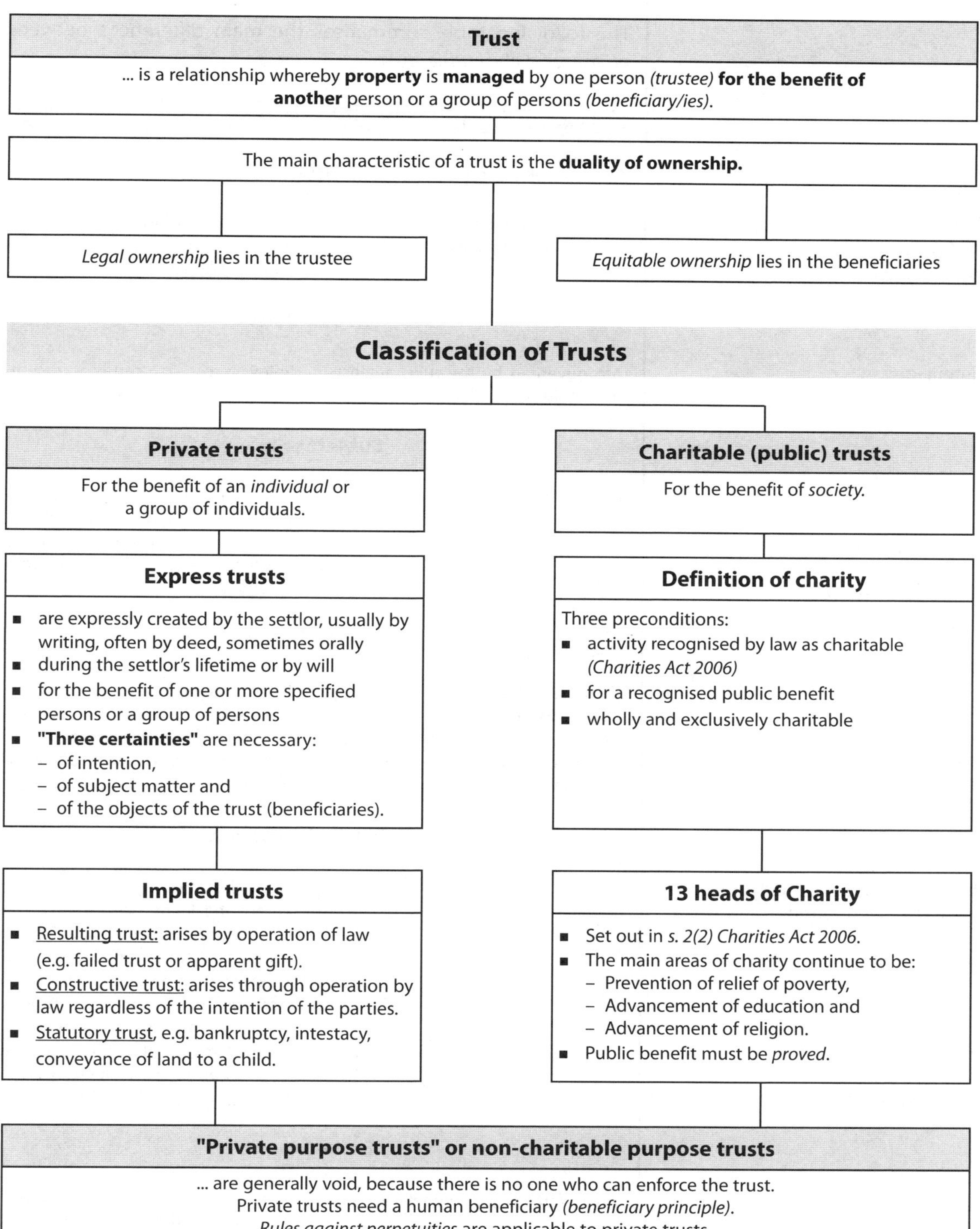
Trust
... is a relationship whereby **property** is **managed** by one person *(trustee)* **for the benefit of another** person or a group of persons *(beneficiary/ies)*.
The main characteristic of a trust is the **duality of ownership.**
*Legal ownership* lies in the trustee
*Equitable ownership* lies in the beneficiaries
Classification of Trusts
Private trusts
For the benefit of an *individual* or a group of individuals.
Charitable (public) trusts
For the benefit of *society.*
Express trusts
▪ are expressly created by the settlor, usually by writing, often by deed, sometimes orally
▪ during the settlor's lifetime or by will
▪ for the benefit of one or more specified persons or a group of persons
▪ **"Three certainties"** are necessary:
– of intention,
– of subject matter and
– of the objects of the trust (beneficiaries).
Definition of charity
Three preconditions:
▪ activity recognised by law as charitable *(Charities Act 2006)*
▪ for a recognised public benefit
▪ wholly and exclusively charitable
Implied trusts
▪ Resulting trust: arises by operation of law (e.g. failed trust or apparent gift).
▪ Constructive trust: arises through operation by law regardless of the intention of the parties.
▪ Statutory trust, e.g. bankruptcy, intestacy, conveyance of land to a child.
13 heads of Charity
▪ Set out in *s. 2(2) Charities Act 2006.*
▪ The main areas of charity continue to be:
– Prevention of relief of poverty,
– Advancement of education and
– Advancement of religion.
▪ Public benefit must be *proved.*
"Private purpose trusts" or non-charitable purpose trusts
... are generally void, because there is no one who can enforce the trust.
Private trusts need a human beneficiary *(beneficiary principle).*
*Rules against perpetuities* are applicable to private trusts.

## 5. Differences between private and charitable trusts

The following table summarises the main differences between *private* and *charitable* trusts.

| Vocabulary | Private trusts | Charitable trusts |
|---|---|---|
| | **Purpose** | |
| *hier:* fördern<br>als Ganzes<br>beträchtlich | Created for the benefit of specified persons or groups of persons. | Created to further a purpose that will benefit society as a whole or an appreciable part of ist. |
| | **Regulation** | |
| unterliegen<br>Ausnahme | Are governed by the rules against perpetuities. | Enjoy, to a certain extent, exemptions from these rules. |
| | **Subject to tax** | |
| befreit<br>Grundsteuer<br>Einkommensteuer | Affected by taxes. | Are wholly or partly exempt from many taxes and enjoy reduced rates. Its income, used for charitable purposes, is largely exempt from income tax. |
| | **Preconditions** | |
| nur/bloß<br>Plan | "Requires the three" certainties, otherwise the trust will fail, e.g. if the persons who are to be beneficiaries are not defined with sufficient certainty. | If the objects are undoubtedly charitable, the trust will not fail merely because those purposes are vague; the court can order a scheme for the application of the property. |
| | **Special features** | |
| *frz.:* "cy près que possible" (so nah wie möglich) – wortgetreu<br>unzweckmäßig<br>undurchführbar<br>mittels<br>Stiftungsaufsicht | | Underlies the cy-près doctrine: where the literal execution of the trust is or becomes inexpedient or impractical, the court will adapt the property to some charity purpose *as near as possible* to the original purpose named by the donor. This is done by means of a scheme for the application of the property by the Charity Commission or the court. |
| | **Enforcement** | |
| | Are enforced by the beneficiaries. | Are enforced by the Attorney General on behalf of the Cown. |

## V. Trusteeship

Treuhänderschaft

Most of the law concerning trusts and trusteeships originally evolved from the decisions of the Court of Chancery but much of it is now contained in the *Trustee Act 1925* and in the *Trustee Act 2000*.

sich entwickeln aus

The **trustee** is the central figure in the administration of the trust. In order to protect the trust property, to give effect to the settlor's instructions and to promote the interests of the beneficiaries, he has a series of important obligations to meet.

### 1. Appointment, removal and retirement of trustees

Ernennung – Entlassung – Pensionierung/Ruhestand

Generally any person who has the capacity to hold property – e.g. not a minor – can be a trustee. Trustees are usually **appointed** by the settlor or testator in the instrument or will that is creating the trust It is one of the maxims of equity that a trust will not fail for want of a trustee. Thus, if a testator creates a trust by will but does not name trustees, or if those who are named refuse to act (disclaimer), the testator's personal representatives (who will be explained in more detail in chapter 11, section II) must act as trustees until others are appointed.

mangels

Verzicht/Ablehnung – Erbschaftsverwalter

There is no general rule as to the number of trustees who may be appointed, although it is unusual to appoint only one person as a sole trustee except in the case of a trust corporation. Where the trust is of land, there may not be more than four trustees, except where the land is held for charitable, ecclesiastical or public purposes. A trust corporation is a corporate body empowered to act as a trustee. As a corporation is not a human trustee, there is no problem with the trustee dying or retiring. Common examples of trust corporations are the trustee departments of banks or insurance companies.

alleinig – Treuhandgesellschaft

juristische Person/Körperschaft

Versicherungsgesellschaft

A trustee can be **removed** by virtue of a special power in the trust instrument, under the provisions of *s.36 of the Trustee Act 1925* (which determine that a trustee may be replaced by a new trustee under certain circumstances, e.g., if he remains abroad for over a year) or, in extreme cases, by the court.

ausdrückliche Ermächtigung

bestimmen

Moreover, the termination of trusteeship is possible by **retirement** which is governed primarily by *s.39 Trustee Act 1925*.

Aufgabe/Pflicht – Ermächtigung/ Befugnis
Ermessen/Spielraum

## 2. Duties and powers of a trustee

A *duty* must be exercised, although the trustee has discretion as to precisely how it is exercised, e.g. a trustee has a duty to invest, but a discretion in what to invest in.

A *power,* by contrast, is discretionary but if it is a discretionary trust (see above in this chapter, section IV.1.a) at the end), the trustee may be obliged to exercise discretion.

### a) Duties

äußerste Sorgfalt

A trustee has to carry out his duties with utmost diligence. If not, the trustee may be *personally liable for breach of trust* (see below). Some duties arise automatically from the relationship between trustee and beneficiary, while others are imposed and regulated by statute. Central to the trustee's functions is the *fiduciary duty* which is imposed by equity.

#### *aa) Duties on appointment*

Bedingung
genau erfüllen
Verlust
zufällig
Fehleinschätzung
unterstützen/begünstigen/ schützen/sichern
Darlehen zurückfordern

There are four duties on appointment:

(1) **Understanding the terms of the trust**, confirming his appointment and ensuring that the property has been vested in him. If a trustee is careless or fails to comply strictly with the terms of the trust, he may be personally liable for losses. Trustees will not, however, be liable for mere accidental losses or errors of judgment.
(2) **Safeguarding the trust property** (e.g. its proper investment, its accurate inventory or its safe custody).
(3) **Calling in loans** (if necessary, the repayment must be enforced by a legal action).
(4) **Investigating pre-existing breaches of trust.**

#### *bb) Administrative duties*

The following three administrative duties are central for a trustee:

(1) **to keep accounts and provide informations** (e.g. when a beneficiary reaches 18 years of age, he should be informed of his interest under the trust),
(2) **to take reasonable care** (trustee's duty of care),
(3) **to invest** the trust funds.

Regarding the trustee's **duty of care (2)**, he must take the same care of trust property as an ordinary business person would take of his (or her) own property. Moreover, a professional trustee is expected to show a higher degree of care than a lay trustee. A professional trustee must exercise the special skills that he professes to have. And a trust company with specialist staff will be judged differently to an unpaid family trustee.

Sorgfalt
„ordentlicher Kaufmann"
Laien ...
Fähigkeit/Können – erklärtermaßen haben (muss)

*Example – Bartlett v Barclays Bank Trust Co Ltd (1980)*

The beneficiaries claimed against the trustee alleging **breach of trust**. As trustee, the defendant had a controlling interest in a private company, but he was not represented on the board or at its meetings and he had relied on information dispensed at annual general meetings. The board had engaged in two hazardous property speculations and, although one had been successful, there had resulted an overall loss to the trust fund.
***Held:*** that the trustee was liable for the loss, as he had failed to discharge **the higher duty of care** owed by a professional corporate trustee or even to act as a reasonably prudent businessman would have acted in his own affairs.

behaupten
Vorstand
verbreiten
sich beteiligen/unternehmen
gefährlich/riskant
Gesamtverlust
erfüllen – schulden

As trustees' duties were mainly governed by 19th century case law, the *Trustee Act 2000* redefined the **standard of care** of a trustee. According to *s.1* a trustee shall exercise such care as is reasonable having regard in particular (1) to *any special knowledge* or experience which he has or holds himself out as having (2) if he acts in the course of a business or profession, to *any special knowledge* or experience which is reasonable to expect of a person acting in that business or profession.

**Investing (3)** is another major element in the administration of a trust. Investments should be aimed to protect the fund from inflation and to generate income for any one with a life interest. Therefore the trustee has to act impartially.

erwirtschaften
unvoreingenommen

Although it is common practice to insert an express investment clause into the trust instrument, *Part II of the Trustee Act 2000* widened and regulated the duty and ability to invest.

*S.3 of the Trustee Act 2000* gives trustees a general power to make "any kind of investment that they could make if they were absolutely entitled to the assets of the trust". The intention was to allow all trustees to take advantage of the wide range of investments available in the modern economy. It also sought to avoid the complexity of the *Trustee Investments Act 1961*.

Generalvollmacht

| | |
|---|---|
| geeignet/richtig/sachgemäß | *S.5 of the Trustee Act 2000* requires the trustees to obtain and consider proper investment advice from a suitable source. |

auf Vertrauen beruhend

### *cc) Fiduciary duties*

As the duty of a trustee is to act in the best financial interest of the beneficiaries, the fundamental fiduciary duties could be summarised under the heading **no personal financial considerations.** They have to put aside their personal interest and views e.g. when considering whether to invest in a certain fund.

These fiduciary duties comprise the following principles:

- **no business competition**
- **no profit**
- **no purchase of trust property**
- **no payment**

Entschädigung/Entlohnung – berechnen/in Rechnung stellen – entschädigen – Auslagen – Ausgaben – anfallen

A trustee is only entitled to remuneration for his activities if this is authorised in the trust instrument or approved by all beneficiaries or by the court. Otherwise a trustee cannot charge for his time and trouble, but he may be reimbursed for his out-of-pocket expenses, i.e. the trustee is only entitled to be reimbursed out of the trust fund for any expenses properly incurred in the performance of his duties (e.g. insurance premiums, fees paid to brokers or money spent on repairs).

Ermessen(sfreiheit)

## b) Powers (or discretions)

Vielfalt – gewähren/einräumen

A variety of fiduciary powers is partially conferred on trustees, some by statute (e.g. under *Part II of the Trustee Act 1925, ss.12–19*) and other powers may be stated expressly in the trust instrument. Some of the main powers will be considered below.

(Lebens-)Unterhalt

### *aa) Maintenance*

The *trust income* should be used to provide for the maintenance or benefit of a *minor* beneficiary as long as he is not entitled to the income from the trust fund. It is common practice for the trust instrument to give the trustees such a power expressly. The statutory power of maintenance is set out in *s.31 for the Trustee Act 1925*.

### *bb) Advancement*

Förderung/*hier:* Vorschuss

The trustees have the power to pay some or all of the money to a – minor or adult – beneficiary before his entitlement under the trust (advancement). The source of the funds given is different from maintenance and the age of the beneficiary does not play any role here, as the focus is not on the day-to-day expenses, but on a particular, permanent and substantial long-term provision. This power will arise either from the trust instrument or under *s.32 of the Trustee Act 1925*.

day-to-day: alltäglich/laufend

### *cc) Delegation*

Übertragung einer Vollmacht

As a trustee is likely to have been selected for his personal qualities, experience and knowledge, the duty of personal service implies that a trustee cannot delegate his trust powers and duties. Under *s.23 of the Trustee Act 1925*, however, there is a list of exceptions to this rule. These exceptions include, for example, the right to employ a solicitor, a banker or a stockbroker to effect transactions in connection with the trust property. The costs of these agents are paid out of the trust estate (see above).

personal service: *hier*: höchstpersönliche Aufgabenerfüllung

stockbroker – effect: Aktienmakler – ausführen

estate: *hier*: Vermögen

**Diagram 52**

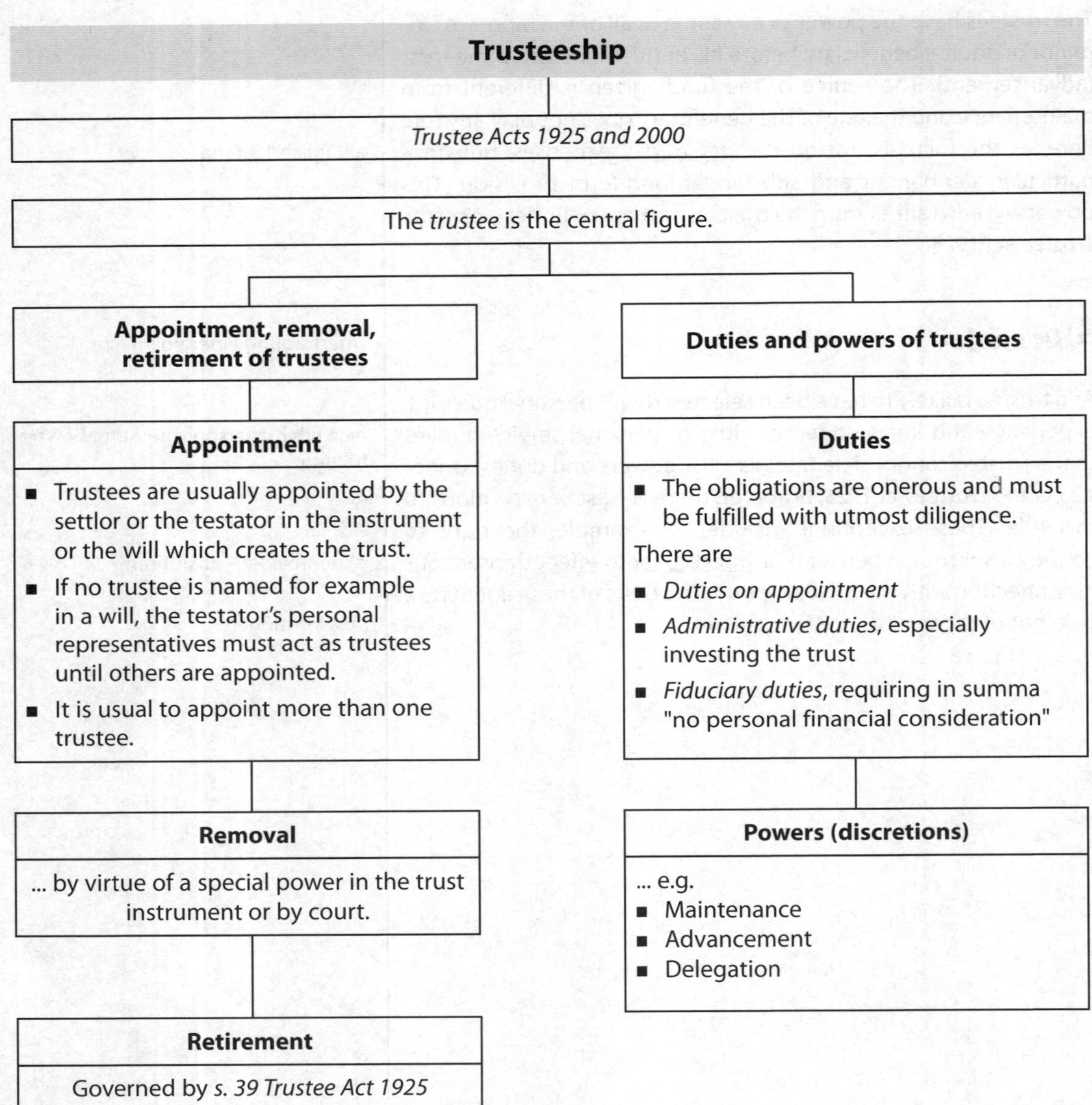
Trusteeship
Trustee Acts 1925 and 2000
The trustee is the central figure.
Appointment, removal, retirement of trustees
Duties and powers of trustees
Appointment
Trustees are usually appointed by the settlor or the testator in the instrument or the will which creates the trust.
If no trustee is named for example in a will, the testator's personal representatives must act as trustees until others are appointed.
It is usual to appoint more than one trustee.
Duties
The obligations are onerous and must be fulfilled with utmost diligence.
There are
Duties on appointment
Administrative duties, especially investing the trust
Fiduciary duties, requiring in summa "no personal financial consideration"
Removal
... by virtue of a special power in the trust instrument or by court.
Powers (discretions)
... e.g.
Maintenance
Advancement
Delegation
Retirement
Governed by s. 39 Trustee Act 1925

## VI. Breach of trust and remedies

Treuebruch – Rechtsmittel/-behelf

### 1. Liability for breach of trust

A trustee is *in breach of trust* if he **fails to observe the duties** laid on him by equity and by the trust instrument. A breach may be *fraudulent* (e.g. wrongly taking trust property) or *negligent* (e.g. failing to review investments at proper intervals). Unless there is a variety of possible breaches, most fall within one of the following three broad categories:

arglistig – fahrlässig

weit/umfassend

- gaining an unauthorised profit,
- failing to act with care and skill in the administration of the trust,
- misapplication of trust property.

Missbrauch

If the trustee commits such a breach of the trust, he is exposed to personal **liability** in an action by the beneficiary.

### 2. Protection of trustees from liability

The trust instrument will commonly restrict the personal liability of a trustee. An exclusion of liability arising from fraud or intentional wrongdoing, however, is not possible. The wide use of **exclusion clauses** has resulted in a public discussion on the need for professional trustees to provide better **insurance** against potential liability, rather than hiding behind broadly drafted exclusion clauses.

*S.61 of the Trustee Act 1925* gives the **court the discretion to relieve**, in whole or in part, a trustee from liability. The burden of proof lies on the trustee to establish that he acted reasonably and honestly and as prudently as he would have done in organising his own affairs. According to *s.1 of the Trustee Act 2000,* an unpaid trustee is more likely to be released from liability than his professional counterpart.

befreien

### 3. Remedies of the beneficiaries

The principal *right* of beneficiaries is their right to enjoy the interest in the trust property. In the case of a private trust, they have a right to compel the trustees, by action if necessary, to administer the property according to the terms of the trust.

zwingen/erzwingen

The beneficiaries have a number of *remedies* against the trustee and sometimes third parties for *the breach of trust*. When considering remedies, an **action *in personam*** brought against a trustee personally for damages for breach of trust (e.g. a monetary compensation) has to be distinguished from an **action *in rem*** brought to recover the trust property (e.g. restitution of the money).

Entschädigung

Besides the possibility of criminal prosecution of a trustee, for example in case of fraud, there are various types of remedies, e.g.:

- **compensation** for breach of trust (action *in personam*),
- **restitution** of unauthorised profits
- personal **liability** as a constructive trustee to make restitution of trust property
- an **injunction** to restrain a breach of trust

gerichtliche Verfügung

Although **tracing** is usually included in the context of remedies, it is not a remedy as such, but rather a right to trace (i.e. to follow) trust property into the hands of another person. This person then becomes a constructive trustee of it. Tracing allows an action *in rem* that can be advantageous over an action *in personam*, if e.g. the trustee becomes insolvent and the person who has the property is an innocent volunteer.

nachforschen/auf der Spur bleiben

**Tracing** is best understood by way of an example:[34]
Suppose that T, a trustee, holds a valuable painting in trust for the beneficiary B. If T, in breach of trust, sells the painting to X, the question arises as to whether B can sue X for the return of the painting. B has a right of action against T. If X had no notice, actual or constructive, that the painting purchased was held on trust, the painting may be kept by him. X, in this case, falls within the category of a person who *bona fide* (i.e. in good faith) purchased trust property without notice that it was such and is therefore protected. B's only remedy is against T, the trustee for the sale price. If, instead of *selling* the painting to X, T had *given* it, the beneficiary may lawfully claim the painting from X, for the latter is not a *bona fide* purchaser. Therefore the beneficiary can follow (= trace) the trust property.[35]

wertvolles Gemälde

(gesetzlich) unterstellt/konstruiert

gutgläubig/in gutem Glauben

schenken

Let it suffice at the end of this chapter to conclude with the four conditions that allow to assess which conditions must be satisfied before **tracing** is possible:

beurteilen

34 According to *Barker & Padfield*, p. 234; cf. also the diagram in vol. 1, chapter 2, p. 34.

35 As a German law student who knows the *BGB* fairly well, you hopefully have thought of *§§ 932 ff.* and *§ 816*? According to German legal history 'tracing' means: „Wo Du Deinen Glauben gelassen hast, dort musst Du ihn suchen".

(1) There must be a fiduciary relationship;
(2) there must be an equitable proprietary interest;
(3) tracing should not be inequitable;
(4) property must be in a traceable form.

Once it is established that tracing is possible, there are a number of rules as to how tracing can be effected. For more details on tracing please consult our section **Further reading**.

In this chapter we have sought to provide an overview of the legal device in English law known as the *trust*. Trusts come in a variety of forms and different types, but always with one underlying characteristic in common: the **duality of legal ownership** (held by the trustee) on one hand and **the beneficial or equitable ownership** (held by the beneficiary/ies), on the other. The trustee is subject to a package of duties and obligations, as he holds the trust property *on behalf of* the beneficiary(/ies).

The purposes of trusts are expressed in various different German legal instruments such as „Stellvertretung; Testamentsvollstreckung; Stiftungsrecht; Nacherbschaft; Verwahrungs/Hinterlegung; Recht des gemeinnützigen Vereins usw." As we have sought to demonstrate in this chapter, the English concept of trust is complex and has no single counterpart in German law.

Entsprechung/Pendant

**Diagram 53**

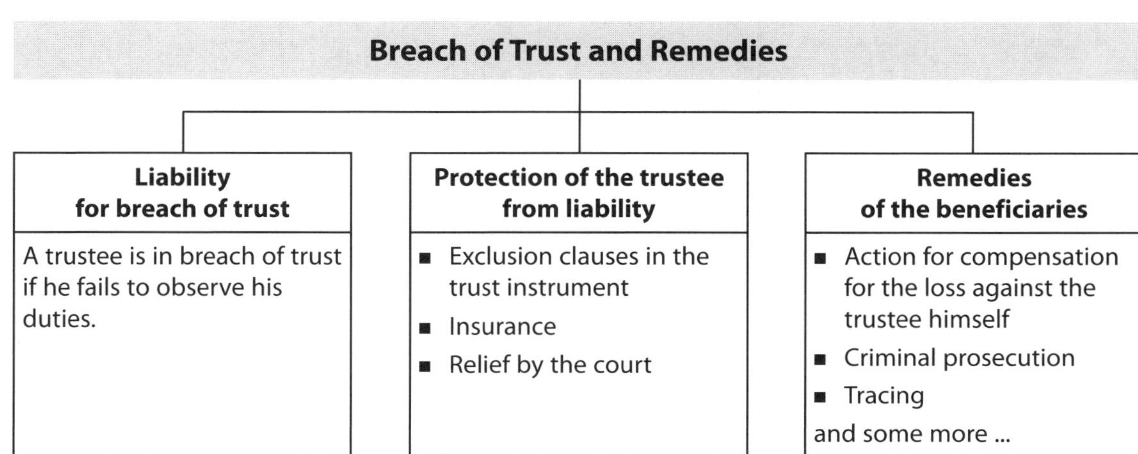

## VII. Further reading & references[36]

*Barker & Padfield*, Law Made Simple; *Chang*, Equity and Trusts; *Cracknell*, Equity and Trusts; *Edwards & Stockwell*, Equity & Trusts; *Geldart*, Introduction to English Law; *Haley*, Equity & Trusts; *Hayton, Matthews & Mitchell,* Underhill & Hayton: Law of Trusts and Trustees; *Hudson*, Equity & Trusts; *Lyall*, An Introduction to British Law; *Oakley*, Parker and Mellows: The Modern Law of Trusts; *Pearce, Stevens & Barr*, The Law of Trusts and Equitable Obligations; *Pettit*, Equity & the Law of Trusts; *Riddall*, The Law of Trusts; *Shears & Stephenson,* James' Introduction to English Law; *Templeman & Cutler*, Equity and Trusts – Casebook; *Templeman & Halliwell*, Equity and Trusts; *Templeman & Doherty*, Equity and Trusts – Revision Work Book; *Wilman*, Brown: GCSE Law.

36 Edition, publisher, place and year of publication are quoted in the bibliography.

# Chapter Ten

# Family Law

## I. Introduction

Family law is predominantly **statute law** supplemented by case law. Statutes have tried to keep pace with the progressive developments and changing social attitudes of the last century. Examples of the important legislative developments in family law are in particular the *Children Act 1989*, the *Child Support Act 1991* as amended by the *Child Maintenance and Other Payments Act 2008*, the *Adoption and Children Act 2002*, the *Civil Partnership Act 2004*, the *Gender Recognition Act 2004* and the *Human Fertilisation and Embryology Act 2008*. However, the statutory provisions relating to divorce and financial settlement have changed little in the last 40 years and case law has largely been responsible for the development of the current matrimonial property regime.

überwiegend/in erster Linie – ergänzen – Schritt halten mit

eheliches Güterrecht

There are three tiers of courts to hear family cases at first instance:[37]

- magistrates' courts (provided that they are constituted as magistrates' family proceedings courts)
- county courts
- the family division of the High Court.

*hier:* Eingangsgericht – verhandeln (to hear a case)

Abt. f. Familiensachen b. Amtsgericht

Amtsgericht (Zivilsachen)

Abt. f. Familiensachen a. Hohen Gericht (1. Instanz für schwierigere Zivilfälle)

Some proceedings can be heard in any of these courts, but others must be heard in a particular court. For instance, divorce proceedings cannot be heard in a magistrates' family proceeding court, they must be heard in a divorce county court; child abduction and other cases with an international dimension must be heard in the High Court. Proceedings under the *Children Act 1989* and cases of domestic violence under the *Family Law Act 1996* can generally be heard in any of the courts named above.

Verfahren

Entführung

Similarly to German family law, English family law can broadly be divided up into four main areas: (1) **marriage law** (marriage, civil partnership, and cohabitation), (2) **family property**, (3) **law on divorce** and (4) **children and parents**.

allgemein

Eherecht – Ehe/Eheschließung

eingetragene Lebenspartnerschaft – nichteheliche Lebensgemeinschaft/eheähnliche Gemeinschaft – Scheidungsrecht

In this chapter, we will take a closer look at the areas mentioned under 1), 3) and 4). We have decided not to include a separate section on family property, as the ownership of spouses or civil

37 The second instance constitutes the Court of Appeal, and the third instance the Supreme Court. The various courts are described in vol. 1, chapter 2 II, p. 38 ff.

partners during a marriage or civil partnership mainly falls under **property law** (see chapter 8) and contract law (see vol. 1, chapter 6). Questions arising from the death of a spouse or civil partner are dealt with the **law of succession** (see chapter 11).

However, we should mention briefly **Matrimonial Home Rights**, which are laid down in *s.30 of the Family Law Act 1996*. They prevent e.g. a spouse being excluded from his or her home even if the other is the sole owner of the matrimonial property.

## II. Marriage law

Marriage has traditionally been defined in English law as "the voluntary union for life of one man to one woman to the exclusion of all others" *(Hyde* v *Hyde (1866))*. This definition, however, is nowadays inaccurate if you consider the high number of divorces: marriage is indeed still a voluntary union, but cannot necessarily be regarded as lifelong.

ungenau

Beside the age-old institution of marriage there is the newly introduced status of civil partnership, which is more or less equivalent to marriage. There are other forms of partnership that may or may not lead to marriage, such as engagement and cohabitation. We will briefly introduce you to the latter forms below.

uralt

Verlobung/Verlöbnis

### 1. Engagement

Since the *Law Reform (Miscellaneous Provisions) Act 1970*, an engagement is no longer a contract which needs consideration to be valid. There is now no right of action for *breach of promise*. Before the *Law Reform Act* abolished this right, a party (usually the woman) could sue for damages for breach of contract if the other party refused to marry. Generally, engaged couples do not have the same rights as married couples.

Gegenleistung

Klagerecht – Bruch des Eheversprechens

Engagements are usually formalised by the man giving the woman an engagement ring. The ring remains the property of the woman should the engagement be broken unless, at the time it was given, the man made clear that, in the event of the marriage not taking place, the ring was to be returned or because of other implied condition to the contrary (e.g. the ring is a family heirloom).

Verlobungsring

es sei denn

im Fall, dass

Erbstück

## 2. Cohabitation

Today, an increasing number of couples – around two million compared to about ten million married couples in England and Wales – live together without marrying or entering into a civil partnership (see the definition in *s.62(1)(a) Family Law Act 1996*). In many cases, these *unmarried couples* wrongly assume that they are in the same position and have the same rights as married couples. In some areas, married and unmarried couples are indeed treated in the same way (e.g. *Rent Act 1977*; *Family Law Act 1996* which gives cohabitants the same rights as spouses to apply for a non-molestation order). In many other respects, however, particularly relating to financial obligations, these rights differ. For example, there is no obligation for one cohabitant financially to support the other, and when one of them dies without leaving a will, his/her cohabitant will not inherit anything automatically. Also, there are no tax advantages for an unmarried couple.

eingehen

Partner in nichtehelicher Lebensgemeinschaft – gerichtliche Verfügung gegen sexuelle Belästigung

Steuervorteil

What happens to property when an unmarried couple splits up? This is a complex question and academically the subject of much discussion. Details, however, would go beyond the scope of the book, but the **law of trusts** (see chapter 9) can help to identify possible solutions to these questions.

sich trennen

In order to remove the perceived unfairness that exists for cohabitees, there have been recent calls for reform, such as the proposed *Cohabitation Bill 2008* or a *Private Member's Bill* from the year 2009 based on the former. Neither bill proceeded further in Parliament; they are, however, interesting in that they show an increasing awareness of the need for reform in this area.

wahrnehmen/erkennen

Gesetzesentwurf/-vorlage

## 3. Marriage

Marriage is not (only) a contract which can be created and terminated at the will of the parties. It is an arrangement in which the state has an interest. For this reason, there are legal rules governing its creation and dissolution. The legal effect of marriage is to give the parties various rights, obligations and privileges. In an international context, marriage is considered to be a human right (see *Article 12 of the European Convention for the Protection of Human Rights*).

auf Wunsch von

Auflösung

Heiratsfähigkeit

### a) Capacity to marry

eine gültige Ehe eingehen
einhalten/befolgen/erfüllen
nichtig/ungültig
die folgenden Voraussetzungen festlegen

To contract a valid marriage, the parties must have the capacity to marry and must comply with certain legal formalities, otherwise the marriage may be void. *S.11 Matrimonial Causes Act 1973* provides the following requirements:

Mindestalter

#### *aa) Minimum age*

Einwilligung/Zustimmung
Elternpflicht/elterliche Verantwortung/Sorgerecht – Vormund

Both parties must be over the age of 16. If one of them is aged 16 or 17, consent must normally be given by both parents with parental responsibility or by the guardian. If consent is refused, the court can grant consent instead; this is, however, rarely the case.

verbotene Verwandtschaftsgrade

#### *bb) Prohibited degrees of relationship*

aufgelistet
novellieren/ändern – enge Verwandte
Enkelin
Enkel

The prohibited degrees are set out in the *Marriage Act 1949 as amended*. Of course, close relatives are not allowed to marry, e.g. a man cannot marry his mother, daughter or granddaughter and a woman cannot marry her father, son or grandson. Also other relatives are not allowed to marry; the complete list is set out in the *Marriage Act 1949.*

#### *cc) Not already married*

vorherig

Bigamie/Doppelehe

If the previous marriage has ended through death or divorce, each partner is free to marry. However, a person who marries for a second time during an existing marriage commits the crime of bigamy. A bigamous marriage is void.

verschiedenes Geschlecht

#### *dd) Partners of different sexes*

je(weils)

The parties to a marriage must be respectively male and female. In contrast to countries like the Netherlands, Canada, Belgium or Spain same-sex marriages are not permitted in England, but same-sex partners can enter into a **civil partnership** (see below, *Civil Partnership Act 2004*).

jmd. etw. möglich machen

Another issue worth mentioning in this context is the situation of **transsexuals**. The *Gender Recognition Act 2004* enables a person to obtain a Gender Recognition Certificate showing that his or her legal sex is the acquired gender.

### b) Preliminary formalities and ceremony

*etwa*: im Vorfeld der Eheschließung nötige Formalität

There are different formalities for a marriage, depending on the marriage being celebrated in the Church of England (*church wedding*) or without the Church (*civil marriage*), respectively.

Zivilehe – beziehungsweise

As it is in the public interest that people should know whether or not other people are married, **civil marriages** are generally solemnised in a register office. However, the *Marriage Act 1949* permits that they can also be celebrated in any venue approved for the purpose of civil marriage (e.g. a hotel or a castle) with the grant of a superintendent registrar's certificate or, exceptionally, of a Registrar-General's licence. Attendance in person at the respective register office, the paying of an administrative fee and the declaration that there are no impediments of marriage all form part of the preliminary formalities.

feierlich begehen
Standesamt
Örtlichkeit – freigegeben/zugelassen
höherer Standesamtbeamte
allgemeines Standesamt – persönliche Anwesenheit
Ehehindernisse

Once these formalities have been satisfied, the ceremony can take place. It is public and secular, but may be followed by a religious ceremony in church. The parties must declare that there are no lawful impediments and they must exchange vows in the presence of at least two witnesses.

weltlich/nicht kirchlich
Gelöbnis/Gelübde
(Trau-)Zeuge

**Church of England marriages** can be solemnised after the publication of banns or after the completion of one of the formalities for the civil marriage mentioned above. Most religious marriages usually take place, however, after the publication of banns. The ceremony is solemnised by a clergyman under the rites of the Church of England in the presence of at least two witnesses.

kirchliches Aufgebot
Geistlicher

## 4. Void and voidable marriages

anfechtbar

A **void** marriage means that no marriage has ever legally existed and that the parties retain their single status. A **voidable** marriage is regarded as legally valid until a court order annulling the marriage is obtained. The law of nullity is laid down in the *Matrimonial Causes Act 1973*.

behalten
Gerichtsbeschluss/-entscheidung
annullieren – Annulierungsrecht

### a) Void marriages

Marriages will be void *ab initio* if:

- one of the parties is under 16,
- the parties are within the prohibited degrees of relationship,
- at the time of marriage either party was already legally married,

*lat.*: von Anfang an
einer von beiden

die Eheschließung vornehmen – unter Missachtung – vorsätzliche Unterlassung – Trauschein

- the parties are not of different sexes,
- the parties have intermarried in disregard of certain required formalities (such as wilful omission to obtain a marriage certificate).

### b) Voidable marriages

According to *s.12 of the Matrimonial Causes Act 1973*, a marriage is voidable for the following reasons:

vollziehen/durchführen – wegen/aufgrund von

Weigerung

Antragsgegner/Beklagter

Nötigung – Irrtum

Unzurechnungsfähigkeit

Geistesstörung

Geschlechtskrankheit – ansteckend

schwanger

einstweilig/vorläufig

erteilen/herausgeben

Geschlecht

- it has not been consummated owing to the incapacity of either party to consummate it,
- it has not been consummated owing to the wilful refusal of the respondent to consummate it,
- either party did not validly consent to it, whether in consequence of duress, mistake (in respect of the identity of the other party), unsoundness of mind or otherwise,
- at the time of the marriage either party, though capable of giving a valid consent, was suffering (whether continuously or not) from a mental disorder within the meaning of the *Mental Health Act 1983*,
- at the time of the marriage one party was suffering from venereal disease in a communicable form,
- at the time of the marriage the man did not know that the woman was pregnant by another man,
- an interim Gender Recognition Certificate has, after the time of marriage, been issued to either party,
- the respondent is a person whose gender at the time of the marriage has become the acquired gender under the *Gender Recognition Act 2004*.

## 5. Civil Partnership

anmelden/eintragen lassen/beurkunden

insofern als/soweit

geradezu/fast/so gut wie

Civil partnerships were created by the *Civil Partnership Act 2004*. The right to register their partnership is only available to people of the same sex. The requirements of minimum age, not being already married and not being within the prohibited degrees of relationship are the same as in the case of marriage. Civil partnerships can be compared to marriages insofar as the civil partners acquire rights, obligations and privileges which are virtually the same as those possessed by married couples.[38]

38 In the UK 7, 169 same sex-couples were registered in 2008, compared to 6, 281 in 2009; cf. www.statistics.gov.uk and http:\\www.statistics.gov.uk/pdfdir/cpuk0810.pdf (23 May 2011).

## 6. Effects of marriage (and civil partnership)

Wirkung/Folge

The legal consequence is that reciprocal obligations fall upon both parties. Some of the rights and duties of spouses (and civil partners)[39] are laid down by statute, while others are provided by the common law.

wechselseitige Verpflichtungen – *hier*: gelten für
festlegen/bestimmen

### a) Financial obligations

Every spouse has a duty to maintain his or her partner during the marriage (and in some circumstances after marriage). If the other party fails to provide such maintenance, the spouse can obtain financial provision orders from the court. However, such applications during marriage are rare.

unterhalten
*hier*: Ehe
Unterhalt leisten
*etwa:* Bescheid zur finanziellen Regelung

Although the old rule by which a deserted wife was entitled to obtain credit against her husband's account as an "agent of necessity" was abolished in 1970, a wife who lives with her husband is entitled to pledge the husband's credit for buying necessary household goods. This authority is based on the presumed consent of the husband that she is his agent. This presumption may be rebutted by the husband informing the trader not to give credit to his wife, or by showing the court that the wife had a sufficient supply of the goods in question, or that she had a sufficient housekeeping allowance to pay for them herself.

verlassen – berechtigt
Konto – Geschäftsführer ohne Auftrag
mit (seinen = ihren) Schulden belasten
Berechtigung
vermutetes Einverständnis – Stellvertreter – widerlegen
Händler/Kaufmann
ausreichender Vorrat
*hier:* Haushaltsgeld

### b) Property rights

As each party to a marriage has a separate legal personality, each party may own property solely or jointly. The rules governing property ownership are the same as those which apply to everyone. The position changes, however, on divorce. The particular rights of one spouse on death of the other are dealt with in more detail in chapter 11.

Rechtspersönlichkeit

### c) Child custody

Sorgerecht für das Kind

Parents who are married have automatic parental responsibility in law for their children (*s.2(1) Children Act 1989*). Thus, both parents normally have custody of their children until they are 18, although

*etwa*: gesetzlich verankerte (umfassendere) elterliche Fürsorgepflicht

39 For reason of simplification we will not distinguish between civil partners and married couples from here on.

it can be lost earlier if e.g. the children marry. They can apply for residence and contact orders and other orders under the *Children Act 1989*.

Aufenthalt – Umgang

There are other persons who have parental responsibility without the need to apply for it, e.g. an unmarried mother, a mother and her civil partner who is a parent by virtue of *s.42 Human Fertilisation and Embryology Act 2008*, and in other cases.

kraft/gemäß

Then there are persons who can acquire parental responsibility according to *s.4 Children Act 1989*, e.g. an unmarried father, a step parent or a female non-biological parent in a same-sex female relationship.

Stiefelternteil

Spouses have a duty to provide maintenance for any child of the family. Both parents have, moreover, duties, depending on the age of the children e.g. to educate their children, which usually means sending them to school, to protect them from dangers in the home and from many other dangers which could harm their health physically or mentally.

## d) Further rights

Spouses and former spouses can seek remedies under the *Family Law Act 1996* and under the *Protection from Harassment Act 1997* to protect themselves and their children from violence in the home (domestic violence). There is a right for a spouse in criminal law to refuse to give evidence against the other. Inheritance between parties to a marriage are exempt from inheritance tax, to give but a few examples.

Rechtsschutz begehren

Zeugnis verweigern

Diagram 54

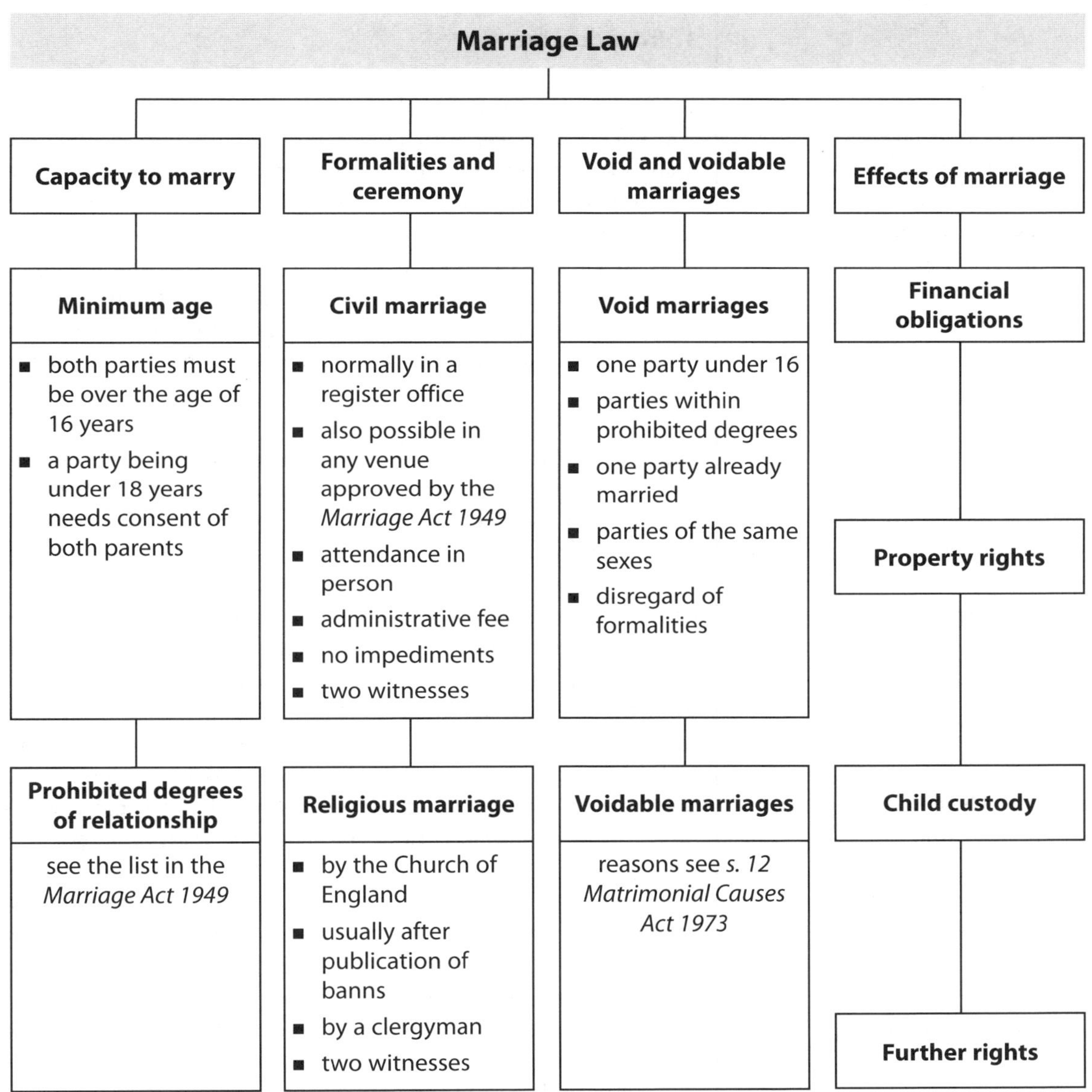
Marriage Law
Capacity to marry
Formalities and ceremony
Void and voidable marriages
Effects of marriage
Minimum age
both parties must be over the age of 16 years
a party being under 18 years needs consent of both parents
Civil marriage
normally in a register office
also possible in any venue approved by the Marriage Act 1949
attendance in person
administrative fee
no impediments
two witnesses
Void marriages
one party under 16
parties within prohibited degrees
one party already married
parties of the same sexes
disregard of formalities
Financial obligations
Property rights
Prohibited degrees of relationship
see the list in the Marriage Act 1949
Religious marriage
by the Church of England
usually after publication of banns
by a clergyman
two witnesses
Voidable marriages
reasons see s. 12 Matrimonial Causes Act 1973
Child custody
Further rights

Scheidungsrecht

## III. Law on divorce

### 1. Introduction

Nichtigkeit
Gerichtsentscheidung – vereinfacht ausgedrückt – Scheidungsantrag
voraussetzen/erfordern
beenden – Scheidungsurteil
vergleichsweise Beilegung/Vereinbarung

**Divorce** must be carefully distinguished from nullity of marriage. The effect of a decree of nullity, broadly speaking, is that the marriage is treated as if it had never existed. A petition for divorce – the parties in court are called *petitioner* and *respondent*, respectively –, however, postulates the existence of a valid marriage, which the court is asked to terminate. Thus, a divorce decree ends the legal status of a marriage which previously existed between the parties. Thereafter the responsibilities towards the former spouse are usually regulated under the terms of a financial settlement.

Lehre/Doktrin – Ehevergehen
Ehebruch – böswilliges Verlassen *(Eherecht)*
Verschuldensprinzip
endgültig scheitern/zerrüttet sein
Zerrüttungsprinzip

Divorce of this kind was first introduced into English law by the *Matrimonial Causes Act 1857* and, from then until 1969, it was based upon the doctrine that some matrimonial offence (such as adultery or desertion) must have been committed by one spouse before the other could obtain a divorce decree. This doctrine can be compared with the "**principle of fault**" which was also applied in ancient German divorce law. A break with this doctrine was made by the *Divorce Reform Act 1969* – eight years earlier than in Germany –, which has now been replaced by the *Matrimonial Causes Act 1973* as amended by the *Matrimonial and Family Proceedings Act 1984*. The position is now that there is only a single ground on which a petition for divorce can be presented, namely that the marriage has broken down irretrievably ("**principle of irretrievable breakdown**").

äußern – betreffend
eine beträchtliche Zeit lang
in Kraft setzen/realisieren
Anzeichen

Many believe that the current law on divorce is unsatisfactory. Particular dissatisfaction is voiced as regards the methods of establishing that a marriage has **irretrievably broken down**. These are the so called "5 facts" that will be introduced below in more detail. There have been calls for reforms for a considerable time; thus the *Family Law Act 1996* was to bring a new law on divorce but this part of the Act has not been implemented. Since the reform was abandoned, there have been no active signs that the governmant intends to attempt reforms again.

unangemessenes Verhalten

**Dissolution** of a civil partnership is very similar to divorce, except that *adultery* is not one of the specific *facts* on which dissolution can proceed. However, adultery may well give rise to grounds for dissolution based on *unreasonable behaviour* (for both facts, see the following section 2).

## 2. Ground for divorce – "the five facts"

Scheidungsgrund

There is *only one* ground for a divorce and that is, as mentioned above the fact that "the marriage has broken down irretrievably" (*s.1(2) Matrimonial Causes Act 1973*). However, the **irretrievable breakdown** must be proven by the petitioner by establishing one or more of the **five facts**, as set out in *s.1(2) of the Matrimonial Causes Act 1973*. This illustrates that, to a certain extent, the doctrine of matrimonial offences has survived until this day.

vorbringen/nachweisen

| *Example – Buffery v Buffery (1988)* |
|---|
| It was found by the judge that the marriage had irretrievably broken down. The couple had nothing in common, never went out together and were unable to communicate with each other. However, none of **the five facts** could be made out.<br>***Held:*** that a divorce could not be granted. Even if the marriage had broken down irretrievably, a divorce could only be granted where one of **the five facts** was made out. The couple would have *to separate for two years* in order to get divorced. |

bewilligen/gewähren

On the other hand, even if one of these facts is established, the court will not grant a divorce if it remains unconvinced about the breakdown of the marriage. Further, there are circumstances in which a divorce cannot be obtained, known as "**bars to divorce**". For instance, the *Matrimonial Causes Act 1973, s.3(1)* states that it is not possible to petition for a divorce until the parties have been married for one year. In such cases it is possible to seek a *decree of judicial separation* under *s.17*; and in other situations *judicial separation* can be a preferred option where there are religious convictions against divorce. Another bar is, for example, financial hardship (*s.5*), which can only be used in cases based on 5-years' separation.

bleiben – nicht überzeugt

Scheidungshindernis

beantragen/ersuchen

gerichtliche Aufhebung der ehelichen Gemeinschaft/ gerichtlich angeordnetes Getrenntleben

The **five facts** which can be used to establish **irretrievable breakdown** of a marriage are as follows:

### a) Adultery and intolerability

Adultery is voluntary sexual intercourse between two persons, one or both of whom is married, but not to each other. The petitioner must prove that the other spouse committed adultery *and* that he finds it intolerable to live with the respondent – i.e. to end a marriage the act of adultery would be insufficient on its own. Note furthermore that an attempt at adultery is not sufficient.

Geschlechtsverkehr

miteinander

unzumutbar/unerträglich

Einheit/Ding/Gebilde
sich auf etwas beziehen/ zusammenhängen mit

Adultery and intolerability are two separate entities; thus, intolerability does not have to relate to adultery. This principle was demonstrated in the following case.

| *Example – Clearly v Clearly (1974)* |
| --- |
| The wife committed adultery. The husband forgave her and they were reconciled. However, this was short-lived and the wife left the husband again. The husband then petitioned for divorce. ***Held:*** that there had been *adultery* and that, because of the wife's conduct during the unsuccessful attempt at reconciliation the husband found it *intolerable* to live with her. A divorce was possible on the **adultery fact**. |

versöhnen – von kurzer Dauer

***Note:*** If the husband and wife have lived together for more than six months and the adultery has not been repeated, the husband would not be able to rely on that adultery as a basis for divorce.

sich stützen auf

unangemessenes Verhalten

### b) Unreasonable behaviour

The petitioner must show that the respondent has behaved in such a way that the *petitioner cannot reasonably be expected to live with the respondent*. The particular sensitivity of the spouse concerned is taken into account in this case. The key question in this context that arises is as follows: "Would any right-thinking person come to the conclusion that this husband has behaved in such a way that *this* wife cannot reasonably be expected to live with him?" *(Livingstone-Stallard v Livingstone-Stallard (1974))*.

Nachweis/Beweis
Gewalttätigkeit – Trunkenheit – zwanghafte Eifersucht
bescheiden/unauffällig
Heimwerker
kitzeln

The court would expect to see evidence of very unreasonable behaviour, such as violence, drunkenness or obsessive jealousy. However, behaviour that, at first sight, may seem rather unobtrusive can, in fact, lead to divorce. In *O'Neill* v *O'Neill (1975)* the husband was a DIY (do it yourself) fanatic and he took eight months to replace the toilet door. In *Lines* v *Lines (1963)* a husband required his wife to tickle his feet for hours every evening; here, too, it was held that unreasonable behaviour fact was proved. Divorce petitions are often based on the cumulative effect of one spouse's behaviour.

| *Example – Bannister v Bannister (1980)* |
|---|
| The husband had not taken his wife out for two years. He did not speak to her unless it was unavoidable. He stayed out at night without telling her where he was going. He led an entirely independent life, ignoring his wife. She petitioned for divorce based on the *unreasonable behaviour* fact. ***Held:*** that the basis of the *Matrimonial Causes Act 1973 s.1(2)(b)* is not *unreasonable behaviour* but behaving in such a way that the petitioner "cannot reasonably be expected to live with the respondent", a significantly different concept. In this case, the wife had made out a clear **case of behaviour** such that she could not reasonably be expected to live with the husband and, therefore, she had proved irretrievable breakdown of the marriage. |

unvermeidbar

An issue which has troubled the courts is blameless behaviour, i.e. without fault. The cases concerned are often such where the behaviour is caused by a medical condition. In *Katz* v *Katz (1972)* a wife was able to get a divorce from a husband who suffered from manic depression and whose behaviour greatly disturbed the wife.

plagen/Kummer machen – schuldlos

## c) Desertion

Verlassen/"Fahnenflucht"

Desertion requires that the respondent has deserted the petitioner for a continuous period of at least 2 years immediately preceding the presentation of the petition.

durchgängig/durchgehend
unmittelbar vorausgehen

Desertion involves:

- the fact of separation for at least 2 years,
- an intention to desert the petitioner,
- no consent by the petitioner to the desertion, and
- no just cause for the desertion.

enthalten/umfassen
Trennung
verlassen/im Stich lassen
kein ersichtlicher Grund

## d) 2-years' separation with consent

The petitioner must show that the parties have *lived apart* for a continuous period of at least 2 years immediately preceding the presentation of the petition, and the respondent consents to a decree of divorce. If the respondent does not consent, and if no other facts are available, the petitioner must rely on the 5-years' separation fact (see below).

getrennt leben
Scheidungsurteil

After separation, the spouses normally live in separate houses, but it is possible to live separate lives under the same roof. *S.2(6) of the Matrimonial Causes Act 1973* distinguishes between house and household. Thus, the parties are to be treated as *living apart* "unless they are living with each other in the same household."

*Example – Naylor v Naylor (1961)*

ehelicher Streit – ablegen

In March 1960, during a quarrel with the husband, the wife cast off her wedding ring and thereafter the parties lived separate lives, but both remained in the matrimonial home. The husband used one small room for sleeping, the wife performed no wifely services for him and there was a complete absence of any communal or family life. The wife intended to leave her husband.

*hier*: verrichten

***Held:*** that the wife had **deserted** the husband, even though the parties were still living under the same roof, because they were leading entirely separate lives and residing separately from each other.

Thus, it is possible to obtain a divorce even though the spouses are living under the same roof because they are living in such a way that they can be said to have established separate households.

*Living apart* does not necessarily mean physical separation of the parties, as the following case illustrates.

*Example – Santos v Santos (1972)*

The wife petitioned for divorce under *s.1(1) and (2)(d) of the Matrimonial Causes Act 1973*. She had left her husband in late 1966 but on three subsequent occasions returned to the husband and occupied the same bed as he did. These visits together did not exceed six months.

***Held:*** that the phrase *living apart* imports something *more than physical separation*. "... the relevant state of affairs does not exist whilst both parties recognise the marriage as subsisting". However, it is sufficient that one of the parties recognised that the marriage was at an end (even if this is the petitioner) and it is not necessary for that party to communicate his recognition to the other.

beinhalten
Sachlage
noch bestehen

Erkenntnis

### e) 5-years' separation without consent

It is sufficient under this heading to show that the parties have *lived apart* for a continuous period of at least 5 years immediately preceding the presentation of the petition.

Überschrift

### f) Procedure

It is interesting to note that the vast majority of divorce cases proceed without the spouses having to attend the court for a hearing. Most divorces are undefended and since the introduction of the special procedure in 1973, the divorce can proceed on paperwork alone. Where there are minor children, the court considers the arrangements for them, but this does not usually lead to any delay in the divorce process as such.

große Mehrheit/überwiegende Mehrheit
Gerichtsverhandlung – unverteidigt
Verzögerung

Cases of defended divorces are rare because they are expensive and often unpopular with lawyers. Furthermore, it is quite difficult to obtain legal aid to defend a divorce. If either spouse wants to divorce, there is not much point in trying to get the court to prevent it.

Prozesskostenhilfe
nicht viel Sinn ergeben

## 3. Legal consequences and effects of divorce

### a) In general

On the granting of the decree absolute of divorce, the marriage is dissolved. Each party is now free to remarry. However, divorce itself has no effect on the spouses' legal relationship with their children. Upon a decree of divorce, the court may make orders in relation to residence, parental contact, maintenance, property and financial issues, if the parents cannot agree on these matters. These rights of the children on family breakdown are laid down in the *Children Act 1989,* which will be introduced briefly in the following section IV along with child support.

*hier*: Erlass – rechtskräftiges Scheidungsurteil
*hier*: bei/mit
Wohnsitz – elterliches Umgangsrecht – Unterhalt
zusammen mit – Kindesunterhalt

On divorce it is the norm for the divorcing couple to distribute and reallocate their property and financial assets, whether it be the family home, a pension, investments or other assets.

Regel
umverteilen/neu verteilen – finanzielles Vermögen/Eigentum

prozessieren

Betonung – Vergleich/Beilegung
als letzter Ausweg/„wenn alle Stricke reißen" – *etwa:* Güterausgleichsregelung – Verfahren für Scheidungsfolgesachen

Most couples do not litigate about property and finance, but reach agreement with or without the help of a lawyer. Thus the **emphasis is on settlement**. Court proceedings are used only as last resort. If the parties cannot reach agreement, financial provision and property adjustment orders can be sought on divorce in **ancillary relief proceedings** under Part II of *Matrimonial Causes Act 1973* and the *Civil Partnership Act 2004*.

einmalige Pauschale/Zahlung

Rentenanteilsregelung

It is possible to apply for maintenance and lump sum orders without there being a divorce or judicial separation. However, the court's powers are limited. For instance, the court cannot make a pension order unless there is a divorce, or a property adjustment order unless there are judicial separation or divorce proceedings.

## b) The orders available for the benefit of spouses

Ermessensfreiheit/-befugnis
laufend

The courts have wide discretionary powers to redistribute property between the spouses and to require ongoing financial support (maintenance).

rechtshängiger Unterhalt
*etwa*: Bescheid zur finanziellen Regelung – Abfindungszahlung/ Zahlung eines Pauschbetrages

The main orders available are:

- maintenance pending suit (this lasts during the divorce process)
- financial provision orders: in form of periodical payments or lump sum payments
- property adjustment orders
- pension orders

richterliches Ermessen – Errungenschafts-/Zugewinngemeinschaft

The system governing disputes over matrimonial assets on divorce in England is based on **judicial discretion**. There is no community of property regime as there is in some European countries, e.g. Germany, whereby each spouse on martial breakdown is entitled to a fixed share of the matrimonial assets, unless agreed otherwise.

## c) Factors to be taken into account

anwenden
Schlussstrich/sauberer Schnitt/klare Regelung

The court must apply the **statutory guidelines** (*s.25*) and the **"clean break"**[40] **provision** laid down in the *Matrimonial Causes Act 1973*, as interpreted by case-law. That is to say that the court must consider all the circumstances of the case.

Wohl

*First* consideration must be given to **the welfare of any minor children** of the family (*s.25(1) Matrimonial Causes Act 1973*).

40 Der Begriff "clean break" kommt aus der Chirurgie. Gemeint ist hier eine abschließende Regelung, die die finanziellen Beziehungen der Eheleute dauerhaft beendet.

However, this first consideration does not mean that the welfare of the child overrides all other considerations.

*hier*: überstimmen/verdrängen

*Example – Suter v Suter and Jones (1986)*

The wife had remained in the home with the minor children of the family. The husband was content for the home, the main asset of the parties, to be transferred to her. The co-respondent Mr Jones lived at the house with the wife, but did not contribute anything to the expenses of it. At first instance, the court ordered the husband to pay periodical payments to the wife of an amount that, together with her wages, was enough to pay all the household expenses.

***Held:*** that the judge in first instance was wrong. He had made the order to ensure the children had a roof over their heads, but this was not the only consideration. It would not be unreasonable for the co-respondent to make a contribution and the reduced award did more justice to the husband.

Lohn/Gehalt

jmd. eher gerecht werden

The factors the courts should consider under *s.25(2) Matrimonial Causes Act 1973* are set out below. The weight which is attached to these factors varies according to the facts of each case.

*hier*: variieren je nach Fall/abhängig vom Einzelfall sein

- **income, earning capacity, property and financial resources** of both parties,
- **financial needs, obligations and responsibilities** which the parties have, or are likely to have,
- **standard of living** enjoyed by the family before the breakdown of the marriage,
- **age** of the parties and **duration of the marriage**,
- any **disability** of either of the parties, physical or mental,
- **value of any lost benefits** (such as a pension) which cannot be acquired because of the termination of the marriage,
- the **contribution** each party made to the welfare of the family; see the following case:

*Example – Gojkovic v Gojkovic (1990)*

The couple turned a property into a hotel. The wife worked hard to make the hotel successful while the husband was involved in other business activities. When they divorced, the husband had £4 million in family assets and the wife had very little. The husband offered the wife a maisonette worth £295,000 and a lump sum of £532,000 on a **"clean break" order** calculated to meet the reasonable needs of the former wife by the wealthy husband. The wife wanted a larger lump sum so that she could buy and run her own hotel. The judge found

umwandeln

Wohnung über 2 Stockwerke/größere Wohnung – Einmalzahlung/Pauschalsumme – Anforderungen erfüllen

Rechtsmittel/Berufung einlegen

Eigenmittel – *hier*: was sein Angebot – bezwecken sollte

abweisen

nahezu mittellos

that the wife had made *exceptional contributions* which were equal to those of the husband and awarded her a £1 million lump sum. The husband appealed, arguing that the order was excessive, that the judge had been wrong in allowing his wife to buy a hotel and that all the court needed to provide was self-sufficiency for his wife, which is what his offer aimed to do.

***Held:*** that dismissing the appeal, the court was concerned with an exceptional **degree of contribution** by the wife from a time when the parties were virtually penniless until the end of the marriage. There was nothing wrong in allowing the wife to continue as an active business woman by enabling her to buy and run a hotel within the context of *s.25 of the Matrimonial Causes Act 1973.*

erwägen – angemessen/sinnvoll

Empfänger

The courts should consider whether it would be appropriate to award either a lump sum payment, or periodical payments but only for such time as the court considers sufficient in order for the recipient to become financially independent of the other party.

unbillig/ungerecht

- **conduct** of each of the parties "whatever the nature of the conduct and whether it occurred during the marriage or after the separation or dissolution or annulment of the marriage" (added by the *Family Law Act 1996*) if in the opinion of the court it would be inequitable to ignore it.

*hier:* eindeutig und grausam

jdn. abstechen

*hier:* negativ beeinflusst von/beeinträchtigt von

Since *Wachtel* v *Wachtel (1973)* the courts should only take conduct into account when "obvious and gross", i.e. a certain amount of **extremity of conduct** e.g. stabbing or shooting one's spouse. In the following cases, the spouses' claim for ancillary relief was affected by their conduct:

gefühllos

verhöhnen/verspotten

*Example – Kyte* v *Kyte (1988)*

The wife behaved callously when the husband, a manic depressive, made two suicide attempts. On the first, she was present and only called assistance at the last moment, on the second she encouraged him, giving him the tablets and alcohol with which to kill himself and jeering at him when he failed to carry out his intentions.

***Held:*** that the court found as a fact that the wife wanted the husband dead so that she could inherit his money, and share it with her lover.

| *Example – Evans v Evans (1989)* |
|---|
| The wife had been convicted of soliciting others to murder the husband. |

dringend/inständig bitten

Further, in *K* v *K (1990)* the court stated that "the court must look at the whole picture, including the conduct during the marriage and after the marriage, which may or may not have contributed to the breakdown ... or which in some other way makes it inequitable to ignore the conduct of each of the parties." *Miller* v *Miller (2006)* confirmed that there must be **extremity of conduct**.

## d) Factors of general application for financial orders

*hier:* generelle Gültigkeit/allgemeine Geltung

In many cases the needs of the child and the primary carer of the child dominate; often there is not enough money to meet them. In the "big money cases", however, the court is not so preoccupied with needs and there is more emphasis on the other factors in *s.25*. Two recent cases dominate this area. In the landmark case *White* v *White (2000)* the court stated that the objective of the list in *s.25(2) Matrimonial Causes Act 1973* should be **fairness.**

Hauptversorger der Familie
(die Bedürfnisse = needs) stillen/befriedigen/abdecken
Betonung/Gewicht
Grundsatzentscheidung

| *Example – White v White (2000)* |
|---|
| The Whites had assets of roughly £4.5 million when their marriage ended after 33 years together. Mr White had run farms and Mrs White had assisted in the business and raised the children.<br>***Held:*** the primary objective in ancillary relief cases is to achieve **fairness**. The court must first meet the **needs** of the parties. If the assets exceed the needs of the parties, the court must consider all of the **factors** in *s.25(2)* and, in particular, the **contributions** of the parties. When considering those, there was to be no bias in favour of a money-maker and against the interests of a home-maker or child-carer. Indeed, where assets exceeded needs, there needs to be a good **reason to justify departing from the yardstick of equality**. In this case there was good reason to give Mr White a little over 50 %, and that was that his family had provided them with an important sum of money to start their farming business. |

übersteigen

Voreingenommenheit – Geldverdiener – der Partner, der Haushalt und Kinder versorgt

abweichen – Gleichheitsgrundsatz

Later the courts held that this concept was elusive *(Miller v Miller and McFarlane v McFarlane (2006))*. In these cases the House of Lords had the opportunity to consider once again the difficult question "How to achieve **fairness** in the division of property following a divorce?"

schwer fassbar/flüchtig

bei der Verteilung

*Example – Miller v Miller; McFarlane v McFarlane (2006)*

The husband (41) and the wife (36) has been married for less than 3 years, and had no children. At the time of the marriage the husband was an exceptionally successful businessman earning about £1 million a year, and the wife earned £85,000 a year. The matrimonial home was purchased by the husband for £1.8 million and he later bought a second property in joint names in the South of France. During the marriage the husband acquired shares in a new business which subsequently proved to be extremely valuable. The wife gave up work to concentrate on furnishing their two homes. The husband left the wife for another woman, whom he subsequently married.

***Held:*** that the husband was ordered to transfer the matrimonial home (worth £2.3 million) to his wife and to pay her a lump sum of £2.7 million. The court argued that the award should not be limited to putting the wife "back on her feet", but should recognise that the husband had, by marriage, despite its short duration, given her a reasonable and legitimate expectation that she would be able to leave the marriage significantly better off in terms of accommodation and disposable income than when she had entered it. The appeal of the husband was dismissed. The court was entitled to take into account the husband's responsibility for the breakdown of the marriage and the wife's legitimate expectation of a higher standard of living.

purchased: anschaffen/kaufen
subsequently: danach/später
argued: argumentieren
despite: trotz
accommodation / disposable: Räumlichkeit/Wohnung – verfügbar
dismissed: nicht stattgeben/zurückweisen *(Berufung)*

Based on these key cases above, the court has developed a number of important **factors of general application for financial orders**:

- **fairness**,
- **needs** (generously interpreted) generated by the relationship, **compensation** for disadvantages arising from the relationship and **sharing** of the fruits of the matrimonial partnership *(Miller v Miller (2006))*,
- **no discrimination** between wage-earner and child-carer or home-maker,
- a **"clean break"** order should be made where desirable,
- division of assets not based solely on reasonable needs in big money cases, particularly in lengthy marriages,
- departing from equality where justified.

generously interpreted: weit ausgelegt
wage-earner: Erwerbstätige(r)
lengthy: besonders lang andauernd

Cases where these principles have been applied are as follows.

| *Example – Charman v Charman (2007)* |
|---|
| The couple had been married for 28 years when they divorced. The husband had been very successful in business and generated £131 million. The trial judge awarded the wife £48 million and the husband appealed.<br>***Held:*** that – following *Miller; McFarlane* – all the assets a couple had were available for distribution. Where, however, a particular asset had been owned before the marriage, or was a gift or inheritance, that might be a reason for departing from an equal division. In a long marriage, the basic principle was a division of all the assets, regardless of when they had been acquired. In this case there should be a departure from equality due to the husband's outstanding business skills. The trial judge's order had been appropriate. |

trial judge – awarded: Tatrichter (1. Instanz) – zusprechen

departing from: abweichen von

outstanding – business skills: hervorragend – unternehmerische Fähigkeit

One of the most notorious divorces of the last decade is the following:

notorious: stadtbekannt/ berühmt-berüchtigt

| *Example – McCartney v Mills McCartney (2008)* |
|---|
| Paul McCartney married Heather Mills in 2002 and divorced four years later. They had one child together. McCartney's wealth was estimated to be about £400 million.<br>***Held:*** that in this case of a short marriage following *Miller*, the court should share the marital gain (goods acquired by the couple during marriage). However, during the marriage no substantial sums of money had been generated. McCartney had given up work to enjoy married life. So there was no award on that basis. Nor was there any award based on compensation as Mills had not suffered any economic disadvantage as a result of marriage. The only award that could be made was the award that was needed to meet her needs. McCartney was ordered to pay £16.5 million to meet the needs of his wife and daughter. |

wealth: Vermögen

marital gain: ehelicher Zugewinn

award: Zuerkennung/Zubilligung

Whilst the court has a discretion in assessing the amount and duration of periodical payments, the court must first consider whether a **"clean break" order** would instead be more appropriate in the case in point. A "clean break" order (see above) would terminate all obligations.

discretion: Ermessen

case in point: fraglicher/einschlägiger Fall

*Example – Ashley v Blackman (1988)*

Following their divorce, the husband was ordered to pay maintenance to his wife. She was mentally ill and lived on state benefits. The husband remarried and had his second wife and two children to support. He earned a low income. He applied for the maintenance order to his ex-wife to be discharged.
**Held:** that the law was intended to leave scope for those of limited means to be spared the burden of having to pay their former spouses a few pounds a week indefinitely. Any maintenance paid by the husband would be swallowed up in the benefits for his ex-wife. The **"clean break"** provisions were to prevent a divorced couple of acutely limited means from remaining manacled together indefinitely. The provision also aimed to avoid regular fights in court on precise figures that one should pay the other at public expense. A **"clean break"** was applied and the wife's maintenance ended.

staatliche Unterstützung
befreien (von einer Pflicht)
*hier:* Ermessensspielraum lassen
begrenzte Mittel – verschont bleiben
verschlingen
*hier*: bewahren vor
aneinander gebunden/gefesselt sein
Betrag
auf Kosten der Öffentlichkeit

The courts have the power to vary awards at the request of either party. The amounts may be increased or reduced.

ändern – auf Antrag

*Example – Clutton v Clutton (1991)*

After 20 years of marriage, the couple divorced. There was only one child, aged 16, living at home. She had left school and was working. The matrimonial home, which was in the husband's sole name, was transferred to the wife. She had a stable sexual relationship with Mr D but did not intend to live with him or marry him. The husband appealed against the property order.
**Note:** that an order whereby the sale of the matrimonial home was postponed until the youngest child is aged 18 (or some other age) is known as a "Mesher order" *(see Mesher v Mesher (1973))*. An order whereby the sale is postponed until the wife dies, remarries or cohabits with another man is usually known as a "Martin order" *(see Martin v Martin (1978))*. In this case, the matrimonial home was the sole asset of the parties. The husband asked for a "Martin order" on terms that he have *a one third share* of the proceeds of sale. The wife was at first content with a "Mesher order" but later supported the "clean break" of a complete transfer of the house to her on the basis of the long marriage and her limited earning capacity as a part-time typist. The husband had a regular income as a bricklayer.
**Held:** that there was a danger in describing the **"clean break"** as a principle. *S.25A of the Matrimonial Causes Act 1973* does not oblige courts to strive for a "clean break" regardless whether it would be appropriate or not. The husband was rightly not ordered to pay

ständig
*hier:* Beschluss über die Vermögensverteilung
aufschieben/vertagen
einziges Vermögen
Verkaufserlös
*hier:* befürworten
Halbtags-Schreibkraft
Maurer
etw. anstreben

maintenance to his wife, but the judge was wrong to refuse to make a "Martin order". Such an order cannot be said to go against the **"clean break" principle**. Not to have made a "Martin order" deprived the husband of his share in the sole capital asset of the marriage, which was manifestly unfair. The judge should have ordered a charge in the husband's favour in the event of the wife's death or remarriage. A "Mesher order" was not suitable, since there were doubts about the wife's ability to rehouse herself if the house was sold when the youngest child became 18. "Mesher orders" could still be the best solution where the family assets are amply sufficient to provide both parties with a roof over their heads if the matrimonial home were sold, but the interests of the children required that they remain in the matrimonial home.

verstoßen
berauben
offensichtlich
anordnen
wieder behausen/jdm. in einer neuen Wohnung unterbringen
Lösung

In *Wachtel* v *Wachtel (1973)* the court stated that, as a starting point for the calculation of periodical payments, the wife should "receive *one third* of the joint earnings and assets". The parties' incomes from all sources are added together and divided by three. The resulting figure is the amount of income the wife should have. If her own income does not add up to this figure, it is to be made up by a periodical payments order from the husband. This **"one third rule"** is only relevant today in cases where there is only one spouse who is working. Even then it probably has to be tempered with **fairness** *(White v White (2000))*.

Betrag
mäßigen/mildern

The **"one third rule"** has been largely replaced by the courts striving to make an award to wives which would meet their reasonable needs judged on a generous basis where finances permit it.

anstreben

## e) Pre-marital agreements

Married couples can enter into agreements about maintenance, finance and property, but an agreement cannot be conclusive, as the court has the power to vary or revoke the terms of an agreement and can insert new terms (*s.35(2) of the Matrimonial Causes Act 1973*).

zwingend
einbauen/einfügen

**Pre-marital agreements** or pre-nuptial agreements – entered into on contemplation of marriage – are not binding in English law in the contractual sense. Such an agreement, however, is one factor which the court can take into account. Following an important decision by the Supreme Court in the recent case of

bei/anlässlich der Eingehung der Ehe

*Radmacher* v *Radmacher (2010)*, the courts appear to pay more attention to the terms of pre-nuptial agreements and are more likely to hold the parties to the agreement. A German heiress worth £100 million married a French husband. They entered into a pre-marital agreement. The court gave "decisive weight" to the agreement. This area of law is likely to develop further.

die Parteien festhalten an – Erbin

ausschlaggebendes Gewicht

In the case of divorce *pre-marital* agreements concerning financial arrangements are treated differently from *post-marital* agreements.

Since *MacLeod* v *MacLeod (2009)* **post-marital agreements** are now more likely to be upheld by the courts. The closer the timing of the agreement is to the actual separation of the parties, the more likely it is to be upheld. The reason for that is that changes of circumstances that would require a variation by the court (under *ss.34-36 Matrimonial Causes Act 1973)* are then less likely.

## 4. Judicial separation

English family law also considers other situations where a married couple do not wish to live together as husband and wife, but, at the same time, they do not want to obtain a divorce. The reasons for a *judicial separation* instead of divorce are usually religious or the parties are elderly and have no intention to remarry. The petition may be issued on the same *five facts* as a divorce petition as outlined above. However, the petitioner does not need to show that the marriage has irretrievably broken down. The effect of a *judicial separation* under *s.17 Matrimonial Causes Act 1973* is likely to be the same as the effect of a divorce.

in denen/demnach

skizziert/aufgeführt

**Diagram 55**

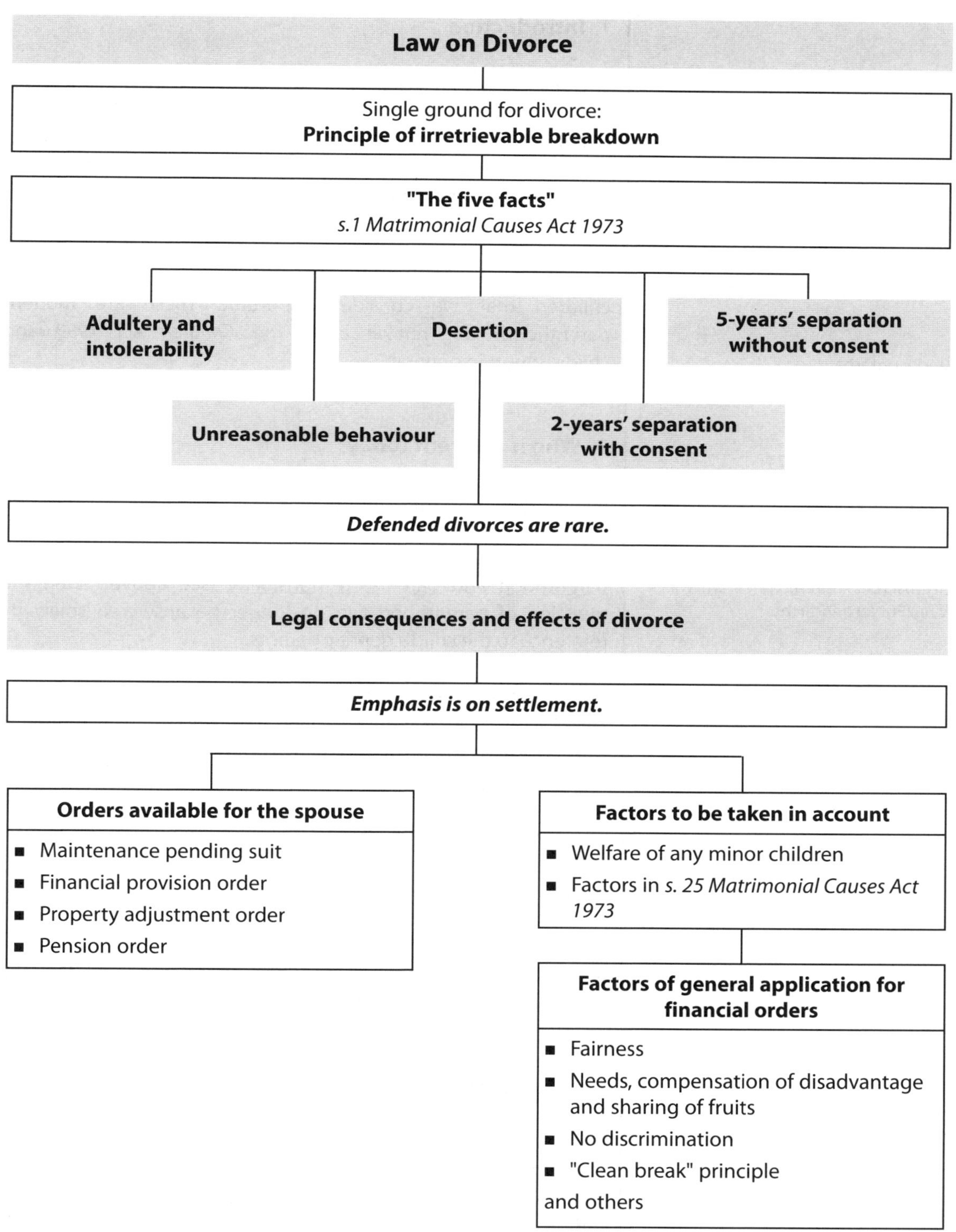
Law on Divorce
Single ground for divorce:
Principle of irretrievable breakdown
"The five facts"
s.1 Matrimonial Causes Act 1973
Adultery and intolerability
Desertion
5-years' separation without consent
Unreasonable behaviour
2-years' separation with consent
Defended divorces are rare.
Legal consequences and effects of divorce
Emphasis is on settlement.
Orders available for the spouse
■ Maintenance pending suit
■ Financial provision order
■ Property adjustment order
■ Pension order
Factors to be taken in account
■ Welfare of any minor children
■ Factors in s. 25 Matrimonial Causes Act 1973
Factors of general application for financial orders
■ Fairness
■ Needs, compensation of disadvantage and sharing of fruits
■ No discrimination
■ "Clean break" principle
and others

## IV. Children and parents

### 1. Introduction

Streit(igkeit) beilegen

The *Children Act 1989* radically reformed the law in this area and is the most important statute on resolving disputes. In this *Act*, a child is defined as "a person under the age of 18", who can also be called a "minor" or "infant". We have already seen above (vol. 1, chapter 5) the rights and duties that minors may have, as well as their capacity to contract (vol. 1, chapter 6).

Überblick geben über/skizzieren

Kindesunterhalt

This chapter can only outline certain selected issues regarding children that we consider important. These are modern parenthood, the relevance of the *Children Act 1989* and child support in general.

### 2. Who is a parent today?

künstliche Befruchtung

Elternschaft – elterliche Verantwortung/Fürsorge/Pflicht

In the light of assisted reproduction and civil partnerships the question of who is a parent is more complex today than it may seem at first sight. We also have to distinguish between parenthood and parental responsibility (see above). Even the question of parenthood can no longer be answered solely by reference to the child's genetic parents.

Leihmutterschaft

*S.33 of the Human Fertilisation and Embryology Act 2008* makes it clear that it is the woman who gives birth who is the child's (legal) **mother**. This is so even if she is carrying an embryo using a donated egg (surrogacy).

Vaterschaft

vermuten

The **father** of the child is the genetic father. Paternity will be presumed if:

- the father is married to the mother at the time of the birth,
- the father is registered as the father of the child on the child's birth certificate,
- if circumstances are proved which strongly indicate that the father is the father of the child.

Otherwise a man can only prove his paternity by applying to the court for biological tests to be carried out.

Under the *Human Fertilisation and Embryology Acts 1990 and 2008* things have become more difficult: there are two situations where a man who is not the genetic father is nevertheless the child's legal father.

It is also possible for a couple who have used a surrogate mother to apply for a parental order which will end the parental status of the surrogate mother. Details regarding this complex area are beyond the scope of this book.

Leihmutter

It is important to explain the concept of *parental responsibility* which is not to be confused with *parenthood*. Thus, *s.3(1) of the Children Act 1989* defines the former: "In this Act, parental responsibility means all the rights, duties, powers, responsibilities and authority which by law a parent of a child has in relation to the child and his property." Concrete examples of such rights are the right to choose the child's religion, to educate the child, to consent to medical treatment for a child, to choose the child's name etc.

## 3. The *Children Act 1989*

This *Children Act* was amended in 2008 in an attempt to bring together all public and private law relating to children into one Act of Parliament and, therefore, it is very wide ranging and detailed. There are over 100 sections and 15 schedules which are too detailed to summarise here, so we cite from James' "Introduction to English Law" as follows on the *Children Act 1989*:

weit reichend
*hier:* Tabelle – zusammenfassen

"Broadly, the Act covers orders with respect to children in

- family proceedings,
- local authority support for children and families,
- care and supervision, protection of children,
- community homes, voluntary homes and voluntary organisations, registered children's homes
- private agreements for fostering children, childminding and day care for young children,
- the Secretary of State's supervisory responsibilities and functions.

The basic philosophy behind this *Act* is that a child should be brought up within his or her family and that local authority support should be provided when necessary to support and facilitate this."

abdecken
Verfahren in Familiensachen
Kommunale Familienkasse
Pflege u. Aufsicht von Kindern/Kinderschutz – städtische und gemeinnützige Heime
Kinderpflege, -betreuung, -tagesstätte
Aufsichtspflicht
groß ziehen/erziehen
erleichtern

## 4. Child support

On divorce, the law's first concern will be with the children and to ensure they are adequately provided for (see *s.25(1) of the Matrimonial Causes Act 1973*). The law on periodic payments for children originally set out in the *Child Support Acts 1991* has been

erstes Anliegen
regelmäßige Zahlung
festlegen/bestimmen

radically reformed by the *Child Maintenance and Other Payments Act 2008.* Some of these changes are in force, but the new scheme is not expected to be fully implemented until 2013.[41]

anwenden/umsetzen

The *Child Support Act* formula is relatively straightforward to apply in cases where the resident parent (with the main day-to-day care) is receiving income support. The calculation until today has been based on the non-resident parent's net income. From 2012, a new statutory maintenance scheme, which is called the future *gross income* scheme, will be based on latest available tax year information from Her Majesty's Revenue and Customs.

einfach/unkompliziert
Hauptsorgerecht
Einkommenshilfe
Nettoeinkommen
Bruttoverdienst

The amount depends on the number of children who qualify for maintenance, the income and circumstances of the non-resident parent and the number of other children living with the non-resident parent.

(unterhalts)berechtigt sein

The new *Child Maintenance and Other Payments Act 2008* aims to encourage parents to come to their own agreement about child maintenance. Such private agreements are possible and also quicker and cheaper than going to court. In addition, stronger enforcement measures have been introduced for parents who fail to pay. When there is no contact between the parents, the correct and only possible way that remains is an application to the new Child Maintenance and Enforcement Commission.

41 The progress of the implementation can be followed on: www.childmaintenance.org.

**Diagram 56**

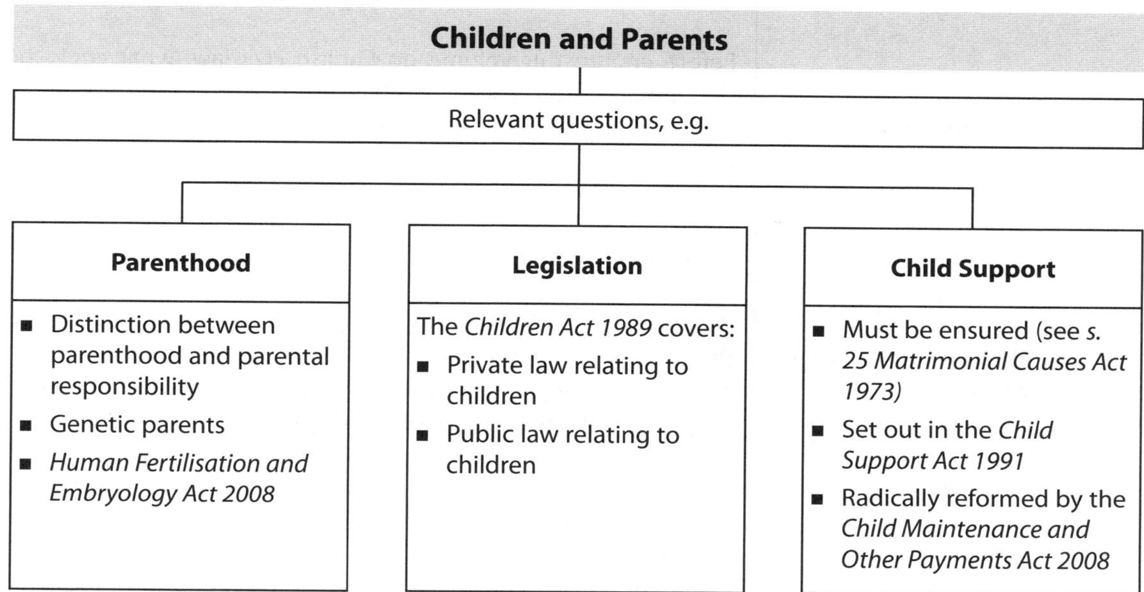


## V. Further reading & references[42]

*Barker & Padfield*, Law Made Simple; *Cretney (Ed.)*, Cretney's Principles of Family law; *Dodds*, Family Law; *Douglas & Lowe*, Bromley's Family Law; *Geldart*, Introduction to English Law; *Herring*, Family Law; *Lyall*, An Introduction to British law; *Shears & Stephenson*, James' Introduction to English Law; *Standley*, Family Law; *Templeman & Dodds*, Family Law – Casebook; *Wilman*, Brown: GCSE Law; *Wragg*, Family Law.

42 Edition, publisher, place and year of publication are quoted in the bibliography.

# Chapter Eleven

## Law of Succession

Erbrecht

unvermeidbar – Tod (juristisch)
Erbe

Before ending this volume on English civil law, what could be better than finishing off with a chapter on the law of succession? As true as it is that death is inevitable, it is also true that "death brings heirs".[43]

### I. Introduction

übertragen
Erwerber – nachfolgen/erben – Veräußerer – Nachfolge/Erbfall
Rechtsnachfolge von Todes wegen

Whenever one person transfers property to another, it may be said that the transferee *succeeds* to the rights of the transferor. In law, the word *succession* has a special meaning that is the transfer of property on death (i.e. **succession on death**).

es ist selbstverständlich

Verstorbene(r) – üblich sein
anbieten/vorsehen/liefern
testamentarische Erbfolge
Testament
gesetzliche Erbfolge – hinterlassen
testamentlos/Sterben ohne Hinterlassung eines Testaments

It goes without saying that a person who is dead cannot own property or exercise rights over property. The legal consequence of this inevitable fact is that other persons will succeed to the property owned or possessed by the deceased. This is common to all legal systems, and most legal systems provide two possibilities which govern succession on death. On the one hand, we find **testate**, i.e. testamentary succession or succession by will. On the other hand, we find legal or **intestate succession** where a person leaves no will and thus he is said to die intestate (intestacy).

beeinflussen/sich auswirken

As with family law (see previous chapter), the English law of succession has been greatly impacted by statute law. We will now be looking at that latter aspect in more detail in this chapter.

anwendbar
grenzüberschreitend

*lat.:* Belegenheitsstatut
was ... angeht

ansässig/wohnhaft/beheimatet

*hier*: Internationales Privatrecht

When does English law of succession affect us? It is applicable, for example, in transnational cases when a deceased of German nationality leaves a house or leaves land in England (principle of the "lex rei sitae", i.e. the law applicable is that of the place where the land is located). In terms of personalty (i.e. assets other than land; see chapter 8, p. 85), English courts would apply English law where the deceased died domiciled in England & Wales. The German courts, however, would apply German law on grounds of the nationality of the deceased *(Art. 25 EGBGB)*. Further details on questions regarding conflict of laws would go beyond the scope of this book, however.

43 German law proverb: „Sterben bringt Erben".

There are two main features of English law of succession, which are distinctively different from German law of succession – the concept of the **personal representatives** and the **concept of trusts**. The former concept will be explained here below in section II, the latter forms a separate chapter (chapter 9).

besonderes Merkmal

Erbschaftsverwalter/persönlicher Vertreter des Erblassers – Rechtskonzept der Treuhand

## II. Administration of estates

Nachlassverwaltung

Concerning the administration of estates, one striking difference between English law and German law is that, unlike German law, English law distinguishes between the administration of an estate[44] and its distribution.

augenfällig/eklatant/beachtlich

Erbmasse/Nachlass(-vermögen)

One characteristic feature of English law is the fact that a deceased's property does not go automatically and directly to the person to whom it had been left by will or who will receive it under the intestacy rules. Abolished in 1925, the **concept of heir** – as we know in German law – does not exist any longer under English law. This is also why the term *heir* is hardly used any longer today and, overall, the term *beneficiary* is used, instead.

Regeln der gesetzlichen Erbfolge

Begünstigter

Since 1925 the property vests, in the first instance, in the deceased's **personal representatives.** These are the testamentary **executor**(s) appointed in the will, or where there is no will or no executor appointed in the will, **administrator**(s) appointed by the probate court.

übergehen –zunächst

Nachlassverwalter

Nachlassverwalter

Nachlassgericht

Executors may deal with the estate immediately following the death of the deceased. However, in order to deal with certain assets, such as land, it is necessary to apply to the probate court for a **grant of probate**. This is usually a formal exercise involving presenting the will, paying any inheritance tax and giving details of the value of the deceased's estate. A beneficiary may be appointed executor, and often more than one is appointed. Banks and solicitors can also be appointed executors.

Beurkundung über die Testamentsgültigkeit und Bestimmung der Erbschafts-/Nachlassverwalter – Formsache – Erbschaftssteuer – Gesamtwert des Nachlasses

Where there is no will, or the will did not appoint executors, one or more of the persons entitled to the estate may apply to the probate court for the **grant of letters of administration**. These appoint the persons applying to be the administrators of the estate, and therefore they become the deceased's *personal representatives*, but only with effect from the date that the letters of administration are granted. Before the receipt of the grant they can not act, but

Feststellung des fehlenden gültigen Testaments und des Erbschafts-/Nachlassverwalters

44 "Estate" in the context of succession means all the property owned by the deceased at the time of his death.

regularly the bank of the deceased allows the paying of the funeral expenses before the application is filed by the deceased's family. The procedure for applying for letters of administration is similar to probate, except that there is no will involved.

Beerdigungskosten

It is the task and responsibility of the *personal representatives* to pay, out of the money in the estate, any debts of the deceased, including funeral expenses, inheritance tax and the costs of obtaining any grant of probate or letters of administration. Then they are required to distribute the estate according to the terms of the will or the rules of intestacy. This could be, for example, to distribute legacies of bequests as intended by the will, or to sell the estate and distribute the proceeds.

The distribution of legacies by the personal representatives is set out fully in section IV below.

## III. Intestate succession (intestacy)

### 1. Intestacy Rules

unbewegliches Vermögen – bewegliches Vermögen – übergehen auf/zufallen – Verwandtschaft
einen Unterschied machen
*hier:* Erbmasse/Nachlass(-vermögen)

Before 1926, under the rules of intestate succession in English law, realty and personalty (cf. above, chapter 8, p. 85) were treated differently. The realty passed to the heir and the personalty to the next of kin. Under the *Administration of Estates Act 1925*, no distinction is drawn between realty and personalty in the administration of the estate of an intestate person.

Intestate succession is governed by the *Administration of Estates Act 1925 as amended.* There are no major differences compared to German law in the area of intestacy.

Kosten der Erbschaftsverwaltung
*hier:* Nachlassschulden – Verwertungs-/Veräußerungstreuhand – Verkaufserlös

After paying funeral expenses, testamentary expenses and debts, the personal representatives hold the estate *on trust for sale*, and then distribute the proceeds of sale according to the following rules:

Five main groups of people are to be considered:

überlebender Ehepartner
Nachkomme(nschaft)

von denselben Eltern abstammend
Verwandtschaft entfernteren Grades

(1) surviving spouse,
(2) surviving issue,
(3) surviving parents,
(4) surviving brothers and sisters of the whole blood, and
(5) surviving relations of remoter degree.

*Issue* is an old term for lineal descendants: i.e. children, grandchildren, great-grandchildren, great-great-grandchildren etc.

Nachkomme in direkter Linie
Enkel

## 2. Rights of a surviving spouse

Following the *Civil Partnership Act 2004,* all references in this chapter to husband/wife or spouse or marriage should be read as also referring to civil partner and civil partnership.

Lebenspartner – eingetragene Lebenspartnerschaft

If there are *no* surviving issue, or parents, or brothers and sisters of the whole blood at all, the *complete* estate passes to the **surviving spouse**.

If there *is* issue, the **surviving spouse** takes

- all the personal chattels: that is, chattels such as furniture, cars, household articles or those for personal use, jewellery, and so on, but not chattels used for business purposes, and
- up to £250,000[45] free of inheritance tax, and
- a life interest[46] in half of the remaining estate, which may, at the spouse's option, be redeemed for a capital payment. The other half then goes to the issue (children) *on a statutory trust* (which will be described below).

Erbschaftssteuer
lebenslanges Recht an
Wahl/Wunsch – einlösen – Kapitalzahlung/-abgeltung – Nachlasstreuhand bei gesetzlicher Erbfolge

If there is *no* issue but other relations, the **surviving spouse** obtains

- all the personal chattels (as above),
- up to £450,000 free of inheritance tax, and
- half of the remaining estate absolutely. The other half goes to parents or, as the case may be, is held *on a statutory trust* for brothers and sisters of the whole blood.

je nach Lage des Falles

## 3. The statutory trusts

Under the terms of the *statutory trusts*[47] property is held by *trustees* for the members of a **class of beneficiaries,** for example the children of the intestate who are living at the intestate's death. If there is more than one beneficiary in a class, they are beneficially entitled *in equal shares*. The statutory trusts are the same for other

Erblasser ohne Testament
als Begünstigte berechtigt
zu gleichen (An-)Teilen

45 This net sum is fixed if the intestate dies on or after February 1, 2009. This sum is regularly increased. Between 1993 and 2009, it amounted to £125.000.

46 Life interest = the right to receive the income from an asset; here: from half of the estate.

47 See chapter 9, p. 127.

relatives, e.g. brothers and sisters of the whole blood or of half blood.

Bedingung/Voraussetzung
Minderjährigkeit
„Repräsentations- u. Stammesprinzip"

There are two qualifications to these rules:
(1) minority and
(2) the principles of representation and distribution per stirpes.

berechtigt
volljährig werden

(1) No child or other issue is entitled until he or she attains full age (i.e. 18 years) or marries under that age.

nach Stämmen

Nutzen ziehen
Aufteilung
pro Kopf
*hier:* Nachlass(gegenstand)
Familienzweig
Gesamtmenge

(2) The principle of representation deals with the situation where a child of the intestate has died before the intestate himself. If that deceased child left children, those children *as a class* (i.e. the intestate's grandchildren) will be entitled to the deceased child's share (and so on if any further generations are involved). Any share will be divided equally, per stirpes. The class includes all the issue of the class members who are living at the moment of the death of the intestate and satisfy the conditions under (1), but no person takes a benefit if their parent is living at the time of death of the intestate. It is rather distribution per stirpes than per capita: the principle of representation applies separately to each *branch* of the intestate's family. The assets are shared according to the branches of the family and not by counting the overall number of beneficiaries.

The following example may illustrate this:

> **G**eorge dies intestate having had three children, **J**ames, **E**mily and **M**ary. James has died before his father and James's only child, **R**upert, has also died, but Rupert had two children who are now living namely **D**onald and **F**redrick. Emily is alive and Mary has died in her father's lifetime. Mary had two children, **H**arry who is still living and **B**eatrice who has died leaving two children, **J**ustin and **A**melia.

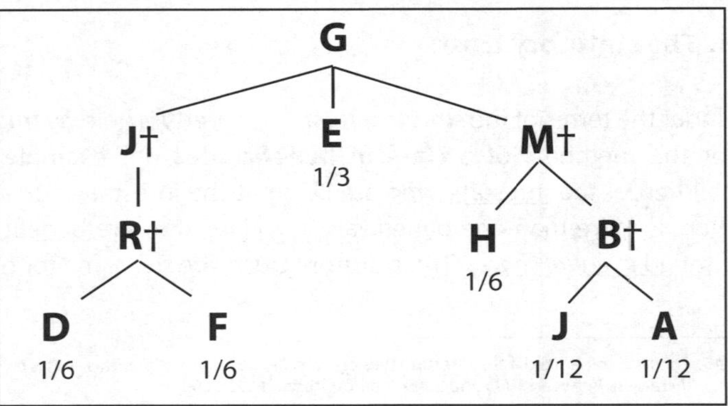

Under the intestacy rules, George's estate is divided into three shares. Donald and Fredrick share one of those 1/3 shares between them, Emily receives 1/3 herself and Mary's 1/3 is divided as to 1/2 of that 1/3 for Harry and the other 1/2 of the 1/3 is divided equally between Justin and Amelia – provided, of course, all of the beneficiaries who take a share satisfy the conditions as to age or marriage etc.

Teil

vorausgesetzt

Besides *statutory trusts* (see above), the concept of trusts also plays an important role in the law of succession. Thus, the testator can have a trust created by his will or during his lifetime. It would go beyond the scope of this introduction, however, to explain the different variations in this area, which can often be highly complex.

## 4. Rights of the surviving children

The **surviving children** include all children, whether legitimate, legitimated, adopted or illegitimate.

ehelich
für ehelich erklärt – adoptiert – nicht-ehelich

Their rights may be summarised as follows:

- If there *is* a surviving spouse, *the* **surviving child** is entitled as above. The other half of the remaining estate will be held *on a statutory trust* for the children. When the surviving spouse dies, the half in which the spouse had a life interest will be held *on a statutory trust* for the children. When the child has reached full age (18 years), he or she becomes entitled in full to his or her share of the capital.
- If there is *no* surviving spouse, the remaining estate is held *on a statutory trust* for the **surviving children**. All children are entitled to equal shares in it. For the case of full age, see our comment above.

zu gleichen Teilen berechtigt

## 5. Rights of surviving parents

Where there is *no* issue and *no* surviving spouse, the **surviving parents** take the whole estate in equal shares. If only one parent is alive, he or she is entitled to the whole estate.

## 6. Rights of surviving brothers and sisters of the whole blood

If there *is* a surviving issue or a surviving spouse or a surviving parent, the **surviving brothers and sisters** will receive *nothing*.

If there is *no* spouse, issue or parent, the estate is held *on a statutory trust* for brothers and sisters of the whole blood, including the issue of deceased brother or sister, thus nephews and nieces.

Neffen und Nichten

## 7. Rights of surviving remoter relatives

entfernter Verwandter

If there are *none* of the relatives mentioned above, **surviving remoter relatives** will be entitled as follows:

(1) brothers and sisters of the half blood,
(2) grandparents,
(3) uncles and aunts, who are brothers and sisters of the whole blood of a parent of the intestate,
(4) uncles and aunts, who are brothers and sisters of the half blood of a parent of the intestate.

halbbürtig (= ein gemeinsamer Elternteil)

Persons mentioned under (2) take the whole estate in absolute terms. In the cases of (1), (3) and (4), the estate is held *on a statutory trust*, as in the case of surviving children. They all take nothing if the intestate leaves a surviving spouse or closer relatives.

*hier*: „ohne wenn und aber"

**Diagram 57**

## Intestate Succession (Intestacy)

... when a person leaves no will at all, he (or she) is said to die *intestate*; the *rules of intestacy* according to the *Administration of Estates Act 1925 as amended* are as follows:

**Rights of surviving ...**

### Spouse

- If there is *nobody*: *complete estate* passes to him/her.
- If there *is* issue:
  - all personal chattels,
  - up to £250,000 free of inheritance tax, and
  - *life interest* in half of the remaining estate.
- If there is *no* issue, but other relatives:
  - all personal chattels,
  - up to £450,000 free of inheritance tax, and
  - half of the remaining estate *absolutely*.

### Children

- If there *is* a surviving spouse:
  - the other half of the remaining estate held *on a statutory trust* for the children.
- If there is *no* surviving spouse:
  - the remaining estate held *on a statutory trust* for the children.
- All children are entitled to *equal shares*.

### Parents

- If there is *no* issue and *no* surviving spouse:
  - they take the whole estate in *equal shares*.
  - if only one parent is alive, he or she is entitled to the *whole estate*.
- If there *are* surviving spouses or children:
  - nothing!

### Remoter relatives

- If there *is* anyone of the above mentioned closer relatives or spouses: nothing!
- If *none* of these are alive, they will be beneficiaries in the following order:
  - brothers and sisters of half blood *(on statutory trust)*,
  - grand parents (whole estate absolutely),
  - uncles and aunts (whole blood) *(on statutory trust)*,
  - uncles and aunts (half blood) *(on statutory trust)*.

### Brothers and sisters of the whole blood

- If there *are* surviving spouses, issue or parents:
  - nothing!
- If there are *none*:
  - the estate is held *on statutory trust* for brothers and sisters or their children.

testamentarische (gewillkürte) Erbfolge

## IV. Testate succession (wills)

### 1. Introduction

etwas bestätigen
letzter Wille/Testament
darlegen

Testate succession ("testamentum" in Latin meaning something attested, i.e. the last will) arises where the deceased has made a will, setting out how his estate should be distributed.

übergehen

In English law, the right of a person to make a will showing to whom his personal property should pass was recognised relatively early.

Grundeigentum
Lehnsrecht – zufallen/übergehen
gesetzlicher Erbe
(testamentarisch) hinterlassen – Grundbesitz
kirchlich
*hier:* Gerichtsbarkeit/rechtliche Zuständigkeit

In medieval times, a person had no right to dispose of freehold land, as the strict feudal law laid down that the land had to devolve to the heir at law. Later, the *Statute of Wills 1540* permitted a freeholder to devise land (i.e. to leave the land by will). Just as with birth and marriage, death also had a direct connection with the Church. In Norman and medieval times, the ecclesiastical courts exercised jurisdiction over wills of personal property, including leaseholds.

übertragen
von da an/seitdem
herleiten
kanonisches Recht/Kirchenrecht

The *Court of Probate Act 1857* transferred this jurisdiction to the ordinary civil courts, where it has stayed ever since. Many of the rules applied today, however, are derived from the early Church courts, which applied canon law, not common law.

*hier:* Rechtsnatur

### 2. The nature of a will

Verteilung/Übertragung

A **will** is a declaration, made by a person in his lifetime, of his wishes concerning the disposition of his property after death.

falls nicht – wirksam werden
Erblasser/Testamentsverfasser
*hier:* errichten – widerruflich
Verfügung
Rechtsnachfolger/Erbe

Unless there is a clear intention to the contrary, a will **takes effect from the time of death** of the testator, not from the time it is made; a will is said to be revocable by testator until his death. Thus, if for example, A makes a disposition of "All my property to B.", successor B will be entitled to receive *not only* the property that A had at the time he was making the will, but *also any other property* A may have acquired *between that time and his death*.

(*jur.*) Auslegung

In contrast to German law (cf. *§§ 2084, 133 BGB*), it is not the intention of the testator which is at the heart of the construction of a will in English law (the intentional or purposive approach), but instead the **ordinary meaning of the testator's words** (the literal or grammatical approach). It is also true that, based on the circumstances and context in which the will was made, English jurisdiction tends to take into account the intention of the testator. In construing a will the court aims to ascertain the intention of the testator. It has been established, however, that the required formalities must accompany the expression of testamentary intentions. Any intention which is not expressed in accordance with those requisite formalities will be ignored and regard will be paid only to the words used by the testator.

Rechtsprechung
erkunden/herausfinden/erforschen

erforderlich/unerlässlich – etw. beachten/Beachtung schenken

Please consult our **further reading** section for more details on the interpretation of a will, an area of immense complexity.

### 3. Testamentary capacity

Testierfähigkeit

The general rule is that any person of *full age* and *legal capacity* (thus, not a minor or a person of unsound mind) may make a valid will. If someone intends to show that a testator was no capable – through unsoundness of mind or for any other reason – of making a valid will, the fact of the testator's incapacity must be clearly proved.

Geschäftsfähigkeit
unzurechnungsfähig

*hier:* wegen Unzurechnungsfähigkeit

eindeutig/klar

### 4. Formalities

Formvorschrift

A will is usually a formal declaration of intention. The formal requirements for making a will are governed by the *Wills Act 1837* as amended.

Willenserklärung

#### a) Writing

Schriftform

The will must be *in writing* – but not necessarily handwritten as in German law *(§ 2231 BGB)* - and *signed* by the testator or – and, here, it differs from German law - by some other person in his presence and under his direction. It must clearly appear that the testator intended, by his signature, to give effect to the will. *In writing* includes handwriting, print and typescript in English law. A notarised will as in German law does not exist.

schriftlich

(An)Weisung

Handschrift – Druck – Maschinenschrift
*etwa*: notariell beurkundetes Testament

#### b) Signature and witnesses

Unterschrift – Zeuge

The signature must be made, or acknowledged, by the testator in the presence of two or more *witnesses*. Acknowledgement will, for example, be necessary if the testator has signed before asking the witnesses to attend. Each witness must either attest and sign the will or acknowledge his signature in the presence of the testator.

anerkennen/bestätigen

zugegen/anwesend sein – bestätigen

erleichtern
Platzierung/Position (auf dem Testament)
namens/im Namen von

The *Administration of Justice Act 1982* relaxes the law governing the position of the testator's signature and the acknowledgement of this signature by an attesting witness. The result of the new *s.9 of the Wills Act 1837* is that the signature by – or on behalf of – the testator can be anywhere on the will, provided that the testator intended, by his signature, to give effect to the will.

ordnungsgemäß/formgerecht ein Testament errichten
am Ende
unten
hinweisen auf
*Lord Justice*: Richter an einem Gericht höherer Instanz
erfüllen/befolgen

| *Example – Wood* v *Smith (1993)* |
|---|
| After duly executing his will a testator made another will two days before his death by writing it in his own handwriting and it began with the following words: 'My will by Percy Winterbone'. He did not sign his name at the foot of the will. However, two attesting witnesses signed the will at the bottom and, when one of them pointed out that the testator had not signed it, he replied: 'Yes I have. I have signed it at the top. It can be signed anywhere.' Had this document satisfied the requirements of *s.9 of the Wills Act 1837*?<br>***Held:*** that it had indeed, since it did not matter that the testator had written his signature before writing the dispositive provisions. Scott L.J. explained that the testator had indicated in clear terms that he regarded his name written by him as his signature and that established that he had complied with the terms of *s.9(a) of the Wills Act 1837*. By writing 'My will by Percy Winterbone', it was also established that the testator had intended to give testamentary effect to the document and that satisfied the requirements of *s.9(b)*. |

Seemann

Apart from that, there is no equivalent in English law to the German „Nottestament" (cf. *§§ 2249, 2250 BGB*) apart from the exception for soldiers and sailors mentioned here below.

## 5. Wills of soldiers and sailors

Legionssoldat
formlos – unmittelbar bevorstehend
Rechtsbeistand – in der Nähe
(dienender) Soldat
Seefahrer – Matrose

It was a rule of Roman law that legionaries "in expeditione" might make *informal wills*, for a soldier may often be in imminent fear of death and he may have no legal advice near by. This rule has passed into English law in the form of *s.11 of the Wills Act 1837*, which provides "that any soldier being in actual military service, or any mariner or seaman being at sea, may dispose of his personal estate"without any formalities whatever.

The *Wills (Soldiers and Sailors) Act 1918* extended the privilege to realty. The three privileged testators may make a will even though they are not of full age. They may make informal wills. Even an oral declaration will be sufficient.

| *Example – Re Wingham (1949)* |
|---|
| The deceased, a member of the Royal Air Force, was sent to Canada in 1943 for training as an airman. He wrote out and signed a document, which he described as a will, but which was not attested. Later the year and during his training he was involved in an air accident in Canada and died from the injuries he received.<br>An informal will may be made by a soldier on actual military service (see *s.11 of the Wills Act 1837*); *s.5 of the Wills (Soldiers and Sailors) Act 1918* extends this privilege to members of the Royal Air Force. Relying on these sections, the document was put forward as the deceased's will.<br>***Held:*** that it could be admitted to probate. Bucknill LJ said "the tests are (a) was the testator 'on military service'; (b) was such service 'active'? In my opinion, the adjective 'active' in this connection confines military service to such service as is directly concerned with operations in a war which is or has been in progress or is imminent". Applying these tests, he concluded that the deceased was so engaged, although he was not in the theatre of war. |

Flieger/Pilot

Flugunfall

anerkannt

*etwa*: zu prüfen ist

unmittelbar bevorstehend

## 6. Classes of testamentary dispositions

Kategorie – letztwillige Verfügung

Testamentary dispositions, i.e. gifts by will, of personal or moveable property, including leaseholds, are called *legacies or bequests*. Gifts of real property (freehold land) are called *devises*.

*vgl.* deutsches Vermächtnis

letztwillige Verfügung über Grundbesitz

### a) Legacies

A legacy (or bequest) may be a *general* legacy, a *specific* legacy, a *demonstrative* legacy or a *residuary* legacy.

Gattungsvermächtnis – Einzelvermächtnis – beschränktes Gattungsvermächtnis – letztwillige Verfügung über den bewegl. Restnachlass (nach Abzug der Schulden u. Belastungen)

#### *aa) General legacy*

This is a gift, not of any particular thing, but of something which is to be provided out of the testator's general estate. The classic example is a gift of a sum of money, e.g. "I give £2,000 to my daughter L". Other examples are: "I leave a car ..." or "... a horse ..." or "... a boat ...".

#### *bb) Specific legacy*

This is a gift by will of specified personal estate/property. For example "I leave my Rolls Royce ..." or "I give my horse 'Pilgrim' to Grace" or "I leave my boat 'Old Love No. I' to my darling Valentine ...".

#### *cc) Demonstrative legacy*

Mischform

This is a hybrid between a general and a specific legacy. In its nature this gift is *general*, but at the same time it is directed to be satisfied *primarily* out of a *specified* part of the testator's estate, normally a sum of money to be paid out of a particular fund, for example "I leave £1,000 out of my 6.5% Federal Government Bond ...".

Bundesanleihe

#### *dd) Residuary legacy*

letztwillige Verfügung über den beweglichen Restnachlass (nach Abzug der Schulden und Belastungen)

This is a gift of the residue of the estate, or part of it, left over after all other gifts have been made and debts and administrative costs have been paid.

### b) Devises

Devises may be *specific* or *general*. The essential nature of any devise is, as mentioned above, that it deals solely with the **real property** of the testator.

einzig/ausschließlich

#### *aa) Specific devise*

letztwillige Einzelzuwendung (unbewegliches Vermögen)

A specific devise is a gift by will of specified real estate/property. The gift must be part of the testator's estate at his death and must be described in such a way as to sever or distinguish it from the rest of the estate. Thus "My house, No. 6 Downing Street, London" or "My cottage in Mullion, Cornwall" are specific devises. Such a devise passes all benefits and burdens which the testator had in the property.

absondern/trennen/teilen – abgrenzen/unterscheiden

Nutzen – Lasten

#### *bb) General (residuary) devise*

letztwillige Verfügung über Restnachlass (unbewegl. Vermögen) – nach Beschreibung

A general devise, or more accurately known as a residuary devise, is a gift of real property by description. Thus, gifts of "all my farms in the Lake District to A" or "all my real property to B" are residuary devises.

Under *s.37 of the Wills Act 1837*, a residuary devise includes any real estate over which the testator has a power of appointment, and such a devise shall operate as an execution of that power, unless there is a contrary intention expressed in the will.

Einsetzungsbefugnis
wirken

## 7. Effects of the classification

The distinction between the several forms of legacies and devises is important because the nature of the gifts will determine whether they are liable to ademption or abatement etc.

etw. unterliegen – *hier:* Widerruf – Kürzung/Minderung

### a) Ademption of specific legacy or devise

If a specific item to be given by will to a legatee is not in existence or no longer belongs to the testator at the time of the testator's death, the gift is revoked and the legatee receives nothing.

Vermächtnisnehmer
widerrufen

### b) Abatement

Abatement occurs when there is not enough property to satisfy all beneficiaries after the creditors of the deceased have been paid. The consequence will be that some of the legacies will have to be reduced or even repudiated altogether. Residuary gifts abate first, then general legacies, and then specific legacies. A demonstrative legacy will not abate unless the fund out of which it is to be paid is itself exhausted. In that case the demonstrative legacy will be treated as a general legacy and will abate with them.

Gläubiger
zurückweisen – herabsetzen/mindern
Fonds
erschöpft/aufgebraucht

### c) Income and interest

Specific legacies and devises normally carry with them all the income or profits accruing from its subject matter after the testator's death.

sich ansammeln/anfallen – Gegenstand

### d) Expenses

The beneficiary has to pay any expenses incurred to the personal representative by his administration of the subject matter of a *specific* legacy or devise. By contrast, any expenses incurred by administration of other assets are payable out of the residuary

entstandene Kosten

estate; they are not payable by the general or demonstrative legatees.

Widerruf

## 8. Revocation

ausdrücklich – stillschweigend durch das Verhalten

A will may be revoked either expressly or by implication by the conduct of the testator.

### a) Express revocation

Testamentserrichtung

An express revocation has to be made in exactly the same way as the making of a will, which means: in writing, signed and witnessed.

### b) Implied revocation

Testamentsnachtrag

#### *aa) By later will or codicil*

Bestimmung/Klausel/Paragraph
einfügen
es sei denn, dass – im Widerspruch dazu

A will usually begins with a clause revoking all previous wills. If such a clause is not inserted, the later will (or codicil) does not revoke the former will, except in so far as it is inconsistent therewith. Thus, if a testator in a first will leaves a specified named house to A, and, in a later will, leaves the same house to B, the house goes to B. If, however, the testator in his first will leaves £1,000 to A, and, in a later will (which does not contain a revocation clause), leaves £1,000 to B, both A and B will receive legacies of £1,000.

ergänzen – ändern

If a will is amended or varied by a codicil, it is necessary to have the written codicil signed and witnessed. A codicil[48] is a supplement or variation to an existing will. The same rules as to capacity and formalities apply to a codicil as they do to an existing will.

| *Example – Re White (1991)* |
|---|
| During the variation of his will the latter was signed by witnesses in the proper manner. Unfortunately, the testator failed to sign again. The question arose whether the variation was valid, in accordance with the requirements of the *Wills Act 1837 ss.9, 15, and 21*. The testator, who died on 26th February 1985, made his original will on 2nd January 1981. He attempted to alter the will |

48 For example, to change the executors, to add new gifts to the will or to delete certain gifts from it.

on 14th December 1984. Z and another person witnessed the alterations and, in the presence of the testator and at his request, placed their signature near the original signature of the testator and beneath the words 'alterations to will dated 14.12.84 witnesses'. However, the testator did not sign the will again. Z claimed that the amendments were invalid (the alterations to the will made it less beneficial than the original will).
***Held:*** that the amendments were invalid because: (1) for alterations to be valid under *s.21 of the Wills Act 1837*, they must be effected "in like manner as ... required for the execution of the will". However, the alterations in this case were not signed by the testator or by someone under his direction; (2) the question arises of whether what took place on 14th December 1984 amounted to the creation of a valid will.
The answer here was that it did not because the formal requirements of *s.9(a), (b) and (d)* had not been complied with. In particular, regarding *s.9(a)* the new will was not signed by the testator, as the signature already existed at the time of the alleged re-execution. As to *s.9(b)* the testator did not by his existing signature, intend to give effect to the new will, and as to *s.9(d)* there was no conclusive evidence that the witnesses were attesting the will as opposed to merely attesting the alteration.

Änderungen – auf sein Verlangen

hinauslaufen auf

erfüllen/einhalten

Neuausfertigung

zwingender Beweis

***bb) By destruction of the will***

Vernichtung

A will is only revoked in this case if it is intentionally destroyed by the testator or by someone else in the testator's presence under his direction. It may be destroyed by burning, tearing or any other means, but it must be done with the clear intention to destroy the will. Thus, a will destroyed accidentally would still be valid. In such a case, the personal representatives would refer to other material, such as a copy of the will or oral evidence, to find the testator's intention.

widerrufen/zurücknehmen

zerreißen

zufällig

mündlicher Beweis/Aussage

| Example – Re Adams (1990) |
|---|
| After her will had been returned to her by solicitors so that she could destroy it, the testatrix had heavily scored parts of the will with a ballpoint pen, including her signature and the witnesses' signatures, which were therefore almost impossible to read.<br>***Held:*** that the will had been 'otherwise destroyed' within *s.20 of the Wills Act 1837*. It had therefore been revoked and it could not be admitted to probate. |

Erblasserin – durchstreichen

Kugelschreiber

späte/nachfolgend

***cc) By subsequent divorce***

Erbschaftsverwalter/-in

A divorce or nullity of marriage revokes any gift to the former spouse, and revokes the appointment of the spouse as executor or executrix, but does not revoke the will itself. If another person or other persons are also named as beneficiaries in the will, it would remain valid, and only the gift to the former spouse would be invalid. If the spouse was the only beneficiary, the testator's estate would be distributed under the rules of intestacy (see above).

***dd) By subsequent marriage***

im Hinblick auf die bevorstehende Eheschließung

A will of the deceased is revoked by a subsequent marriage but it will not be revoked if it is made in contemplation of marriage. Thus, it is not sufficient to state in the will that the testator intends to marry. The will would still be revoked by a subsequent marriage, unless the name of the intended spouse was also stated and the testator intended that the will would not be revoked by the marriage.

## 9. Example of the structure of a will

A typical will would read as follows:

"This is the **last will** and testament of me", full name, address, occupation:

- "I hereby **revoke** all former wills…" (Clause of revocation)
- "I **desire** my body may be buried"
- "I **appoint** my wife (name) to be the sole executrix and trustee…" (Appointment of an executor)
- "I **give** the following legacies …"
- " I **give** the following devises …"
- Establishment of a trust
- Administrative provisions
- Testimonium clause: declaration, date, testator's signature
- Attestation clause: declaration, the two witnesses' signatures, addresses and occupations

Beglaubigung(svermerk)
Zeugnis(vermerk)

**Diagram 58**

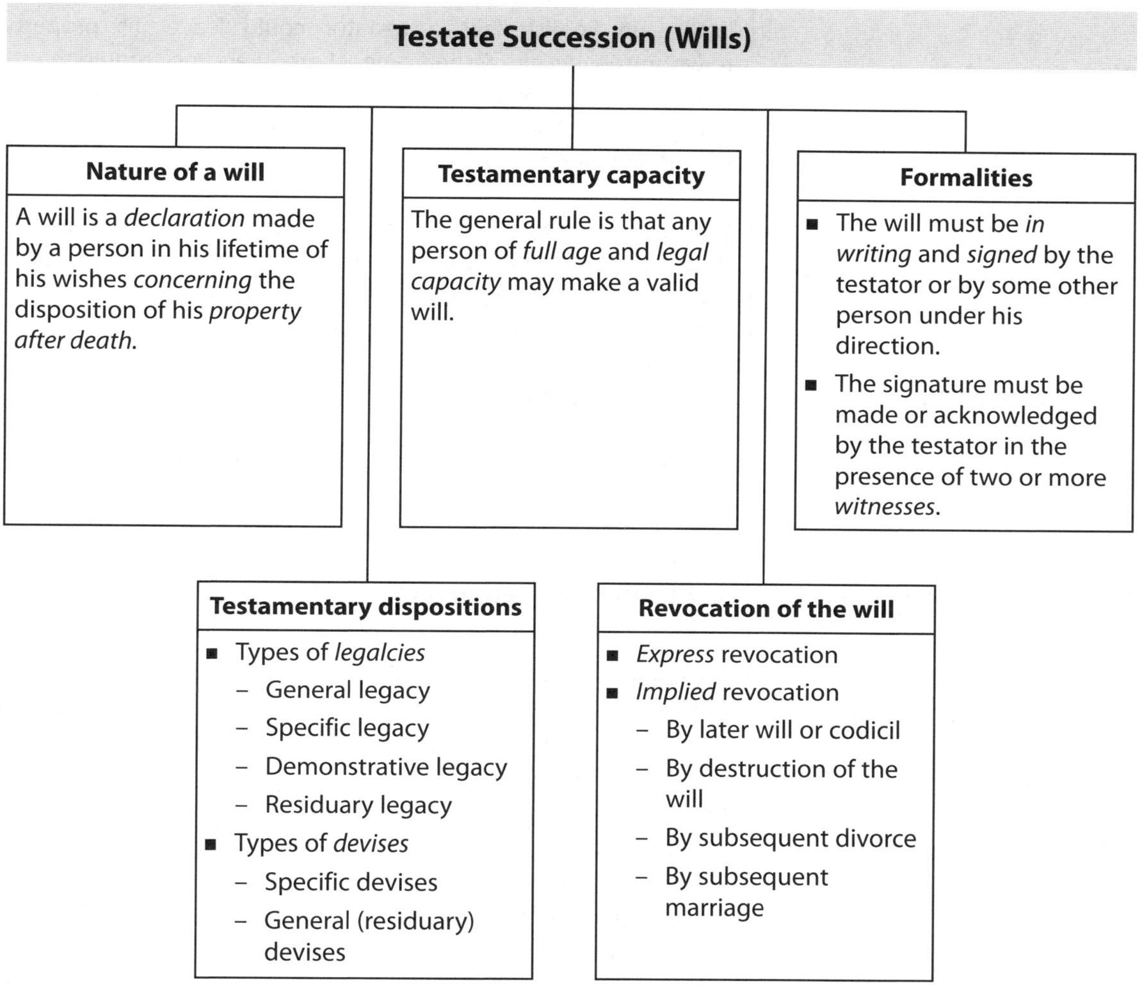

## Testate Succession (Wills)

**Nature of a will**

A will is a *declaration* made by a person in his lifetime of his wishes *concerning* the disposition of his *property after death*.

**Testamentary capacity**

The general rule is that any person of *full age* and *legal capacity* may make a valid will.

**Formalities**

- The will must be *in writing* and *signed* by the testator or by some other person under his direction.
- The signature must be made or acknowledged by the testator in the presence of two or more *witnesses*.

**Testamentary dispositions**

- Types of *legalcies*
  - General legacy
  - Specific legacy
  - Demonstrative legacy
  - Residuary legacy
- Types of *devises*
  - Specific devises
  - General (residuary) devises

**Revocation of the will**

- *Express* revocation
- *Implied* revocation
  - By later will or codicil
  - By destruction of the will
  - By subsequent divorce
  - By subsequent marriage

## V. Family provision

gerichtlich festgesetzte Versorgung unterhaltsbedürftiger Familienangehöriger aus dem Nachlass

The basic concept of family provision is comparable to the German right of compulsory portion as far as regards the concept and idea as such; the structuring and enforcing of English legislation concerning family provision, however, differs significantly from its German equivalent.

Pflichtteilsrecht

## 1. Introduction

Unlike German law and other civil laws of the continent (and Scots law) – in English law, a testator could leave his property to whomsoever he wished and there were no requirements to provide for his family. The testator could give his entire estate to charity and leave his family penniless. This was true for the period between 1836 until 1938.

an wen auch immer
*hier*: (vor)sorgen für
Wohltätigkeitsorganisation – mittellos/vermögenslos

With the *Inheritance (Family Provision) Act 1938*, amended by the *Intestates' Estates Act 1952*, this period of testamentary freedom came to an end. Henceforward, the court was given the power to vary a will on application of certain persons. Further and more extensive powers were given to the courts by the *Inheritance (Provision for Family and Dependants) Act 1975*.

Erbschaft
von da an
auf Antrag von
Unterhaltsberechtigter

This legislation imposes a considerable limit on testamentary freedom.

## 2. Persons entitled to apply for family provision

*etwa*: Personenkreis, der aus dem Nachlass Versorgungsansprüche bei Gericht beantragen kann

According to the *Inheritance (Provision for Family and Dependants) Act 1975*, the court has a discretion to make an award out of the deceased person's estate to dependants who have not received "reasonable financial provision", i.e. adequate financial support from the deceased's estate, because of the will or the application of the intestacy principles. The following persons may apply to the court for family provision:

(1) the spouse of the dead person,
(2) former spouses who have not remarried,
(3) the children of the deceased, whether they be illegitimate, adopted, or treated as a child of the family,

Ermessen – e. Betrag festsetzen
angemessen/vernünftig
bei Gericht etw. beantragen

| *Example – Re Callaghan (1984)* |
|---|
| After his father's death, P and his mother lived in a house given to P's mother by P's grandfather. C moved into the house as a lodger and married P's mother treating P as his own son. When P married the families remained close and P's children treated C as their grandfather. When C became seriously ill, he nominated P as next of kin and P and his wife cared for him. C died intestate. Under the rules of intestacy, C's estate (value £31,116), mainly the house given to P's mother, passed to C's sisters. P applied for financial provision |

Untermieter
(nächststehender) Angehöriger/ Verwandter – ohne Testament
finanzielle Unterstützung

> from the estate under *s.1(1)(d) of the Inheritance (Provision for Family and Dependants) Act 1975* as a person 'treated by the deceased as a child of family'. C's sisters argued that a 'child of the family' could only be a minor or dependent child, which P was not when C met P's mother.
> ***Held:*** that *s.1(1)(d)* should not be construed narrowly and did include an 'adult child'. The word 'child' related to the relationship between the deceased and the applicant and the treatment referred to in *s.1(1)(d)* was not limited to treatment of a minor or dependent child. After C had married P's mother, there was sufficient evidence that C had treated P as an adult child of the family. C had no obligations to his sisters whereas he was under a considerable obligation to P; moreover, C's estate originated from P's mother. P would be awarded a lump sum of £15,000.

eng auslegen

Antragsteller

Pauschalbetrag

(4) cohabitants (an unmarried couple) — Lebensgefährte
(5) any other persons who, immediately before the death of the deceased, were being maintained by the deceased. — unterhalten/unterstützen

## 3. The test of reasonable financial provision

In the case of a surviving spouse or civil partner the term *reasonable financial provision* is defined in *s.1(2)(a) of the 1975 Act* as follows: "Such financial provision as it would be reasonable in all circumstances of the case for a husband or wife to receive, whether or not that provision is required for his or her maintenance." This is called "**the surviving spouse standard**".

Lebensunterhalt

In the case of applicants other than the spouse or civil partner, the provision is governed by *s.1(2)(b) of this Act*: "Such financial provision as it would be reasonable in all circumstances of the case for the applicant to receive for his maintenance." (called the "**maintenance standard**"). In this case, financial provision is limited to what is needed for actual maintenance of living.

There is no specific definition of *maintenance* in the *Act* but there are many definitions delivered by the courts themselves. According to Templeman & Spedding, to define maintenance, one should refer to the statement found in *Re Borthwick (1949),* which is still relevant today. In this case, it was said that, "Maintenance does not only mean the food the applicant puts in her mouth, it means the clothes on her back, the house in which she lives, and the money which she has to have in her pocket, all of which vary

bloßes Verpflegungsgeld

according to the means of the deceased .... Maintenance cannot mean mere subsistence."

Antragsfrist

### 4. Time limit for applications

Antrag

An application for financial provision – which is to be filed to the *personal representatives* – must be made within **six months** from the date on which a valid grant of probate or letters of administration is first taken out.

Leit-/Richtlinie

### 5. Guidelines for the court

regelmäßig wiederkehrende Zahlung
Zahlung eines Pauschalbetrags

Vergleich/Regelung – Versorgungsanordnung

(Geld-)Mittel

Beitrag

(Aus)bildungsbedarf

The court can make an order for periodical payments or lump sum payments from the estate. Moreover, the court may transfer certain property, such as the family house, or make settlements of other property. Before making a provision order, the court has to consider a number of circumstances: the value and the size of the estate and the provision already made for the applicant, the applicant's resources and the applicant's conduct towards the deceased. In the case of a spouse, consideration would be given to age, duration of marriage and the contribution made by the applicant to the family and its welfare. In the case of young children, educational needs would be considered and, in the case of older children, the ability to maintain themselves to a reasonable standard. Moreover, the court would take into consideration statements (if any) by the deceased as to the reasons why certain provisions were made or not made.

## VI. Further reading & references[49]

*Borkowski*, Textbook on Succession*; Cracknell*, Succession: The Law of Wills and Estates; *Geldart*, Introduction to English Law; *Kerridge*, Parry and Kerridge: The Law of Succession; *King*, Probate Practitioner's Handbook; *Lyall*, An Introduction to British Law; *Shears & Stephenson*, James' Introduction to English Law; *Templeman & Spedding*, Succession (Casebook, Revision Work Book, Textbook); *Wilman*, Brown*:* GCSE Law.

49 Edition, publisher, place and year of publication are quoted in the bibliography.